SERMONS,

ADAPTED TO THE

CELEBRATION OF THE HOLY SACRAMENT

OF

THE LORD'S SUPPER.

BY

THE REV. CHARLES BRADLEY,

VICAR OF GLASBURY, BRECKNOCKSHIRE, AND MINISTER OF ST. JAMES'S
CHAPEL, CLAPHAM, SURREY.

LONDON:
PRINTED FOR HAMILTON, ADAMS, AND CO.,
AND J. HATCHARD AND SON.
1842.

LONDON:
PRINTED BY G. J. PALMER, SAVOY STREET

CONTENTS.

SERMON I.

CHRIST FORETELLING THE TREACHERY OF JUDAS.

St. Matthew xxvi. 20, 21, 22.—Now when the even was come, he sat down with the twelve; and as they did eat, he said, Verily I say unto you, that one of you shall betray me. And they were exceeding sorrowful, and began every one of them to say unto him, Lord, is it I?

Page 1.

SERMON II.

THE SWORD OF JEHOVAH SMITING HIS SHEPHERD.

Zechariah xiii. 7.—Awake, O sword, against my Shepherd, and against the man that is my Fellow, saith the Lord of hosts. Smite the Shepherd, and the sheep shall be scattered: and I will turn mine hand upon the little ones.

Page 21.

SERMON III.

THE TOKEN OF THE COVENANT.

Genesis ix. 14, 15.—It shall come to pass, when I bring a cloud over the earth, that the bow shall be seen in the cloud, and I will remember my covenant.

Page 40.

SERMON IV.

THE CHRISTIAN WORSHIPPING IN GOD'S TEMPLE.

Psalm v. 7.—As for me, I will come into thy house in the multitude of thy mercy, and in thy fear will I worship toward thy holy temple.

Page 59.

SERMON V.

THE CHRISTIAN LONGING TO SEE GOD IN HIS TEMPLE.

Psalm lxiii. 1, 2.—O God, thou art my God; early will I seek thee. My soul thirsteth for thee, my flesh longeth for thee, in a dry and thirsty land where no water is; to see thy power and thy glory, so as I have seen thee in the sanctuary.

Page 77.

SERMON VI.

THE RISEN JESUS APPEARING TO HIS DISCIPLES.

St. John xx. 19, 20.—Then the same day at evening, being the first day of the week, when the doors were shut where the disciples were assembled for fear of the Jews, came Jesus and stood in the midst, and saith unto them, Peace be unto you. And when he had so said, he shewed unto them his hands and his side. Then were the disciples glad when they saw the Lord.

Page 95.

SERMON VII.

CHRIST PROCLAIMING HIS FINISHED WORK.

St. John xix. 30.—He said, It is finished.

Page 111.

CONTENTS. v

SERMON VIII.
THE CHRISTIAN TAKING UP HIS CROSS.

St. Mark x. 21.—Come, take up the cross, and follow me.
Page 130.

SERMON IX.
THE HOLINESS OF GOD.

Psalm xxx. 4.—Sing unto the Lord, O ye saints of his, and give thanks at the remembrance of his holiness.
Page 147.

SERMON X.
THE FAITHFUL SAYING.

1 *Timothy* i. 15.—This is a faithful saying, and worthy of all acceptation, that Christ Jesus came into the world to save sinners, of whom I am chief.
Page 166.

SERMON XI.
THE OFFERINGS OF CAIN AND ABEL.

Genesis iv. 3, 4, 5.—It came to pass that Cain brought of the fruit of the ground an offering unto the Lord; and Abel, he also brought of the firstlings of his flock and of the fat thereof. And the Lord had respect unto Abel and to his offering, but unto Cain and to his offering he had not respect.
Page 183.

SERMON XII.
THE MARRIAGE SUPPER OF THE LAMB.

Revelation xix. 9.—Blessed are they which are called unto the marriage supper of the Lamb.
Page 204.

SERMON XIII.

THE VIRGIN MARY'S JOY.

St. Luke i. 46, 47.—And Mary said, My soul doth magnify the Lord, and my spirit hath rejoiced in God my Saviour.

Page 222.

SERMON XIV.

THE LORD'S SUPPER AN EMBLEM AND MEMORIAL.

St. Luke xxii. 19, 20.—And he took bread, and gave thanks, and brake it, and gave unto them, saying, This is my body which is given for you; this do in remembrance of me. Likewise also the cup after supper, saying, This cup is the new testament in my blood which is shed for you.

Page 243.

SERMON XV.

THE SONG OF SIMEON.

St. Luke ii. 28, 29, 30.—Then took he him up in his arms, and blessed God, and said, Lord, now lettest thou thy servant depart in peace according to thy word, for mine eyes have seen thy salvation.

Page 262.

SERMON XVI.

THE LORD'S SUPPER A SHEWING FORTH OF HIS DEATH.

1 *Corinthians* xi. 26.—As often as ye eat this bread and drink this cup, ye do shew the Lord's death till he come.

Page 282.

CONTENTS.

SERMON XVII.

THE LORD'S SUPPER A FEAST AND A COMMUNION.

1 *Corinthians* x. 16, 17.—The cup of blessing which we bless, is it not the communion of the blood of Christ? The bread which we break, is it not the communion of the body of Christ? For we, being many, are one bread and one body; for we are all partakers of that one bread.
Page 299.

SERMON XVIII.

THE APPREHENSION OF CHRIST.

St. John xviii. 4, 5, 6.—Jesus therefore, knowing all things that should come upon him, went forth, and said unto them, Whom seek ye? They answered him, Jesus of Nazareth. Jesus saith unto them, I am he. And Judas also which betrayed him, stood with them. As soon then as he had said unto them, I am he, they went backward, and fell to the ground.
Page 316.

SERMON XIX.

THE CHRISTIAN ENQUIRING FOR HIS ABSENT LORD.

Song of Solomon i. 7.—Tell me, O thou whom my soul loveth, where thou feedest, where thou makest thy flock to rest at noon; for why should I be as one that turneth aside by the flocks of thy companions?
Page 333.

SERMON XX.

FELLOWSHIP WITH GOD.

1 *St. John* i. 3.—Truly our fellowship is with the Father, and with his Son Jesus Christ.
Page 353.

SERMON XXI.

THE HOLINESS OF CHRIST.

Hebrews vii. 26.—Such an High Priest became us, who is holy, harmless, undefiled, separate from sinners.

Page 375.

SERMON XXII.

CHRIST CONTEMPLATING HIS FUTURE BLESSEDNESS.

Psalm xvi. 9, 10, 11.—Therefore my heart is glad and my glory rejoiceth; my flesh also shall rest in hope; for thou wilt not leave my soul in hell, neither wilt thou suffer thine holy One to see corruption. Thou wilt shew me the path of life; in thy presence is fulness of joy; at thy right hand there are pleasures for evermore.

Page 394.

SERMON XXIII.

THE FOUNTAIN OPENED.

Zechariah xiii. 1.—In that day there shall be a fountain opened to the house of David and to the inhabitants of Jerusalem, for sin and for uncleanness.

Page 416.

SERMON I.

CHRIST FORETELLING THE TREACHERY OF JUDAS.

St. Matthew xxvi. 20, 21, 22.

"Now when the even was come, he sat down with the twelve; and as they did eat, he said, Verily I say unto you, that one of you shall betray me. And they were exceeding sorrowful, and began every one of them to say unto him, Lord, is it I?"

We can hardly read these words without placing before our minds the scene they describe. It is an affecting scene, brethren. And its chief interest lies perhaps in the view which it gives us into the thoughts and feelings of those concerned in it. We take pleasure in looking into the heart of any one we love, and here is laid open to us the heart of him we love best, the blessed Jesus; and the hearts of those he loved best, his dear disciples. And these hearts are laid open to us at a time when they are filled to the full with thought and feeling.

Our Lord was now eating his last meal with his disciples. He had gathered them around him to take a final leave of them, and to institute among them his holy supper; but there was a traitor among them, and as though this were a pollution he could no longer silently endure, he abruptly tells them of it; he gives fresh sorrow to these already sorrowful men, by proclaiming one of them his future betrayer.

The account given us of this scene naturally divides itself into two parts—our Lord's prediction of the treachery of Judas, and the effect of that prediction on those who heard it.

I. " He sat down with the twelve ; and as they did eat, he said, Verily I say unto you, that one of you shall betray me." There is *the prediction ;* and it discovers to us

1. *The close and constant view which the Lord Jesus seems to have taken of his final sufferings.*

We all know that he saw these sufferings before him, but we generally conceive of him as looking at them occasionally only, and then, as it were, afar off, only dimly discerning them; in the same way as a traveller may see at intervals, and at a distance before him, some dark, troubled river he is soon to pass. But the truth probably is, that his last sufferings were never for one moment out of his thoughts. They had been in his mind as God ages before, revolved and meditated there, and now he is man, they enter his human mind, and hold possession of it. He refers to them when we least expect him to do so, and he foretells circumstances connected with them, which clearly shew that he saw them not confusedly and in a mass only, like objects seen at a distance, but clearly, distinctly, in all their number and with all their aggravations. Here he predicts, and not for the first time, the treachery of Judas, and a few minutes afterwards, the denial of him by Peter, and the forsaking of him by all his disciples.

And knowledge like this must have added greatly to his daily misery. We are saved the pain of anticipation by our ignorance of our coming sorrows, but our suffering Lord could not fly from the anticipation of his. His foreknowledge brought them within reach of his mind, and they were of a nature that impelled his mind to look at and grasp them.

2. We may see next in this prediction *the naturalness of our Lord's mind.* By this I mean its resemblance to our own minds; its participation with us in the ordinary workings and feelings of our nature.

Look into your own hearts, brethren. If you have ever really loved a fellow-creature, and that fellow-creature has inflicted on you some painful injury, you have forgiven the injury perhaps, but in spite of yourselves, you cannot wholly forget it. The remembrance of it will still occasionally recur to you, and will be most likely to recur when you might suppose it the least likely—in those seasons when your love for your friend is called into the liveliest exercise. Think of that touching interview which took place between Joseph and his brethren when he made himself known to them. Not a reproach escapes him for the wrong they had done him, but yet he cannot keep it from his mind nor even from his lips. Again and again, while his heart is really melting with love for them, he reminds them of it. And now turn to the Saviour.

Never did his love for his disciples appear so drawn forth as at this period. He was about to part with them, and his whole soul seems overflowing with the love he bore them. Naturally and beautifully does St. John begin his narrative of this scene with speaking of his love. "Having loved his own," he says, "which were in the world, he loved them unto the end." And how does he shew this love? He rises, we are told, from supper, and stoops down, and washes their feet. This over, he seats himself again amongst them, and exactly at this strange moment, in the midst of this scene of tenderness and, we might have said, nothing but tenderness, he says to these wondering men, "One of you shall betray me."

And turn to the sixth chapter of the same evangelist. "From that time," we read, "many of his disciples went back and walked no more with him." Our Lord, touched doubtless with sorrow at this desertion, turns round and says to the twelve, "Will ye also go away?" Then Simon Peter answered him, "Lord, to whom shall we go? thou hast the words of eternal life; and we believe and are sure that thou art that Christ, the Son of the living God." A noble confession, we may say, nobly given, kindling undoubtedly in the breast of Christ pleasure and love; but what comes out of this love? He thinks immediately of the traitor among them; the betraying kiss comes into his mind; and instead of saying, "Blessed art thou, Simon Barjona; blessed are ye, my faithful disciples, my comforters still in a world that forsakes me;" he says, and almost startles us as he says it, "Have not I chosen you twelve? and one of you is a devil."

And thus he lays open to us his resemblance to ourselves, the entireness with which he has taken our nature upon him. He has not only our outward nature, a human form like ours; and not only our inward nature, a human mind like ours; but that mind is affected as ours is; it works as our minds work and feels as they feel. We have no stranger, brethren, for our High Priest in the heavens. Lifted up above us indeed he is, so high that the throne of the everlasting Jehovah is not higher, but notwithstanding this, he is as really one of ourselves as though he were now walking the earth in our form. His heavenly exaltation has indeed wrought some change in his human mind, as our exaltation to heaven will in some degree change our minds, but it is a human mind still. He is as much a partaker of our nature and of all the sinless feelings of our nature, as he is of the eternity of his Father and the purity of the Holy Ghost.

3. Observe here too *the exceeding tenderness of Christ.*

Bearing in mind the weight of mental anguish he was now sustaining, we might have thought that it would be to him a matter of but little moment whether the men around him loved or hated him. His Father's hand was heavy upon him; it pleased an almighty God to bruise and grieve him; and his griefs, we should have said, are so profound, that the kindness or unkindness, the faithfulness or unfaithfulness, of man, will be alike unheeded by him. As for our deepening sorrows like his by any thing we can do, it would be as easy for us to deepen the gloom of midnight. But look to the fact. It would seem as though any worm of the earth could wound him. One of the vilest worms that ever crept on the earth's surface, is here putting this mighty Sufferer, and in one of his most suffering hours, to new grief. "One of you shall betray me" was not uttered by him in a moment of respite from his misery, or without emotion, as the mere prediction of a fact he cared not for; he said it with all the anguish of Gethsemane and Calvary directly before him, with the sins of a whole world pressing down on him, and the terrors of his cross well nigh overshadowing him; and said it as though he could not refrain from saying it, as though even in this situation the treachery of one bad man could inflict on him an anguish he was not able to conceal. He was "troubled in spirit," St John says, agitated and visibly so, when he "testified and said, One of you shall betray me."

We talk of feeling and tenderness, brethren, and there is the semblance of these things in our world, but here is the reality. And how cheering the thought, that this tenderness dwells in the very heart where we would most wish it to dwell! not in the heart of one with whom we have nothing to do, but in the heart of him with whom we have the most to do; in his heart, the Christian says, who is my Redeemer and Sanctifier, my daily Comforter, "my Companion, and Guide, and familiar Friend." It is tenderness that is even now in existence and in operation, and I am the object of it. It is mixed up with the love my exalted Lord bears to me; it mingles itself with all his dealings towards me. I feel it often in the comforts he sends to gladden me, and I have felt it too in the afflictions and sorrows wherewith he has chastened me. He could as soon forget his everlasting throne, as soon lay aside his holiness or existence, as lay aside his tenderness, or, if I am one of his, withdraw it from me. With his servant David, I shall say at the last when he has raised me to his kingdom, "Thy gentleness, O Lord, hath made me great."

4. We are reminded also here of *the wonderful self-denial of our Lord;* his amazing command over his own feelings and conduct.

It is clear that although Judas had been now for three years constantly with him, he had never treated him differently from the other disciples. There had been nothing in his conduct toward him at all peculiar, nothing most certainly that had marked him out to his companions as a treacherous or even a suspicious man.

On the first view, this may appear a trifle. We sometimes behave alike to our best friends and our worst enemies, but we do not always know who our enemies and our friends are; men deceive us. Not so however with the Lord Jesus. He "knew from the beginning who should betray him." The very first glance he ever had of Judas, revealed to him his betrayer. The man never once appeared before him, but he recognized in him a deceiver; never sat down with him or walked by his side, but he thought of his baseness; never gave him one word, or look, or token, of affection, but he saw concealed beneath it a traitor's heart. And this wonderful forbearance held out to the very last. To think that within a few hours of his condemnation and death, our Lord could sit calmly down at the same table with this perfidious apostle; eat and drink with him as a friend; actually bend down before him, take up his vile feet, and wash them with his own sacred hands; and still more—bear perhaps with his presence at the supper he was instituting, and see him partaking of it; and during all this, never betray any abhorrence of him, never by any one look or gesture bring down suspicion on him:—we cannot think of forbearance like this, and not see in this patient Jesus something more than earthly—a self-command, a long-suffering, a greatness, that at once astonish and delight us. Could you have done this, brethren? You know what you feel, when you are obliged at any time to treat with common civility, for a few short minutes, a man whom you believe to be perfidious. We ministers know what we feel, when we are obliged at the table of the Lord to hold out the emblems of his dying love to those who, we suspect, are hypocritical and base. But here is Christ doing this and far more than this, and amidst feelings of disgust and sorrow, compared with which any painful feelings of ours are as nothing; and doing it in silent, tranquil dignity. "Never man spake like this man," said the Roman officers who were sent to take him; and surely we must say, "Never man acted like him." Look at him in what light we may, we are forced to see that all in him is wonderful; all alike wonderful; love, tenderness, patience, strength, greatness, all passing our comprehension; all indicating a Being raised far above us; all testifying of that suffering Jesus, "Truly this was the Son of God."

But we, in our measure, must resemble him; and not in this or that grace only, but in that combination of graces, which formed the peculiarity of his character. It still forms a main peculiarity of the Christian character. Nature, without the Spirit of Christ, may give to one man feeling and tender feeling, and to another man a great apparent self-command; but we do not often find these things combined in natural men. Their tendency is to clash one with another, and to shut the door of the heart against each other. But the Spirit of Christ comes in and triumphs over this tendency. It makes a man feeling, and it makes him firm. It softens his heart, and it strengthens his heart. Under its influence, he becomes a seeming contradiction—a babe and yet a giant. He can weep with his Lord over what another man would deem a trifle; and, if need be, he can suffer with his Lord a weight of misery that would half break that other man's heart, and suffer it quietly, calmly, as though he suffered not at all. And this is partly that perfection of which St. Paul often speaks; that completeness of character, which he so often presses his fellow-Christians to seek. And when it is thus with us, brethren; when things contrary to our nature begin to rise up within us, and things apparently opposite one to another to meet together in us; when the cold heart begins to warm, and the hard heart to melt, and the tender heart to grow firm; when the man of feeling can reign the lord of his feelings, and the man of strength, without losing his strength, can soften and feel; then may we indeed begin to hope that "the same mind that was in Christ," is at last in us; that we are in his hand and under his teaching; that his Spirit is moulding us into his perfect likeness, and that we shall come forth in his likeness "to the praise of the glory of his grace" in the day of his appearing.

II. We must now turn from Christ to his disciples, and notice *the effect produced on them by his prediction.*

But our fellow-men, brethren, are poor objects

of contemplation after looking at our glorious Lord. To turn to them is like turning from a lofty mountain to a petty hill, or from some wide, splendid landscape, to a pictured copy of it. But yet scripture holds up our fellow-men to us for our contemplation, and the faint traces it enables us to discover in them of our Master's likeness, often surprise, delight, and encourage us.

In the men before us, we may observe

1. *Their simple faith in their Lord's prediction.*

It must have been very startling to them. It announced something as about to happen, which really seemed most unlikely to happen. They knew that the Jews were seeking his life, and he had at last produced something like a conviction in them that his life would be taken, but none of them had in consequence forsaken him, or wavered in the least in their adherence to him. Here they were, gathered together around him, with hearts warmer than ever with love for him, and all in appearance ready at any moment to die for his sake. And yet when he abruptly says to them, "One of you shall betray me," no doubt is expressed or even felt as to the truth of his words. Confounding as they were, with the simplicity of little children they believe them.

And this was not the usual way of these men. At other times they could scan and question their Master's words as doubtingly and rudely as others.

But they were not now in their usual mind. Their Master's thrilling conduct towards them in washing their feet, and perhaps the unusual solemnity and affection of his demeanour, seem to have sobered them. They have now no heart for the indulgence of self-conceit and cavilling. They feel, and think, and speak, like Christian men; like disciples almost worthy of such a Lord.

And there are seasons perhaps in the life of every Christian, when something like such a change as this comes over him. It may be in deep affliction, or under signal mercies, or perhaps simply beneath the power of God's holy word, but, be the cause what it may, the man becomes sobered, subdued. His proud foolish heart feels for a time as though all its folly and pride had left it. He lies down at his Saviour's feet, and is content to lie there, and wishes he could lie there for ever, believing all he says, submitting to all he does, with his self-will broken, his self-dependence crushed, his high imaginations all cast down, every thought within him " brought into captivity to the obedience of Christ." O that such moments would last! Blessed to you and me, brethren, have been the mercies or trials which have brought them; and blessed will any thing be to us, which brings them again.

2. Notice further *the warm love of these disciples for Christ.* We discover this in their sorrow.

It was a thought they hardly knew how to bear that he should in any way be taken from them. Ignorant as they partially were of his real character, and basely as they afterwards deserted him, yet they could not hear of his departure from them without deep sorrow of heart, without indeed emotion so strong as even to silence and apparently overwhelm them. "Now," says Jesus to them, "I go my way to him that sent me, and none of you asketh me whither goest thou; but because I have said these things unto you, sorrow hath filled your heart."

Imagine these men then, in this state of mind, hearing their Lord declare that he was not only eating his last meal with them, and then going directly afterwards to prison and to death, but that he was to go there a victim to treachery, and the treachery of one of their number; that not only were the nails and spears of his enemies to enter in a few hours the form they were gazing on, but the perfidy of one of his few companions, one of themselves, to pierce his soul;—conceive them hearing and believing this, and you will not want to go far for the origin of their sorrow. "They loved their Master," you will say, " and because they loved him, the thought of his thus suffering and his being thus betrayed into suffering, grieved and distressed them; they were exceeding sorrowful."

And you know nothing of Christian feeling, brethren, if you cannot readily enter into their sorrow. Once get into your hearts a real love for the Lord Jesus, and it will not always be the evil of sin, or the misery it brings, or the danger attending it, that will make you weep over it; it will often be the dishonour it does to your dying Lord. And this feeling will not be confined to your own sins, it will extend to the sins of those connected with you—your families, your relatives, your friends, your neighbours. You will see in them so many injuries done, and done in a blaspheming world where they ought least to be done, to your holy Master, and the thought of them will cut you to the heart. " I thank God," you will say, " that it is not I; but it is one of mine;" and you will be sorrowful, brethren, and " exceeding sorrowful," like these troubled men. And when the sin is your own, what will you be? Ask him who has himself dishonoured his Saviour's name, what you will be. He will tell you that you can scarcely know what the bitterness of sorrow is, till you experience this. He will say that he can think with calmness of his worldly losses and worldly troubles, of his buried friends and withered comforts, but he cannot think with calmness of a dishonoured Saviour. " Betray him?" he says, " Yes, I have done it. I have brought shame in this vile world on his blessed name, and the remembrance of it dries up my spirit. O could I wipe off the stain, my whole life should be a life of weeping. It must be a life of weeping. I shall go softly all my years in the bitterness of my soul."

Brethren, there is no happiness, there is much misery, for any of you who love the Lord Jesus, and yet get into sinful ways. You may be poor, and yet be happy; you may scarcely know where to lay your heads, and be happy; you may be friendless and solitary in the world, and be happy; you may be ill treated and despised in it, and be happy; you may stand by the grave of all that was dear to you on earth, and even there be happy: but sin against the Lord Jesus Christ; for money, or pleasure, or pride, or any thing, betray him in this land of his enemies; and there is no happiness for you; you have a misery to go through greater than any you have ever yet experienced; years will roll over your heads before you will know real, quiet, settled happiness again.

3. But there is one thing more to be noticed in these apostles, and that the most striking of all— *their great self-distrust.*

It might have been supposed that love like theirs, so sincere and warm, would at once have impelled them to pronounce impossible the crime their Lord predicted; that they would have acted in this case, just as they acted a little afterwards, and declared with one voice and one common feeling of indignant determination, that they would die with their Master, but not prove false to him. But mark the fact. " One of you shall betray me," says Christ, and what follows ? There is no attempt to repel the charge; not a single voice says " No." And there is no looking about one on the other for the traitor. No man suspects his brother; not one of them suspects even Judas; each man suspects himself. As soon as their astonishment and grief would let them, eleven out of these twelve men begin to cry out, " every one of them," and say unto him, " Lord, is it I?" Only one in the whole company is silent, and he the guilty one, the very man who was meditating the crime. He too said the same, but when? afterwards, when he felt himself obliged to say it or draw on himself suspicion.

A beautiful picture, brethren, of Christian humility; and the more beautiful, because exhibited to us in such half humbled, such half sanctified men. Shall I say, we may learn from it that there is no sin so great, or so much opposed to his present feelings and inclinations, but that the Christian may be brought to fear he may fall into it? Every real Christian here knows this. He is well acquainted with the fear of sin, and almost wishes he were better acquainted with it. He can trust his Redeemer's grace to preserve him from every sin, but he cannot trust himself: he knows that there is not a single sin, from which, without this grace, he is for a single moment safe. "I am frail enough and vile enough," he says, " for any thing. Left to myself, I could be a Judas to-morrow." Such a man looks with admiration at these fearful disciples, and says within himself as he looks at them, " Let me be as they are. Lord, make me also self-suspicious, fearful before thee. Let me be ever ready, as they were, to say unto thee, Is it I."

This is not unbelieving, it is holy language, brethren, and language that undoubtedly the Lord Jesus loved to hear from his disciples. He seems to have predicted the treachery of Judas at first in this general way, that he might hear it from them. O that he were hearing it now from every one of us! We are in a situation very like that in which these men were when they uttered it. We are going to sit down, as it were, with our blessed Lord, and to eat of the supper he has provided for us. There were only twelve of them, yet one of them was a traitor. There are many of us. How many traitors there may be among us, we know not. It is a solemn question, but it is one we have not to answer and need not ask. There is another question however which every one who really loves the Lord his Saviour, will surely ask—" Am I in their number? Am I a traitor?" Nay, were that blessed Saviour now to pierce these walls with his voice, and tell us that there is only one such man, only one man within these walls who will betray and dishonour him before he dies, " O, " I would say, " let me be among the first who says within himself when that voice is passed, Lord, is it I?" Most certainly the holiest of us all would be the first to say this; the worst of us all would say it the last.

And, for our comfort, we may regard this also as certain—the most fearful here are among the least likely here to be traitors; the most trembling heart here is the most likely heart here to be honest and sincere before its Lord. The man he will probably delight in the most to-day at his table, is the man who will go there with this feeling the strongest in his soul, " I am a weak, helpless, miserable sinner. Save me, Lord, save me by thy mighty Spirit from ever betraying or dishonouring thee. Thou hast died for this guilty soul of mine; thou hast washed it from sins innumerable in thy blood; thou hast clothed it in its nakedness with the robe of thine own spotless righteousness; thou hast done for it more than my tongue or my heart can tell. O do for it this one thing more—keep all hypocrisy and guile ever out of it; keep all indulged sin ever out of it, especially such sin as may lead me in the end to bring shame on thy gospel and on thee! Let me be the most afflicted, the most sorrowful man that ever went through this world of sorrow to thy kingdom, rather than leave behind me on thy church a blot or a stain."

SERMON II.

THE SWORD OF JEHOVAH SMITING HIS SHEPHERD.

Zechariah xiii. 7.

"Awake, O sword, against my Shepherd, and against the man that is my Fellow, saith the Lord of hosts. Smite the Shepherd, and the sheep shall be scattered, and I will turn mine hand upon the little ones."

We have scriptural authority for applying this passage to the Lord Jesus. Indeed we have his own authority for so doing. In one of his last conversations with his disciples, he applies a part of it to himself. "All ye," he says, "shall be offended because of me this night; for it is written, I will smite the Shepherd, and the sheep shall be scattered abroad."

We must consider, first, the description here given us of him; then, the command of Jehovah concerning him; and then, the consequences which are to follow the execution of this command.

I. In looking at *the terms in which our Lord is here described*, we are struck at once with the natural manner in which they bring together his divine and human nature. He is exhibited to us at the same time in both these natures, and in such a way, as to make us feel that the Person speaking of him is in the habit of contemplating him in both.

And this mode of describing him is of frequent occurrence in the old testament. " Unto us a child is born, unto us a son is given," says Isaiah, but he is a child and a son with these lofty titles on him, " the everlasting Father, the mighty God." He is " a righteous Branch raised unto David," says Jeremiah; but the next moment he calls him " the Lord," Jehovah. Micah tells us that he shall come forth from Bethlehem-Ephratah—he is to have an earthly origin; and then he ascribes to him immediately an eternal existence; his " goings forth have been from of old, from everlasting." It seems as though the Holy Spirit exulted beforehand in that union of the two natures, which was to be accomplished in his person, and wished the ancient church also to foresee and exult in it.

Here he is described in the same two-fold character. He is a man, and yet " the man that is my Fellow," saith the Lord of hosts.

" My Fellow "—the word signifies " My Equal;" and besides that, "My Companion, one near me, an equal by my side." It is expressive of our Lord's divine equality with the Father, and his eternal existence with him. It sets him forth as the sharer in his greatness, and happiness, and counsels, and operations, and purposes; one with him in all he is and does. It intimates exactly what St. John afterwards plainly declared concerning him, " The Word was with God and the Word was God."

But he is man as well as God. Not however originally, naturally man, as he was God. Here is an anticipation of a character he afterwards took on him. He "was made flesh," the scripture says, made man; and this not by putting off his divine nature, but by taking our human nature into union with it; becoming " God and man in one Christ."

And this assumption of our nature was necessary for the work of suffering he had to go through. As God, he is above all suffering, "God blessed for ever." In this character, no sword could reach him. No pang, no sorrow, could ever enter his happy mind. To come within reach of such things as these, he must take on him a creature's nature; and as we were the creatures he was to suffer for, it pleased him to take on him ours. "Forasmuch as the children are partakers of flesh and blood, he also himself likewise took part of the same." And he did this for the express purpose of suffering for us. The Father did not put him in our form, and then determine that he should die for us; he determined that he should die for us, and then he clothed him in our form. "He sent his Son," sent him into our world, made him flesh and blood as we are, "that he might be the propitiation for our sins."

And in this human nature, he is set forth in the text under a third character. He is a Shepherd, and "My Shepherd," says Jehovah.

Here the Lord views him in relation to his church. He is God in himself and man in himself. He would be both were he alone in the universe. But speak of him in this new character, and you bring others immediately upon the scene, and connect him with them.

He is called the Shepherd of his people, because the charge of his people devolves upon him; because he performs towards them a shepherd's part, watching over, providing for, and guiding them. And he is called God's Shepherd, because the flock under his charge is God's flock; a flock committed to him by God, to be rendered back by him to God again. Willingly, joyfully did he take the oversight of it, but he did not put himself into the office; he was appointed to it by his Father; so that when we view him as the Shepherd, "the good Shepherd," "the great Shepherd of the sheep," we have not only his goodness and greatness to rejoice in, we may look higher, if higher we can look; we may regard him as holding a lofty commission from his Father to watch over and care for us; as impelled to act towards us a Shepherd's part, not simply by his own love for us, though surely that were enough, but by the love and obedience he owes to him who appointed him. "I will save my flock," says the Lord by his prophet Ezekiel; and how? "I will set up one Shepherd over them, and he shall feed them, even my servant David," the son of David; "he shall feed them and he shall be their Shepherd." Happy they, brethren, who are fed by him! He leads them often into strange paths, and gives them at times strange food; but there is not one among them who is not thankful to be under his care; not one who would not say, "I must be happy here or happy no where."

II. Let us look now at *the command given by Jehovah* in the text with reference to this glorious Shepherd.

It is couched, you observe, like much of sacred prophecy, in figurative and highly poetic language. The Lord places himself on the throne of a king or the seat of a magistrate, as he utters it. Now they who bear these offices, have often a sword near them as an emblem of their authority, and moreover, if need be, a ready instrument to execute any sentence they may pass on the guilty. Here the Lord describes himself as suddenly addressing the sword near him, and calling on it to smite, not the guilty, but his own high, dear, holy Son, "the man of his right hand;" and this, observe, in the very character he has put upon him, while executing the very office he has given him. " Awake, O sword, against my Shepherd, against the man that is my Fellow, saith the Lord of hosts. Smite the Shepherd." A solemn command, brethren, and solemn indeed are the truths involved in it.

1. We see in it that the sufferings of our Lord were *divinely appointed*, all ordered and foreordained by his Father. The persecuting Jews indeed were willing agents in all they did against him. They did it as voluntarily as ever men did any thing; and they were as guilty in all they did, as though none but themselves had ought to do with it. But what were they? Scripture tells us what they were—instruments to do "whatsoever God's hand and God's counsel had determined before to be done." " That sword is mine,' Jehovah says, " that dreadful sword which is now piercing the heart of my beloved Son. It was I

who awoke it. I gave it its commission to strike. You look on those Jews and tremble as you look on them, and well you may tremble; but I want you to look higher; to see my hand guiding the weapon they are so franticly wielding; to see me overruling their madness, and accomplishing by it my own purposes. I have said, the wrath of man shall praise me, and there it is in its fury praising me in the highest. It is laying a foundation for the loftiest praise I shall ever have. Think not that the hand of man could bring that mighty Sufferer to that cross. No; I have sent him there; he is smitten of me and afflicted."

And our Lord himself seems to have had this truth ever in his mind. In referring to this very prophecy, he alters it, as though unconsciously, making it declare in explicit terms that it was his Father who should smite him; and just before he came to the cross, he calls the bitter cup he was about to drink on it, a cup which his Father had given him.

2. Here too we see that the sufferings of our Lord were *most severe*.

We might infer this from the truth we have just noticed. Man can inflict much misery; it is astonishing how much; but still man's power to afflict is limited. When God therefore calls off our attention from man as the author of our Lord's sufferings, and directs it to himself, we feel at once that our Lord must be a most severe sufferer. He is enduring misery, we see, greater than man ever could inflict, a misery that is the work of a stronger arm.

But the language of the text conveys this idea yet more forcibly. It is a sword, the Lord calls up against his Son; not a rod to scourge or even a rack to torture, but the magistrate's last, most fearful, his fatal weapon—a sword to destroy. And the command given to this sword is not " Wound," but " Smite ;" strike hard; let the blow be mortal.

And mark that word " awake." It seems to imply that up to this hour, the sword of Jehovah had been sleeping; that his justice had never yet been fully called into action; never yet had come forth in its strength or appeared in its greatness. It had cast sinning angels down into hell; for four thousand years it had visited this sinning earth with judgments, turning its paradise into a desert, now raining down fire from heaven upon its cities, and now covering the whole face of it with the waters of the deep; but all this it had done, as it were, slumbering. Now it is to awake, to rise up in its vigour and majesty. An object worthy of it is before it—the man that is Jehovah's Fellow; a man who can bear a blow, and a man who has taken the sins of guilty millions upon him, almost demanding a blow;—it is to strike in the greatness of its strength. "Awake, awake, O arm of the Lord," cry the Jews in their captivity in Babylon; and they explain what they mean by the word—they want that arm, they say, to "put on its strength," to work wonders of power for their deliverance. So here the Lord calls on his sword to awake, to smite with its full force a blow of wonderful vengeance.

3. And this text represents our Lord's sufferings as *surprising*. Indeed the description it gives us of him, seems given us for the very purpose of exciting our surprise at them. "Awake, O sword," the Lord says—against whom? The very Being whom of all others we should have expected him to shield from every sword; the Being who is the nearest and dearest to him; the man that is his Fellow.

And not only this, twice over he tells us that he is his Shepherd; one whom he has placed over his beloved flock and constituted the great keeper and guardian of it.

And to add to our surprise, the Lord seems to afflict him not reluctantly, but willingly; yea, more than willingly, almost eagerly. "Awake, O sword," he says, as though he were glad of this opportunity of smiting him, in haste to seize it; and determined that it shall not be lost. And why this? Shall we say that he is a vindictive God, taking pleasure in suffering? O no, brethren. This is the old pagan notion. We disclaim it with abhorrence.

And yet we may say, there is no doubt but that the Lord is well pleased in this thing "for his righteousness' sake." He delights in the contemplation and display of all his perfections, and this august display of his justice in the sufferings of his Son, is doubtless pleasurable to his holy mind. But we must trace the eager language he utters here, to another source.

He is pre-eminently a God of love. Love rules within him. It is the spring of all he does and all he says. He speaks even in this awful text under its influence. It is this, which impels him to call so abruptly on his sword to smite. His justice indeed is to give the blow, but it is love that wakes up his justice and bids it strike. So says the scripture ; " Herein is love, not that we loved God, but that he loved us, and sent his Son to be the propitiation," a smitten sacrifice, "for our sins." " He loved us"—us poor, miserable, perishing sinners—there all began; that led him to send down his glorious Fellow from his side, and place him in a mortal form in our world. " He loved us," and because he loved us, he was delighted to find, though at his own cost, a victim to suffer for us; and though that victim was his own dear Son, he "spared him not;" he delivered him up for us ; he was well pleased when he saw him bound to the altar, and stricken and slain. "It pleased the Lord," the prophet says, "to bruise him and put him to grief;" and why did it please him? Because, he immediately intimates, in so doing he made "his soul an offering for sin;" he vindicated by the grief he put him to, the honour of his insulted law, and thus opened a way for the indulgence of his love towards the sinners who had insulted it. Their salvation constitutes what the prophet goes on to call "the pleasure of the Lord," the highest pleasure his happy soul knows; and because of this pleasure, he is said to be pleased with, to take a pleasure in, the sufferings that accomplish this salvation.

We can sometimes rejoice in the cross we bear, when we recollect the advantages we shall get from bearing it; and undoubtedly the Lord himself rejoices as he puts our crosses on us and thinks of the blessings which, through his grace, they will work for us. Just so he rejoiced when he laid that heavy cross on his Son. He calls eagerly and joyfully on his sword to smite, knowing that as it smites, it will not only glorify his justice, but magnify his mercy; opening by one blow his kingdom and presence to banished millions, and placing "salvation in Zion for Israel his glory."

And thus the mystery that hangs over the command before us, is partially cleared away. More of it will go, as we look at—

III. *The consequences which are to follow the execution of this command.* These are two.

1. One of them is exactly that which we might have expected. The Shepherd is to be smitten— he to whose sole care Jehovah has entrusted his flock; and the sheep, frightened by the violence they have seen done to him, and driven hither and thither by their enemies, are to be scattered. And so it happened. This prediction was fulfilled to the very letter. No sooner was the sword actually lifted up to descend on our Lord, than his whole church fell, as it were, to pieces; it was scattered to the winds. "All his disciples," we are told, "forsook him and fled."

And thus the Lord in his wisdom often allows things to take, for a time, what we call their natural course in his church. He seems to forget his own purposes; nay, to undo his own work, to frustrate his own designs; and still more, to place the accomplishment of those designs apparently beyond possibility. He wants his sheep, wandering about our world, sought and saved; gathered together, watched over, and led to his kingdom; but there lies the Shepherd who is to do this, slaughtered, and slaughtered at his command. And where is the flock he had begun to form? It is "scattered because there is no shepherd;" it is wandering again on the mountains with none to "search or seek after it." But this does not last long.

2. The smiting of this Shepherd is to be followed by a signal interposition of Jehovah in behalf of his scattered sheep. "I will turn my hand," he says, "upon the little ones."

"The little ones"—an expression of pity and affection, such as a father might use if he saw his children in alarm and danger. It represents to us the feeble and helpless condition of our Lord's followers at the time of his crucifixion. They are as the young lambs of a flock, shivering before the blast; unable to endure its violence, and knowing not where to look for a shelter from it.

"I will turn my hand upon them," the Lord says. He had just turned his hand against their Shepherd, but that was his strange, his unaccustomed work; and the blow being struck, the sword the next moment drops, and his arm is turned another way for another purpose. The God of love appears again in his accustomed character, as a God of love; is occupied again in his accustomed work. His hand is stretched out with eager haste towards his scattered sheep. It is "upon them," the text says, not helping them at a distance, but reaching them, holding them, and working effectually for them. He becomes a present and "very present help" to them in their "time of trouble." "I have smitten your Shepherd," he says, "but fear not, little flock; you are still safe. I will supply his place. He bequeathed you to me before he suffered; you heard him implore me to keep you through my name when he was gone; and keep you I will. No power in earth or hell shall harm you. You shall want nothing that this strong arm of mine can do or give."

And well was this pledge redeemed. These timid disciples of our Lord were strangely kept together, in spite of their unbelief and fears, after his crucifixion, and sheltered from every danger. And we know what the early church soon became. It was a wonder in the world, itself doing wonders. His hand was indeed upon his little ones, gloriously, visibly upon them; and, blessed be his name! it has been upon them ever since. He has sought "that which was lost, and brought again that which was driven away;" and placing again his recovered sheep under their former Shepherd, he has fed them "in a good pasture, and upon the high mountains of Israel" has their fold been. He has made their condition in this evil world, as safe as though there were not an evil in it, and, one by one, he is filling with them his own heaven.

We have now to look at the practical purposes to which we may turn this text.

It may serve, first, perhaps *to strengthen our faith in the holy scriptures.* And in saying this, I do not allude to the predictions we find in it, which were afterwards so exactly fulfilled. I refer rather to that beautiful harmony of thought and expression, which exists between this verse of the old testament and another passage of the new.

There is an extraordinary blending together here of apparently contradictory things—the manhood of our Lord and his Godhead—his office as a Shepherd, and yet his death while filling this office—the danger of his infant church, and, at the same time, its security. Now turn to the tenth chapter of St. John. It contains precisely these same things, blended together in the same strange way. "The man that is my Fellow," says Jehovah here; "I and my Father are one," says Christ there. "My Shepherd," says Jehovah again; "I am the good Shepherd," answers Christ. "Smite the Shepherd," the Lord says here; "I am the good Shepherd that giveth his life for the sheep," says Christ there. "I will turn my hand upon the little ones," is Jehovah's promise in this place; and what says Christ in that? "My sheep shall never perish. No man shall pluck them out of my Father's hand." "Awake, O sword, against my Shepherd," cries the Father, as though he were impatient to have his Shepherd smitten; "Therefore doth my Father love me," says the smitten Jesus, "because I lay down my life."

Now account for this similarity, brethren. It cannot possibly be artificial or designed. It is not enough on the surface for that. It is a similarity of thought and feeling, which art could not reach. There is only one way of accounting for it—both these scriptures came from the same source; they emanated from the same mind. This Jesus of the new testament, and this Lord of hosts of the old, are one and the same Being. This holy book is true. It is what it professes to be, the word of the living God.

Here too we are taught again *the fearful evil of sin.*

There are moments, Christian brethren, when we can scarcely read this text without an inward shudder—it exhibits the great Jehovah to us in a character so awful, and in an attitude so dismaying. He is represented as an offended Judge, calling for and eager for the sacrifice of his own dear Son. And yet we know that he is the same God who holds himself forth to us as "very pitiful and of tender mercy;" "the Father of mercies;" one who "delighteth in mercy;" the kindest, tenderest of all beings. And such as he thus describes himself to be, we have found him to be. Words could not tell the goodness, the grace, the love, we have received at his hands. What then must that evil be, which can place such a Being before us in such a light as this—a God of love taking the character and speaking the language of a God of wrath!

Some of you, brethren, as you hear this, may turn away and say in your hearts, it is all nothing; but a man in his right mind would not say so with you to gain a world. The evil of sin is a reality; the divine justice is a reality, as much so as the divine mercy; the inflexible, unbending character of God's law is a reality; his determination to punish every breach of it every where throughout his wide universe is a reality. The cross of Jesus Christ proclaims all these things to be most solemn realities. It tells you that you will one day have to do with the God that made you, as a Lawgiver and Judge, as surely as you have to do with him now as a Preserver and Benefactor. O for pity's sake, do not meet him in this character unprepared. Acknowledge him in this character, bend down before him in this character, now. Even as a Lawgiver and a Lawgiver you have offended, he is full of mercy towards you. This very text tells you he is. What would have been more easy to him than to have pointed long ago to this world of sinners, and bidden his sword strike here? One blow of it would have destroyed us all. But he turned that dreadful sword another way. To save this world of sinners, he bid it strike his holy Son. And now he has struck him, he sets him forth to us as a great propitiation for our great sins. We are as free to use him as such, to apply for and obtain a full forgiveness through him, as we are to breathe. But ask yourselves, brethren, and ask it again, and never cease asking it to your dying day, " How shall we escape if we neglect so great salvation ?"

We may see lastly here *the perfect safety of all who are indeed resting for safety on our crucified Lord.*

You, brethren, have nothing to fear from this awful God. In the greatness of him whom he here commands to be smitten for you, you may see the sufficiency, the completeness, and more than that—the grandeur and glory, of the atonement he has made for your sins. The holy impatience the Lord here manifests for the accomplishment of this atonement, may shew you something of the complacency and satisfaction with which he now regards it. It cleanses "from all sin." It has not left on you, if you are indeed the true followers of Jesus Christ, a spot or a stain. While it brings delight unutterable to Jehovah's mind, it brings to your guilty souls a full remission. The throne of judgment indeed still exists. It is " established for ever in the heavens," and in the heavens it will stand for ever firm. But it is become to you a throne of grace. A sword there may be still in the hand of him who sits on it, and a sword he will not bear in vain, but you will never feel it. He is no Judge, or if a Judge, he is a satisfied Judge, he is a Father and Friend, to you; and his hand will be upon you only for good.

But how difficult is it sometimes, brethren, to believe all this! or though we believe it, how difficult to realize it, to feel its truth! Other men will not regard Jehovah's displeasure against sin as real; we are often as unwilling or unable to regard our justification before him as real. But what is the gospel for, what are our sabbaths for, what are our sacraments for, but, among other purposes, for this—to bring the full remission, the sure salvation that is in Christ Jesus, before our minds and bid us rejoice in it? May the God of all grace enable you to rejoice in it to-day! As you look on the emblems of his wounded and bruised, his smitten Son at his table, adore him, stand in awe of him—this text and that table itself plainly call on you to do this—but they say as plainly, Trust him; hope in him; let your spirit rejoice in him as God your Saviour. He was angry with you, but his anger is turned away; it is past and gone. He has sworn that he will not be wroth with you any more. And what says the great "Shepherd and Bishop" of your souls, he who is again by his side and knows his purposes? "Fear not, little flock," he says, "it is my Father's good pleasure to give you the kingdom."

SERMON III.

THE TOKEN OF THE COVENANT.

Genesis ix. 14, 15.

"It shall come to pass, when I bring a cloud over the earth, that the bow shall be seen in the cloud, and I will remember my covenant."

A covenant is a contract or agreement. The word is often applied in scripture to the promises God has given us. And this use of it is a touching instance of God's love and condescension towards us. Men form covenants one with another, because men distrust one another; they feel that they cannot rely on each other's word. "And I," says God, bending to our infirmities, "do not ask you to rely on my bare word—here is my covenant for you. If you will not trust me as a merciful God and a promising God, I call on you to trust me as a God solemnly pledged to you, a God sworn and bound to bless you."

The first transaction of this nature we find mentioned in scripture, is that recorded in the chapter before us—the Lord's covenant with Noah. And in this we may notice, first, the time when it was made; secondly, the covenant itself; and, thirdly, the sign or token of it.

I. *The time when it was made*, was just after the flood, and consequently
1. *A time of desolation.*
If you have ever traversed a country which has been ravaged by a flood, you have witnessed a scene that has made you serious. It may not have struck you much at first, but you have felt at last, that scarcely any scene could be more mournful or depressing. But what does Noah witness as he steps forth from that ark? A ravaged world; ruin every where around him; the traces every where of God's displeasure. And if he says, "I will escape from this to some fairer scene," there is no fairer scene, he knows, to be found on the earth; it is all over a desolation.

And it is in the midst of desolation, brethren, that we have the oftenest had revealed to us a present and a gracious God. We have sought him in the hour of ease and prosperity, in the midst of friends and comforts, and scarcely any glimpses of his reconciled countenance could we get; but when we are looking around us on the ruin perhaps of well nigh all that was dear to us, when we can see nothing to cheer us, nothing for a sinking heart to rest or hope in—it is then often that a voice comes to us from heaven, as it came to Noah, and says, "Here am I; hope in me." The Lord tells us it shall be so. "I will allure her," he says of his church, "and bring her into the wilderness, and speak comfortably unto her," comfortably unto her there in the wilderness, far away, as she supposes, from all comfort; where she expects none to speak to her.

And more especially is this the case, if the holiness or terrors of the Lord have been in any peculiar manner impressed on us. A father runs to the comfort of a frightened child; so our heavenly Father is never so ready to come to our comfort, as when the soul is filled to the full with a trembling fear of him. "The secret of the Lord," David says, "is with them that fear him, and he will shew them his covenant."

2. In confirmation of this, observe again, the Lord made this covenant with Noah, *when Noah was humbling himself as a sinner before him.*

Had we seen this man come out of the ark, what should we have expected from him? Tears of joy, it may be, and then a look upwards, and a burst of thanksgiving. He and his family, we should have said, will be lost for a time to every thing but joy and praise. But mark—the first thing Noah does, is to "build an altar unto the Lord." And for what purpose does he build it? Surely, we may say, he will never slay one of those animals which have been so miraculously preserved, and are now so much needed. But Noah does slay, and not one animal only—" he took," the foregoing chapter says, " of every clean beast and of every clean fowl, and offered burnt-offerings on the altar."

What a sense of sin must there have been in this man's soul, to do such a deed as this in such an hour as this! The judgments of the Lord which he has witnessed, have indeed done their work in him. We can conceive of him as coming forth from the ark with solemn and almost trembling steps; as gathering his sons around him and saying, "True, we are saved, but what are we now we are saved? unworthy even to tread this desolated ground. We are just what those men were, whom we saw swept away before us, miserable sinners; and no joy, no praise, nothing for us, till we have cast ourselves down before our holy, our awful God, and in the way of his own appointment, by bleeding sacrifices, sought his mercy."

This, brethren, is genuine Christian feeling and Christian conduct also, whether under judgments or under mercies. They both abase the soul; they both lay God's servants down. They both make them feel anew that they are sinners and need a sacrifice. And in this way we get on ground where the Lord has promised to meet his people, and meet to bless them. " I dwell with him," he says, " that is of a contrite and humble spirit," and for this purpose—" to revive the spirit of the humble, and to revive the heart of the contrite ones." And approaching him thus, we put what he calls honour upon him. We honour at once the Lord's holiness and the Lord's mercy—his mercy by venturing to approach him at all as sinners, and his holiness by shewing that we dare not approach him as sinners but through a propitiation. " And them that honour me," says God, " I will honour." He loves to manifest himself more and more to his people, when his people are doing homage to and glorifying his perfections.

II. But what was this covenant that the Lord God entered into with Noah at this time?

It is remarkable that though detailed in this chapter with much minuteness, it relates only to temporal blessings. Not one spiritual promise does it contain. All it stipulates is, that there shall never again be a general flood or famine on the earth. And yet notwithstanding this, it bears in many particulars so close a resemblance to that everlasting covenant established in Christ between Jehovah and his church, that we cannot look at the one without thinking of the other; we see the same God acting in both on the same principles; making in fact the one almost a type or counterpart of the other.

1. *This covenant had God alone as its author.*

There was no negociation, no treating, between him and Noah before it was made. It proceeded at once from God. Indeed God claims it as entirely his own. Thrice in this chapter he calls it "My covenant." He tells us that it is "the covenant which he makes," and "the covenant which he establishes." Even the bow, the appointed token of it, is "My bow," he says; and when it is seen in the cloud, "I," he says again, "have set it there."

And just as determined is he, that we should ascribe to him as its author, the covenant which saves our souls. The condescension he displays in it, is infinite. He stoops from an inconceivable height when he vouchsafes to covenant at all with a sinner; but he does not leave his majesty behind him as he stoops. He brings his sovereignty and greatness down along with him; and he manifests these by writing, as it were, the covenant he offers to our acceptance with his own hand, and fixing in it at once unalterably the terms of our peace. We want to be treated by him almost as equals, to debate with him, to discuss these terms, to modify one and leave out another; but he says, " No, I will not treat with you as equals. I will be most gracious to you, but it shall be the grace of a lofty and sovereign God. There is my covenant, ordered in all things for your benefit, and sure; reject it, if you will; but if you accept it, you must accept it as it is, in all that you deem its offensive, humiliating character, like rebels accepting a monarch's pardon on a monarch's terms." The psalmist has expressed this, and with much strength, in almost one word; " He hath commanded his covenant for ever;" and then he adds, evidently adoring the sovereignty he has acknowledged, " Holy and reverend is his name."

2. *This covenant was a disclosure to Noah of God's secret thoughts and purposes.* The history describes it as such, for it traces it not simply to God, but to the heart and mind of God. "There shall no more be a flood to destroy the earth," said the Lord to Noah; but how came he to say this? He had before said it to himself. The preceding chapter tells us, " The Lord said in his heart, I will not again curse the ground any more."

And the Lord's covenant in Christ with his church had existed, and existed long in his own mind, before he made it known to us. He had thought of it there, and revolved it there, and delighted in it there, ages before. It is called an " everlasting covenant;" and it is so, if we look backward as well as forward—it was in Jehovah's mind from everlasting. The promises it contains, are nothing more than the unfolding of his long cherished purposes. They are the overflowings of his eternal love towards us. His heart has so long been so full with thoughts of good to us, that it can hold them no longer. He cannot stay till he has accomplished them, but he must tell us beforehand of them; as he says by Isaiah, "Before they spring forth, I tell you of them." And that is a striking declaration he makes by another prophet, " I know the thoughts that I think toward you, thoughts of peace and not of evil." "I know them; I am conscious of them; they are thoughts that dwell in my mind, and are pleasant to me there."

And it is comforting to the soul, brethren, and elevating, to connect thus the divine mercies and promises with the divine mind. The Lord encourages us, you perceive, to do so. " Here is my heart open to you," he seems to say to us, " look into it. You see mercy and love in my dealings with you, but there was love and mercy in my heart towards you before you saw it in my dealings, or even in my promises; and there is more love and mercy there; much that you have not yet seen." David understood this. " I am poor and needy," he says, " yet the Lord thinketh upon me;" "thinketh concerning me;" and you and I, brethren, if we are indeed the servants of the Lord, may say the same. We have been for ages and ages in the divine mind; we are in it now. I may be so poor and mean, so forlorn and friendless, that not a human being may vouchsafe me a thought; but I can look upwards above all human beings, and recollect that I have a place there, in the mind of the great Lord of all. He is thinking of me, and thinking of me for good. What he is saying of me in his heart, I know not; but I know this, that he is saying something of me there, something kind, something pleasant, something blessed, something that would make this sad heart of mine burn within me, did I know it." But another remark—

3. *This covenant with Noah was connected with a sacrifice;* it was indeed founded on one.

We have seen Noah coming forward as a sinner before God with a sacrifice; and we have already traced the peculiar mercy shewn to him at this time, to this sacrifice. The Lord, in consequence of it, spake to him words of comfort from heaven, and revealed to him his purposes. But this history goes farther, and traces these purposes themselves to Noah's offerings. "He builded," we read, "an altar unto the Lord, and took of every clean beast and of every clean fowl, and offered burnt-offerings on the altar;" and then it is immediately added, " the Lord smelled a sweet savour, and the Lord said in his heart, I will not again curse the ground any more." Not that this gracious resolution arose then for the first time in his heart; but he speaks of it as arising then, that we may connect it with this sweet savour and these offerings; that we may associate it with them in our hearts, and not it only, but the covenant which sprang out of it. And why this? We well know why. These offerings had a reference in Jehovah's mind, if not in Noah's, to that one great sacrifice for sin, which he has made the foundation of his covenant of grace. They recognize and declare the same truths—man's guilt; the sacred character of God's law, requiring of man some atonement for his guilt; the necessity man is under of looking out of himself for this atonement; the willingness of God to accept for guilty man an atoning substitute. We accordingly find the Holy Spirit applying the very same language to the sacrifice of the Lord Jesus, that he applies here to these sacrifices. "The Lord smelled a sweet savour," he says here of Noah's offerings, and in the epistle to the Ephesians, "Christ hath loved us," he says, "and hath given himself for us, an offering and a sacrifice to God for a sweet-smelling savour."

And here comes out again that blessed truth we discover almost every where—all the mercies which flow from God to us sinners, flow to us through our bleeding Lord. If he has thoughts of peace towards us, they are thoughts which are interwoven in his mind with our Redeemer's cross; and if he makes with us a covenant of peace, it is a covenant sprinkled with that Redeemer's blood. Even our worldly blessings, our every-day mercies, this history says, "seedtime and harvest, and cold and heat, and summer and winter, and day and night"—every thing that makes the earth fruitful, and every thing that makes it pleasant—they are all given to us and all secured to us, because Christ has died for us. If God keeps famine from our doors, if he covers the earth year after year with smiling plenty, if he restrains the swelling sea within its bounds, so that it " turn not again to cover the earth," I do it, " he says," out of love to you, but it is a love that rests not on any worthiness of yours, but on the offering of my beloved Son once for you all." And as for spiritual and eternal blessings, the blessings of the everlasting covenant, they would never have been ours, they could never have been ours, had not infinite love found in the sacrifice of the holy Jesus a way to make them ours. Think of them as a mountain of blessings—blessings heaped on blessings till they reach the skies;—the Lord Jesus bears up that mountain; he is the foundation it rests on. Or conceive of them as rivers of life and blessedness, flowing through this dry world into an ocean of life and blessedness beyond it;—these rivers all spring from one fountain, the Lord Jesus still. We often wonder that God can heap so much that is good on creatures so sinful. " He bare our sins in his own body on the tree;"—that one sentence explains it all.

III. Let us pass on now to *the appointed token of this covenant.*

And here again we must begin with admiring the divine compassion. Had we been present at this scene and heard the gracious words of Jehovah, these men, we should have said, will never forget them; the time will never come when they will need any thing to remind them of them. But man is a forgetful being; and especially forgetful of God's mercies and promises; and God pitifully remembers man's forgetfulness. " Look at that radiant bow," he says, " which is now spanning the heavens. Let that testify to you and your children of my promises; let that be a memorial of this covenant of mine through all generations." But even this does not satisfy him. With a wonderful condescension, he provides, as it were, for his own forgetfulness, as well as man's; yea, for his own, rather than man's. " That bow," he says, " shall be a token and memorial to myself. It shall never shine, but I will look on it and think of my covenant." Twice over he says this—first, in the text, intimating it, "The bow shall be seen in the cloud, and I will remember my covenant;" and then in the verse following the text, plainly declaring it, "The bow shall be in the cloud, and I will look upon it that I may remember the everlasting covenant."

Is not this, brethren, a stooping down to human infirmity? Here is an infinite God, before whose infinite mind all time with all things in it is every moment present, who could as soon pass out of existence as have one purpose of his pass for one instant out of his thoughts—here is this lofty Being representing himself to us as providing against his own forgetfulness; as so determined to shew perpetual mercy to this sinful earth, that he will set up a sign above it to keep him mindful of his purpose towards it. This is of the same character with his declaration to his church, "Behold, I have graven thee upon the palms of my hands; thy walls are continually before me."

The rainbow had probably existed before. From the first perhaps the holy men of the early world had looked on it with delight and admiration, tracing in its beautiful form and colours a reflection of the beauty and glory of him who made it. Now they were to look on it with new feelings. It was to testify to them of the grace and faithfulness of that glorious Being, and to inspire them with renewed confidence in him.

And of all the objects in nature, it was peculiarly suited for the purpose to which it was now destined. It always appears in a cloudy sky. It comes into sight just when danger to the earth, or seeming danger to it, comes into sight: we generally see it on the face of some lowering cloud. And this ordinary position of it is noticed again and again in the chapter before us. Indeed every time the bow is mentioned, the situation of the bow is mentioned with it. "I do set my bow in the cloud." "It shall come to pass when I bring a cloud over the earth, the bow shall be seen in the cloud." And yet again, "The bow shall be in the cloud." Every dark cloud, as it rises, may be viewed as a threatening to man; it is an intimation to a once deluged world of what God has done and could do again in it. "There," says God, "shall the token of my covenant shine forth. Many of these threatening clouds shall exhibit to the world a pledge of its security. They shall have written on them in the most distinct characters, 'The world is safe.'"

Now what is there resembling this in the Christian covenant? We may turn to the sacrament of the Lord's supper. It is of the same character. It is a memorial to us of our sinfulness and danger, and of the promises God has given us in our crucified Lord of security from that sinfulness and danger. It is too, like the rainbow, a memorial of God's own appointment; and being such, we may safely look on it in the same light in which he holds up this shining bow to us, as a memorial to God himself of his promises. On our part, it is a reminding him of them, a pleading of them before him; and it is like an assuring of us on his part, that he will never forget them. Hence we sometimes call it a seal of God's covenant of grace. Every time it is celebrated among us, it confirms and ratifies anew that covenant, as a seal ratifies the earthly contract to which it is affixed. And hence our church tells us that our Lord " instituted and ordained these holy mysteries as pledges of his love, as well as for a continual remembrance of his death." But we must look higher. St. John speaks of a " rainbow round about the throne" in heaven; and Ezekiel gives us a magnificent description of one he saw there. "Above the firmament there was the likeness of a throne, and the likeness of a man above upon it, and it had brightness round about it." And then he adds, " As the appearance of the bow that is in the cloud in the day of rain, so was the appearance of the brightness round about. This was the appearance of the likeness of the glory of the Lord." With this scripture before us, we need not perhaps hesitate to say that while the Lord's supper is as a rainbow to the church on earth, our bow in the heavens will be the glorified manhood of our Lord.

The bow that shone over Noah, spake of danger passed, of security for ever for sinful man from a merited destruction; and who in the heavens can look on the form that is shining there on the throne of God, and not think of man's passed away danger and man's security? Who there can behold the face of our "King in his beauty," and not feel as he beholds it, How near was I once to destruction, and how far removed am I from it now! Fear we cannot take into heaven with us, but could we take it, one glance at that glorified Son of Man, glorified in the very form in which he died, would drive it from our hearts for ever. And the eternal Father too—how can he look on him and forget his covenant? The mere appearance of Christ in heaven is an everlasting memorial to him of his promises to his church; it is an everlasting appeal to his faithfulness. He needs indeed no such memorial or appeal, but did he need them, there they are for him, and his whole soul rejoices to have them. We can conceive of him as often saying anew to his church as he looks on his Son, "This is as the waters of Noah unto me; for as I have sworn that the waters of Noah should no more go over the earth, so have I sworn that I would not be wroth with thee nor rebuke thee: for the mountains shall depart and the hills be removed, but my kindness shall not depart from thee, neither shall the covenant of my peace be removed."

Happy you, brethren, who have an interest in his covenant; and the design of this scripture is to make you feel your happiness. It brings before us a perfection of Jehovah, which has been the prop and stay, the comfort and joy, of his church in every age of it. It represents him as holding up to us his long tried faithfulness, and bidding us, if we want " strong consolation" amid our sins and sorrows, to seek it there. This is often one of the last of his perfections we feel the power of. A merciful God, a patient God, a God of the kindest and tenderest pity — in all these characters perhaps we have long known him and often rejoiced in him; but here is another character he sustains, as glorious as any of these, and sometimes able to bear up the soul when all these fail it — a faithful God, a God who has given us great, " exceeding great," magnificent promises, and bound himself by a solemn covenant to fulfil them.

Look up to him then, brethren, in this glorious character—a God of truth. Glorious it is. He himself deems it so. He rejoices in it. He has " magnified his word," the psalmist says, " above all his name," and we also must learn to magnify and adore it. Amid the storms of life, we must learn to hope in it. As cloud after cloud comes over us, we must see, if we can, the rainbow that often shines forth on the cloud itself; but if all there be darkness, this we know, there is a rainbow high above round about the throne, and we must think of that. It is ever shining, and ever ensuring to us all that God has promised or we can need—safety in dangers, help in difficulties, comfort in sorrows, supplies in want, "all grace" in this world, and the fulness of joy and glory in another.

But there is one thing we must all remember. The two covenants we have been looking at, much as they resemble each other, have yet this difference—Noah's covenant comprehends all mankind; every man living partakes of its blessings, and without seeking them; we share them as matters of course. The truth is, its blessings are comparatively of little value. God will give them to any one. Even the living creatures around us, "the fowl, and the cattle, and every beast of the earth," enjoy them with us. But not so with God's covenant of grace. Its blessings are unspeakably precious. Even in his sight who has all the treasures of eternity before him, they are precious. He deems them "riches," "unsearchable riches," and he will give them to none but the men he delights in. And who are they? They are the same he calls around him in the fiftieth psalm; "Gather my saints together unto me, those that have made a covenant with me by sacrifice." There these men are, brethren—men who have subscribed to his covenant, accepted it, become parties to it, made a covenant with him. And how have they done this? That word "sacrifice" will shew. It is not by offering to God painful services, and trying penances, and cold, wearisome prayers, and heartless sacraments, and saying within ourselves, "These shall entitle us to his promises." It is by lying down before him in conscious guilt and helplessness, and making the one great sacrifice he himself has provided for us, our all.

SERMON IV.

THE CHRISTIAN WORSHIPPING IN GOD'S TEMPLE.

Psalm v. 7.

"As for me, I will come into thy house in the multitude of thy mercy, and in thy fear will I worship toward thy holy temple."

"God is a spirit," brethren, "and they that worship him, must worship him in spirit;" inwardly rather than outwardly; with the mind and heart. And this is not enough—they must worship him aright with their minds and hearts; with right views of him and right feelings towards him. And what are these? Here is David telling us in this text what they are. "The Lord taketh pleasure," he says elsewhere, "in them that fear him, in those that hope in his mercy;" and here he says as one remembering this and longing to have the Lord take pleasure in him, "I will come into thy house in the multitude of thy mercy, and in thy fear will I worship toward thy holy temple."

We have two qualifications then before us of a right worshipper of Jehovah. The psalmist does not say that these two are all, but they are all he now thinks of. They are the chief; and where these are, all others will be found. They are either included in these, or invariably accompany them. We will consider each of them first apart, and then both of them conjoined.

I. " I will come into thy house in the multitude of thy mercy."

This expression, " the multitude of thy mercy," occurs frequently in the psalms. In most instances however the word " mercy" is used in the plural; " the multitude of thy mercies," David says. Here his meaning is the same. He seems to trace all the multitudinous streams of the divine goodness to one great fountain, and then, as he looks at that fountain overflowing on every side and pouring out its waters in those numberless streams, he calls it a multitudinous fountain; he says, " the multitude of thy mercy." In this, he says, he will come into God's house. He means that he will go there like one who sees himself surrounded with mercies as he goes; passing through a throng of them into God's house, and getting into another throng of them when he has entered it. But we must look more closely into his words.

1. He will go there, he intimates, with *a thankful remembrance of the Lord's great mercies past.*

Our memories, brethren, like every other faculty within us, are depraved; worse than weakened, they are defiled. We remember but too well the things we ought to forget and perhaps would give much to forget, whereas the things we should remember, we let go. And among these are our mercies. When they are first given us, we feel as though we could never forget them. The impression they make on our minds is so deep and pleasurable, that it seems to us impossible for it ever to be effaced; but it is effaced. It goes almost while we are thinking it can never go, and we are absorbed again in present scenes and pursuits. Now to come into God's house as this psalmist resolves to come, is to rise above this infirmity of our nature. It is to come here with a mind looking back into the past, and gratefully retracing the abundant goodness of the Lord towards us in the past. It is to regard ourselves, as we enter these doors, the living monuments of God's mercy, creatures whose every breath has been breathed in mercy, to whom above all other creatures he has shewed " his marvellous lovingkindness." It is to " enter into his gates with thanksgiving, and into his courts with praise ;"

to say within ourselves as we enter them, " Bless the Lord, O my soul, and forget not all his benefits." " What shall I render unto the Lord for all his benefits toward me? I will take the cup of salvation, and call upon the name of the Lord. I will pay my vows unto the Lord now in the presence of all his people, in the courts of the Lord's house."

2. And it is to come here *with a lively sense in our minds of God's great mercy now.*

We talk of his mercy, brethren, but it is often as a child would talk of the wide ocean, who has never seen it. We have no realizing, no soul-affecting perception of it. As for its greatness, an infant has almost as just an idea of the greatness of the sun or stars. Who indeed can measure his mercy? It is like himself, infinite. But what we want is to feel that we cannot measure it, to see that it is vast and infinite. To come here in the multitude of God's mercy is to think largely of his mercy as we come, and to be conscious that we can never think largely enough of it. It is to approach God here as the fountain of all mercy; as one who is as full of mercy as the sun is of light, and whose chief happiness it is to pour abroad the mercy he is so full of. It is to have our hearts penetrated, pierced through, with a sense of his mercy; contemplating it, not as some glorious object at a distance from us, which we are to admire and wonder at, but as something that in Christ Jesus is come near us, stretching itself out to us, taking us within its sphere and influence; a mercy we are to receive, and embrace, and enjoy.

3. And it is to come into God's house *with great expectations from his mercy*.

There is such a thing as believing God merciful, and yet putting ourselves almost out of the pale of his mercy, expecting little or nothing for ourselves from it. Our souls may be so cast down and disquieted within us, that hope may lose for a time all power over us. David seems to have felt this at a distance from God's house; we have felt it perhaps and felt it often within it.

Now to come here in the way this text points out, is to leave behind us all such dejection as this. It is to say, "There is mercy for me in this merciful Being, and I will look up to him for it." It is to regard his house as the place he has appointed to meet his people and bless them, as the place where perhaps he has often met and blessed us, and where it may please him even to-day to meet and bless us again. It is to say, " I am in my Father's house and at my Father's feet, and I will expect him to comfort me there. I wait for thy loving-kindness, O God, in the midst of thy temple." If we cannot leave our burdens behind us, it is to bring them here that we may for a time forget them, or have fresh strength given us to bear them; and to bring our sorrows here, not that we may indulge, foster, and cherish them, but that we may pour them out at the Lord's feet, and, if we can, leave them at his feet—go away without them. The psalmist speaks elsewhere of "hoping in God's mercy;" and it is this hope chiefly which he has in his thoughts now —a looking on this mercy as something which in the midst of our sin and wretchedness we are warranted to hope in, and this, not for supplies of comfort and grace while in God's house only, but all through our future days, regarding it as mercy that will surely follow us all the days of our life, and beyond the days of our mortal life, going down into the grave with us, and bringing us out of it, and abiding with us for ever.

These three things then, we may say, are included in the first part of the text—a remembrance of God's great mercy past, a lively sense of his great mercy now, and large expectations from his mercy yet to come; in other words, thankfulness, confidence, and more especially hope. These, the psalmist says, he will take into God's house with him. They are pleasant companions there, brethren, and pleasant companions any where. But he will not take these alone, he says. Here is another thing in the text, which he will take with them.

II. " In thy fear will I worship toward thy holy temple."

If there is any one thing concerning which we and the scriptures are at variance, it is this, the fear of God. Fear, as we generally experience it, is a humiliating and painful feeling. We suffer under it and are ashamed of it. And because of this, we cannot disconnect the ideas of pain and humiliation from it. As for its having any place in real godliness, it must be, we conceive, if at all, quite in the first stage of it, and must be regarded then as the infirmity and alloy, rather than any essential part, of it. But fear is not necessarily a painful thing. It may be so blended with other feelings and so modified by them, as to become a pleasurable thing, elevating the mind, or if not so, accompanying the mind upwards when other things elevate it, and heightening its sensations of admiration and delight. Who for instance has been among majestic mountains, or in any of the grander scenes of nature, and not been conscious there of a feeling akin to fear rising up within him, and a feeling he would not part with? And if we turn to the scriptures, they speak oftener of a holy fear of God, than of any other grace whatsoever. They call real godliness by this name oftener than by any other. They represent it as forming the sum and substance of real godliness. And we must not say that the scriptures do not

F

mean fear though they use the word; they were not written to deceive us; they do mean fear, or they would not use the word.

"But we have scriptural authority," some of you may say, "for putting fear aside. Perfect love, scripture itself assures us, casts it out." There are few things, brethren, more dangerous than placing one declaration of God's holy word against the general testimony of the whole. To say nothing of other evils attending it, we are sure to misapply and misinterpret the passages we rest on. Perfect love, it is true, does cast out fear, but what fear? The fear which has torment—no other. A servile fear of condemnation and punishment, terrifying the soul—love wars with this and in the end annihilates it; but it fosters, and fosters more and more, that filial fear of offending, which awes and restrains the soul, and while it restrains, delights it. When therefore we read in this text, "I will worship in thy fear," we must not set about explaining away the words; we must endeavour rather to open our minds to them and receive them in their full meaning.

The fear David means here, is that feeling which naturally arises in the human mind from the contemplation of any object immensely superior to ourselves. It is a fear of the same kind, as that which the works of God in nature sometimes inspire, though far deeper in its character and course holier. It flows from a lively perception of his greatness, majesty, and holiness, just as hope flows fron a perception of his mercifulness. It is made up of admiration, and awe, and reverence. It leads to a dread of offending God, and a readiness to bow down to and submit to him. It makes a man feel that it is the greatest honour that can be put upon him, to be permitted to hold communion with this great Being, and the greatest shame as well as loss he can sustain, to be cut off from him. Did it exist alone in the soul, it would alarm, distract, and overwhelm it; but, in the godly soul, it is mixed up with other feelings, and serves only to sober, regulate, humble, and exalt it. And here lies the main difference between what we call servile and filial fear—the one reigns alone in the mind; it is a slave's fear of a master he can neither revere nor love: but the other has reverence and love always associated with it; they share the throne of the mind with it; it is a son's fear of a father he delights in, and honours as well as delights in—a father who loves his children well, but makes them feel that he loves truth and righteousness better than any child in the world.

In this fear, the psalmist says, he will come into God's house, or rather "worship toward his holy temple"—a phrase taken from a custom among the Jews of always turning towards the temple or tabernacle when they prayed. By worshipping in this fear, he means calling this fear into exercise and giving himself up to its influence as he worships; coming before God with this fear in his mind, and cherishing it in his mind; standing in a holy awe and reverence of God, as he worships before him.

We know, brethren, how some men enter God's house—they have no more consciousness of coming into his presence here, than they have when entering their own doors. As for fearing him, they have scarcely known perhaps once in their whole lives what the sensation is; they have not even a distinct notion of it. But to come in God's fear into God's house, is to understand this feeling as well as you understand the feeling of heat or cold, or joy or sorrow. It is to be conscious of fearing God, and to take pleasure in fearing him; never to be happier here, than when, mindful of his presence here, the fear of him comes over you; and never to be more pained, than when carelessness, dulness, or stupidity of soul keeps this fear away.

How deeply David felt this fear, his own words shew. "My flesh trembleth for fear of thee," he says in one psalm; and he did not regard this as an infirmity to be got rid of—he thought it right. "Thou, even thou," he says in another psalm, "art to be feared." " Let all that be round about him, bring presents unto him that ought to be feared." And again, " God is greatly to be feared"—where? in the thunder and in the storm? in the midst of his enemies whom he is striking down with the rod of his wrath? No; "God is greatly to be feared in the assembly of the saints, and to be had in reverence of all them that are about him." St. Paul calls upon us to cultivate this fear. He traces it to the grace of God, and tells us that it renders our service acceptable unto him. "Let us have grace," he says, "whereby we may serve God acceptably with reverence and godly fear." And look up into heaven, brethren. If there is any place in the universe where God is feared, it is there. You may think of it as a world of joy and a world of love, and so it is; but those veiled faces, those cast down crowns, those prostrate angels, that solemn silence reigning at intervals through all those countless hosts before the throne of God—what do they shew? They make us feel that if there is fear any where, there is fear here—here in this world of light, and love, and security, and joy. And listen to the songs of heaven. One moment, mercy is their theme, redeeming mercy; the next, "Fear God and give glory to him." "Who shall not fear thee, O Lord, and glorify thy name?"

III. We have thus looked at these two things apart; let us now view them, as we proposed, *conjoined.*

1. It is plain from the psalmist's language, that *they may be conjoined.* He does not speak of an impossibility when he speaks of bringing them together into the house of God with him. He had doubtless often brought them together there.

We are apt to imagine a contrariety between these things. It perplexes us to conceive of a mind under the influence of hope and fear at the same time, and a hope and fear settling both on the same object. But this is only one of the many mysteries of practical religion. It is all a mystery to a man, till he gets it into his heart and experiences the power of it. These things, instead of warring one with another in the renewed soul, support and strengthen each other. There is not only harmony, there is a close sympathy, between them. They generally languish together and they flourish together. The reason is, it is a view of God's mercy, that kindles hope and nourishes hope in a sinner's breast, and God never manifests his mercy in any high degree to a sinner, without manifesting to him his holiness and greatness with it. His mercy bears on it the impress of his holiness and greatness. It is the great mercy of a great God, and the holy mercy of a holy God; and the soul that discerns, embraces, and hopes in it, must discern with it his holiness and greatness, and come under their influence; in other words, it must fear before him. Hence it is that these two things, and things like them, are so often joined together in scripture. They go together in fact. They are twin graces, springing up together from the same root—the seed of God's Holy Spirit implanted by God himself in the renewed heart.

2. *And it is good for us to have these two things conjoined.* The psalmist's words clearly imply this also. They intimate that it is not only possible for us to come into God's house with them together in our minds, but most desirable and right for us so to come.

To make this plain, we have only to remember that the union of them qualifies us for the service and worship of God in his house. This worship, let it take what outward form it may, must consist essentially in the exercise of certain inward feelings and affections towards him. And these feelings and affections, to render our worship in any degree acceptable and right, must correspond with God's character, must answer to the representations and discoveries he makes to us of himself. In what character then does he manifest himself to us here in his house? First and above all, as a God of mercy; of large, wonderful mercy. His word that is read to us here, and his gospel that he has commanded to be preached here, are read and preached for the very purpose of declaring and setting forth his mercy, and his mercy in its highest glory and greatness. They proclaim him to be "rich in mercy," and this not to a few favoured individuals only, but to "all that call upon him." They invite the most sinful, they encourage the most guilty and miserable, to call upon him, and assure them that none shall call upon him in vain, that "whosoever shall" really "call upon him, shall be saved." He holds forth his own dear Son to us as one whom he himself has made a propitiation for our sins; and he lets us see that through him, sinners are as welcome at his feet as angels, and more welcome, for in them he can indulge and shew forth his mercy more. If we say that our sin has abounded, he says that his grace much more abounds; and if we tell him of "the multitude of our transgressions," he tells us immediately of "the multitude of his mercies" that far surpasses them.

And while all this is going on, something else is going on. He is revealing to us here his majesty and greatness, his holiness and justice: and he does this by the same gospel that proclaims to us his grace. It represents him in the very grace it proclaims, as the most awful Being in the universe, as well as the most merciful. It may seem at times nothing to us for God to give his only begotten Son, and to send him into the world and to the manger and the cross for our sakes; but if he ever revealed himself as a fearful God to his creatures, it was then. The most tremendous words that ever issued from his holy lips, were those that called on the sword of his justice to awake and smite " the man that is his Fellow."

And it is the same too in that sacrament he has instituted, and in his holy gospel commanded us to continue. It testifies to us, just as his gospel does, of his holiness and justice, as well as of his mercy. There are the bread and the wine, reminding us of the human nature of our Lord, the love which found for us a Saviour and made him incarnate for us; but that bread is to be broken, and that wine to be poured out, and why? To bring before us again that breaking to pieces of our Lord's human nature, that pouring out of his precious blood, which infinite justice demanded of him before he could save us. The table of our Lord is a memorial to us of what scripture calls " the rejoicing of mercy against judgment," of mercy's triumph in Christ over justice; but no thoughtful man can go to it without being reminded of what that triumph cost, without being constrained to do homage to Jehovah's justice as he approaches it.

David felt this also, this awfulness of God as a God of mercy; and he felt it even while perceiving and acknowledging his mercy. " There is forgiveness with thee," he says, but wherefore? That thou mayest be hoped in, rejoiced in, loved? No; " that thou mayest be feared;" as though all the wonderful mercy that Jehovah exercises and manifests in forgiving sin, is manifested for this one purpose only, that the sinners whom he pardons, may be brought to fear him.

It is now easy to see why he uses the language in the text. The hope and fear he desires to take into the house and temple of God with him, correspond with the revelation God makes of himself in his house and temple. They glorify him in those glorious perfections he displays there to be glorified. Is he a merciful God? " I will come to him in the multitude of his mercy," David says. And is he a great and a holy God? " In his fear will I worship before him." The want of either of these feelings in his house would be highly dishonourable to him. By the want of fear, we pour contempt on his greatness; and by the want of confidence and hope, we disparage his mercy, in some way or other contracting, narrowing it, making a small thing of it.

But we are not always in God's house. In his temple above, we shall "no more go out." Once in it, we shall dwell in it for ever. Not so however now. We shall soon leave this earthly temple of the Lord, and most of our future hours must be spent far from it, in a world of danger, trouble, and sorrow. I will not say, it matters little what our feelings are here compared with what they are there; but there is the heat of the battle; there our faithfulness to God and our dependence on him are mainly to be tried; and there we are chiefly to honour him. And the state of our minds there, will depend very much on what they are here. We shall be nearly the same men to-morrow in the world, that we are to-day in this church. And if there is any thing which, under God's blessing, can carry us safe through the dangers that beset us in the world, it is the union of these two graces within us, the same graces that qualify us for the services we are engaged in here.. There are rocks on either side of our course. This hope and this fear will keep the soul from striking on any of them. They will save us from unbelief, despondency, and a cowardly shrinking from duty on the one hand, and, on the other, from that carelessness and presumption which are still more perilous. They will keep the heart in a due medium between an unholy security and a torturing anxiety. They will keep it watchful, and they will keep it peaceful. They will save it from all confidence in the flesh, and they will fill it with an invincible confidence in Christ Jesus its Lord. They will make us afraid to take a single step but as he goes with us; they will enable us to take any step, to go any where and do any thing, that he bids us. And if we look higher, they will prepare us for his house and temple above—to fall down and worship before his throne with adoring angels, and to stand before his throne and sing of his salvation with the triumphant multitude of his redeemed.

Let us all seek then and cultivate these holy feelings; each of us enquiring in which he is most deficient, and all of us longing to have our souls brought more and more under the influence of both. What is that religion worth, brethren, which does not pervade and fill the soul? You are often called on to beware of a merely outward religion, a religion that never touches the heart. Beware too of one that touches only half the heart. That is true religion, the religion that "cometh from above," which extends its dominion over all the mind, calling every one of its powers and feelings into exercise and delightful exercise, making the living God the object to which they all turn, and subduing them all to his will and glory.

SERMON V.

THE CHRISTIAN LONGING TO SEE GOD IN HIS TEMPLE.

PSALM LXIII. 1, 2.

"O God, thou art my God; early will I seek thee. My soul thirsteth for thee, my flesh longeth for thee, in a dry and thirsty land where no water is; to see thy power and thy glory, so as I have seen thee in the sanctuary."

THESE words are filled to overflowing with holy thoughts and feelings. David's heart must indeed have been in a happy state as he wrote them. Happy will it be for us, if through the presence of the eternal Spirit amongst us, they should be the means of bringing our hearts into a state resembling it.

I. Observe in them *what the psalmist calls God.* "O God, thou art my God."

"My God"—what a crowd of thoughts does that expression call up in a pardoned sinner's mind! The God who loved me, and found for me when lost in sin a Saviour; the God who has revealed himself to me and taught me to know him, drawn me out of an evil world and brought me near to him; the God who has heaped mercy upon mercy on me, and given me promise upon promise, entering into covenant with me, pledging all his glorious perfections to me, and bidding me regard him and his perfections as my own, to look up to him as though I had a claim on him, and could when I please make use of him as my own;—all this comes into my mind as I call him "my God;" and more than this—he is the God I have chosen for myself, given myself up to, confided in among all the vicissitudes of my mortal life, walked with, and hope to walk with to the end. "My God"—they are two of the happiest words my tongue can utter. I never expect to utter happier words even in heaven.

But mark when David utters them. It is in affliction. The title of the psalm tells us that it was written "when he was in the wilderness of Judah," driven there probably by the rebellion of Absalom.

When we use this language, it is generally in our prosperity; when all around us is sunshine and within us peace; when God draws near to our souls, and we feel him near. In our lips, it is most frequently the language of feeling and happiness. But in David's lips now, it is the language of faith and confidence. He is an outcast and an exile. God is scourging him, rather than smiling on him, and, it would seem, has been hiding his face from him while scourging him. He has no sensible tokens of his loving-kindness; on the contrary, he has sensible tokens of his displeasure; and yet, with a beautiful faith, he looks through the clouds of his displeasure, and sees him still as his God; his own merciful, loving, faithful God. "O God, the God who hast driven me from my throne into this miserable desert and seemest to have deserted me here, I know thee well, who thou art. Clouds and darkness thou hast wrapped around thee, but thou art the same to me as when in Jerusalem I saw thy glory; thou art mine."

We can tell where to find a counterpart to this. The greatest sufferer the world ever bore, called God his God even when asking, in the anguish of his soul, why he had forsaken him. This is real faith, brethren, real confidence. O that you in every dark hour may possess it and feel the support of it.

II. Observe *how the psalmist says he will act towards the God he calls his.*

And there is always this difference between a true servant of God, and those who only think themselves his servants—they will call God theirs, but they feel and act as though they had nothing to do with him. "Thou art our God," they say, and there they stop. Nothing practical comes out of their supposed connection with him. They are like men who tell us that a mine of gold is theirs, and yet go starving through the world, begging for alms. But his true servants cannot leave the matter thus. If he is our God, they say, something must come out of it. His being ours must affect our hearts and influence our conduct. We cannot possess such a treasure and never turn to it, never take from it; always feel and act as though we possessed it not. "Thou art my God," says David; "early will I seek thee."

But why seek him? we may ask. Had he not long ago sought and found him? He most certainly had done so; but when we speak of seeking God, we speak not of something that is to be done once only and then is over; it can never be over. It is not like a man seeking a petty cistern or even a fountain; it is like a man seeking an ocean, and not this or that shore of it, but the whole ocean itself; longing to take in the whole, to traverse, and see, and know it in all its boundless extent. And even this is not going far enough. The ocean and the whole earth with it might be explored; we can even conceive it possible to range through the universe, and leave not a part of it undiscovered or unseen; but God is a Being we can never fully see. None by searching can find him out. Explore and search him for ever, there will be for ever more in him than we have found: we shall still have to seek him, and shall feel as we seek him, that much as we have seen and much as we have enjoyed of him, we have as yet seen and enjoyed nothing. There will still be a fulness of grace and glory in him, we shall seem to ourselves not even to have approached. Hence Moses who had been up with him in the holy mount and had beheld so much of his glory, speaks as though he had never beheld it at all; "I beseech thee, shew me thy glory." And Paul who had embraced Christ and, we should have thought, had received from him all that a sinner on earth could receive, speaks yet of winning him, as if he felt himself still at a distance from him, and had received nothing; had only seen, but never touched him.

But the psalmist says he will seek his God "early." He may have written this psalm in the morning, and then this expression may refer to the morning. God shall have his first thoughts and desires, he says; he will begin the day with him. And language like this is common in the psalms; "My voice shalt thou hear in the morning, O Lord, in the morning will I direct my prayer unto thee." In another psalm, he says that he begins his prayer yet earlier, he anticipates the morning; "I prevented the dawning of the morning, and cried."

But the expression may bear here, and probably was intended to bear, another meaning. David is in affliction; and we know, brethren, where in affliction, if left to themselves, our minds first turn. We seek our friends, and tell them of our troubles, and look to them for help or consolation. Too often, it is not till they have one after another all disappointed, failed, and perhaps wounded us, that we turn in real earnest to our God. "But I," says David, "will turn to him at first. I will not wait for men to disappoint me. He is my God, and early will I seek him. He shall be the first friend to whom I will go in my trouble, not the last."

And then again we are apt to wait in our afflictions for our afflictions to thicken and darken, before we seek help of God under them. "My child is ill," says one, "but it will be time enough to call upon God for him when he is worse." "My affairs are entangled," says another; "I will try to disentangle them, and when I find I cannot, then I will take them to the Lord." "Here is a mournful breach made in my family," says a third, "but I will bear it. It is ready to bow me down with sorrow, but I will sustain it." It is not till the man's heart is half broken with the effort, that he says at last, "Lord, help me. Thou must help me, or I shall sink." Now, brethren, this is not coming up "from the wilderness leaning on our Beloved;" it is an effort to get out of it without him, leaning on our own strength. This is not making use of God as though he were our God and we loved to make use of him; it is like calling in a stranger's aid, and a stranger we would keep from if our necessities did not drive us to him. "But," says David in opposition to all this, "I will turn to my God at once. The first stroke of his rod shall bring me to him." In this sense the word is used in another psalm; "When he slew them, then they sought him, and they returned and enquired early after God."

III. He tells us next *how he will seek God*, or rather how he is even now seeking him—earnestly and most earnestly. "My soul thirsteth for thee," he says, "my flesh longeth for thee."

He speaks of his "soul" as thirsting for God. This is more than if he had simply said, "I thirst for him." It is stronger language. It indicates a desire within him, which he feels to lie very deep within him; no superficial or slight desire, but one which has entered his heart, and filled it, and is working powerfully in it. So Isaiah says, "With my soul have I desired thee; yea, with my spirit within me will I seek thee early."

And then he says, his "flesh" longeth for his God. The desire he feels for him is so great, that his soul, as it were, is not large enough to contain it. It runs over, breaks out of its proper dwelling place, and spreads itself over his bodily frame, making that sympathize with his longing soul, and share in feelings which are not natural to it.

And the apparent confusion of terms here still strengthens his language. His soul, you observe, is described as doing the body's work, and his body as exercising one of the soul's powers. We should have said perhaps, "My soul longeth, my flesh thirsteth;" but David says, "My soul thirsteth, my flesh longeth," and shews us by this intermixture of ideas, how entirely his desire after God had taken possession of him. It had made his soul thirst as the body thirsts; and his flesh long, and long after a spiritual object, as the soul longs.

Is this ideal, brethren? Is there no such thing in existence, as a fervent desire like this for the living God? You do not know who that living God is, nor what a real affection for him is, or you would not think so. A great God cannot be a little loved. Little our love may be and must be for him, measured by his greatness, but not little measured by our capabilities. He requires to be loved with the heart, and all the heart, and soul, and strength; and he must be so loved, or not loved at all. His excellencies are so high and glorious, the mercy he has shewn us in Christ Jesus is so vast, his loving-kindness is so sweet, the happiness and honour of fellowship with him are so transcendant, that if the soul comes at all under their influence, it must come greatly under their influence; and as it grows more acquainted with them, it will have its affections and desires more and more called forth by them; its love and its longing for God will be on the increase, and become, and that soon, the very strongest feelings the soul can know. And all this time, they will often seem to the soul itself weak and poor feelings. Its eye will be on its glorious Lord, and seeing how he ought to be loved and desired, it will stretch itself out so to love and desire him, to meet him with affections proportioned to his excellencies; and failing in this, it will be ready at times to deem all it does feel towards him nothing. Instead of saying with this psalmist, "My soul thirsteth for him, my flesh longeth," it will rather say, "O that my straitened soul could thirst for him! O that I had a heart large enough to love him! Were a fellow-creature the object of the love I bear him, I should call it love; but when I recollect who he is, when I think of his wonderful love to me, and all his infinite, matchless excellencies, I dare not call it so. Lord, teach me to love thee. Give me power to love thee. O enable me really to desire and really to seek thee." And thus the soul often shews, more than the sincerity, the strength and fervour of its affection, by the very complaints that it makes of its want of affection.

IV. We are told also *where David thus seeks and desires God.* It is in a wilderness and a wretched one; " in a dry and thirsty land where no water is."

And this is one of the spots where God has often promised to meet his people, and shew great mercy to them. " He will be to them," he says, " as rivers of water in a dry place." " When the poor and needy seek water," he says again, " and there is none, and their tongue faileth for thirst," he the Lord will hear them, and will open rivers and fountains for them, turning the wilderness into a pool of water and the dry land into springs. David's thirst then is a thirst in the right place. His God has promised to come and refresh him in that dry land, and he is looking out for him there, thirsting and longing for him.

And what are you doing, brethren? There are no parched up wildernesses in our own happy country; but there is many and many a situation in it, which closely resembles them. Some of us perhaps may be at this moment in one of these situations. We could not feel more destitute or more lonely were we in a desert. Nay, the whole world, it may be, seems to us as one vast desert, dry indeed, a "land where no water is" or none for us.

And these are the times when the heart, instead of rising upwards to its God in desire and hope, is often tempted to sink down in wretchedness and despair. Our circumstances are desperate, we say; we have nothing to hope for. But where are you, brethren, while you say this? Exactly where a faithful God has told you, you have much to hope for. You are on the very ground which he has marked out for meeting you, and helping you, and working wonders for you. Your extremity, he says, shall be his opportunity, and now your extremity is come. Need you be told what your feelings ought to be in it? Feelings surely of expectation and desire.

Besides, the Lord may have placed you in that desert for the special purpose of calling up in you such feelings as these. David's thirst for God was not only a thirst where God had promised to meet him, it was a thirst in "a dry and thirsty land," in a land calculated to excite thirst. So in your case. The Lord gave you quiet and abundance, and you half forgot him perhaps in them. You delighted in the cisterns he had filled for you, and he, the source of all your comforts, the great " fountain of living waters," was forsaken. But now these cisterns are empty, broken perhaps before your eyes, or removed far away from you; he has dashed to pieces your quiet and abundance; and wherefore? that your poor earthly soul may no longer cleave to the dust it had stooped to, but shake itself from that dust and rise upwards once again to its God. How did he treat his backsliding Israel? He afflicted them, and in their affliction he "returned to his place," appeared to forsake them; and what did he say of them while he was doing this? " In their affliction they will seek me," and seek me " early." At this very moment he may be saying the same of you. O let him not say it in vain! Let your answer be, " O God, thou art our God; early will we seek thee."

V. The psalmist declares, lastly, *for what purpose he thus earnestly seeks his God.*

And here, familiar as we are with his holy and lofty language, he almost surprises us. He does not long that God may take him out of this miserable wilderness, and restore him to his palace and throne. He does not implore him to turn the heart of his unnatural son and rebellious subjects. No; he seems to say, " Be this, O Lord, as thou wilt have it be. My soul thirsteth, my flesh longeth for something higher. O grant me this—

to see thy power and thy glory, so as I have seen thee in the sanctuary."

Now whether he means that he wishes to see these divine perfections in the wilderness as he had before seen them in the tabernacle, or that he longs to see them in the tabernacle again, his words do not clearly tell us. In either case the tabernacle was in his thoughts, and our object must be to understand what he means by seeing the divine power and glory there.

Power, you all know, cannot, strictly speaking, be seen. We may see its operations and effects, but never itself. Thus a man says, he has just witnessed the power of a storm; he means that he has seen the raging of the sea or some devastation on the land, occasioned by that storm. So when the psalmist speaks of seeing God's power in the sanctuary, he does not refer to any display God had made there of his power itself; nor does he refer, as far as we are aware, to any visible effect or operation of it he had witnessed there. This is his meaning—he had felt God's power there within his own soul, and he longed to feel it again. And the same as to God's glory. Never perhaps with his bodily eyes had he beheld any manifestation of this, but the Lord had revealed to his mind his spiritual glory, the glory of his infinite perfections, and revealed it so clearly and brightly to him, that he felt as though he had seen it. A visible display of Jehovah's visible glory and magnificence could scarcely have affected him more.

But this scarcely harmonizes perhaps with the notions of some of us. We often think that David must have had peculiar and unearthly visions of God afforded him in the tabernacle, as Solomon and Isaiah afterwards had in the temple. He loved it so much and speaks in such high terms of his enjoyment in it, that we are ready to conceive of him in it as in some mysterious place, a place where unseen things became visible to him, and heaven and heavenly glories often burst upon his view. But where is the proof of this? Could we have seen him in that tabernacle, even in some of his most favoured and happy moments there, we should have looked around in vain perhaps for any thing unusual; we should have seen him in an humble structure, worshipping with a multitude of his fellow-sinners just as they worshipped; in a situation in fact very similar to that in which we are now, with even less around him to draw his mind upwards, and less to display to him the divine power and greatness. The simple truth is, he went into that tabernacle thirsting for God's favour and presence, longing to meet his God in it, looking for him in all its sacrifices and ordinances, exercising spiritual discernment as he attended on them and holy and spiritual affections, worshipping God with a spiritual worship; and the result was, he found there the God he sought; the Lord of that tabernacle drew near to his soul and manifested himself to it; he shone forth to him, made him feel as though he saw his face and beheld his glory. The man became as happy, as love, and admiration, and joy, can make a man on this side heaven. No wonder the remembrance of these hours of happiness followed him into the wilderness. No wonder, when his soul thirsts for God there, that he longs to have them renewed.

And is such happiness all gone from the earth? Did it perish with the Jewish tabernacle where David enjoyed it? No, brethren; the power and the glory of God are still seen in many an earthly tabernacle; there is many a happy Christian who will behold them this day, and behold them as really and clearly as David beheld them centuries ago in Jerusalem. We look around our churches and say, where are these things? and where are the men who can discern them? The thousands who fill our churches, see them not, but among those thousands is here and there a heart burning with a secret joy beneath the power of them.

What is that gospel which is preached in our churches, and typified and set forth in our sacraments? It is the clearest revelation of the Godhead earth ever saw. God himself calls it, as though he exulted in it, "his glorious gospel," "the gospel of his glory;" and as he sends it forth, "It is the rod of my power," he says, "the power of God unto salvation." That Saviour too, who is the sum and substance of it, he calls his "power," and exhibits him to us as his "express," exact image, a splendid manifestation of himself, "the brightness of his glory." Now then to understand this gospel aright, is most certainly to see the divine power and glory as David saw them; and to come under the full influence of this gospel, is to have our hearts affected by these lofty things as David's heart was; filled, elevated, and delighted by them.

And O the blessedness this gospel can give! O the wonderful power it does sometimes exercise over man's hard, senseless heart! Which have been the happiest moments some of you have ever known? the moments to which you look back with the fondest remembrance, and long the most to live over again? You could tell us. They have been moments you have spent in God's happy sanctuary, moments in which he has revealed to you there his grace and goodness, his power and glory, in Christ Jesus, and enabled you to say, This gracious, this powerful, this magnificent God is my own.

And how is this happiness to be again attained and enjoyed? We must again long to enjoy it. The same mighty Spirit that kindled years ago a holy thirsting after God in our minds, must revive it in our minds, must kindle it anew. We must come up to God's house as though it really were his house, " the place where his honour dwelleth." We must look for him here, seek him here, and never go away contented unless we have found him here. What are prayers, the best that were ever offered; and sermons, the best that were ever preached; and sacraments, without him? They satisfy the man who has no longing after God within him; they are all he cares for; he rests in them; his poor earthly soul has no conception of any thing higher; but so many stones would as soon satisfy a hungry man, or so many empty vessels satisfy a thirsty man, as these things, if God is away, satisfy a hungry and thirsty soul. Our desires must rise above these things. While our prayers ascend, we must long for him to whom they ascend, to shine forth. While we listen to his word, we must pray that it may come to us not in word only, but " in demonstration of the Spirit and in power." While we kneel at his table, we must look for him to come among us at his table, and make himself known to us in breaking of bread. There must be the early seeking and the earnest thirsting, before there can be the happy seeing and enjoying.

And what says this psalm? Here is David

thirsting for his God, and evidently, while thirsting, finding him. We can see as we read it, that his God has met him in that dry land, and opened for him, almost before he is aware, the promised rivers and fountains there. He looked for him perhaps to bring him again to his holy mountain and make him joyful in his house of prayer, but he has made him joyful and exceedingly joyful in that wilderness. The psalm is one of the happiest this book contains. And it tells you, brethren, that you too may be happy. Seek the God that is your God, early, it says, and he will soon be with you. Let your soul thirst for him, and he will abundantly satisfy it. Long for a sight of his power and glory in his sanctuary, and in his sanctuary you shall have it. You shall feel again that " his loving-kindness is better than life," and with joyful lips your mouth shall praise him. As you sit here, you shall feel that you could abide here in his tabernacle for ever; and when you go away, you shall go away with this thought burning within your inmost souls, we shall soon be in his temple above, where we shall indeed see his face and behold his glory.

SERMON VI.

THE RISEN JESUS APPEARING TO HIS DISCIPLES.

St. John xx. 19, 20.

"Then the same day at evening, being the first day of the week, when the doors were shut where the disciples were assembled for fear of the Jews, came Jesus and stood in the midst, and saith unto them, Peace be unto you. And when he had so said, he shewed unto them his hands and his side. Then were the disciples glad when they saw the Lord."

THE forty days our Lord spent on the earth after his resurrection, appear to have been all peaceful. There was no reason why they should be otherwise. He had paid, and paid to the full, his people's ransom on the cross, and his only business on the earth now was to prove to them, not to the world, that he was indeed risen and living. We accordingly find him going no more among the men who had persecuted him, and who would have been ready as ever to persecute him again we see him always among those who loved him, imparting joy to them, and doubtless receiving in some measure joy from them. We have him before us in the text with a whole company of these happy men. St. John speaks of them generally as " the disciples;" St. Luke says, they were "the eleven and others with them."

I. Let us notice *the time when he appeared to them.* It was " the same day at evening," the text tells us; the day of his resurrection, but quite at the close of it. We may say then,

1. *It was not till he had appeared before to others.*

Mary Magdalene had seen him many hours ago; so had the other women; Peter also; and at last the two disciples on their way to Emmaus; but the day was nearly ended, and these, his chosen friends and disciples, had seen him not.

It is painful, brethren, to be thus passed over by the Lord. It is painful to know that he is lifting up the light of his countenance upon others, while we ourselves cannot obtain a glimpse of it. We do not like an earthly friend to visit others and pass us by; much less this great heavenly Friend. But this is sometimes the Christian's portion, and his portion after long and intimate acquaintance with his Saviour. John had lain in his bosom, the other disciples had been for three years his constant companions; but they are a whole day without a sight of him, while almost from the first dawning of that day, one after another had come to them joyful from his presence.

2. And he came too *at a time when they did not expect him.*

"The doors were shut," we read, "where the disciples were assembled." They looked not for him, or, we may be sure, they would have left them open. They seem also to have barred him out, as well as to have given up the hope of seeing him. Yet "the same day at evening came Jesus and stood in the midst;" came, observe, not only unlooked for, but when it seemed impossible he should come, and when they were in fear of other and hostile visitors—"the doors were shut for fear of the Jews."

And often has he surprised his people in a similar way. "There is no sight of him for me," one and another of them has said. "I have waited for him long, but he has not visited me; and I know he will not." The doors of the heart are, as it were, closed in despair against him; we shut ourselves up in sorrow and darkness. But the evening brings him. In the beautiful language of the prophet, "at evening time, it is light.;" the evening time, when light is the last thing to be expected. He surprises us by some unlooked for visitation of his goodness, some really startling manifestation of his favour towards us. We feel ourselves in his presence, and wonder to feel ourselves there, we thought him but an hour before perhaps so far away.

And what does this say to us? It calls upon us to cultivate a waiting spirit, an expecting spirit. We must not think ourselves forgotten, it says, when we are for a time passed by; but recollect that it is only for a time; our turn will come; and till it comes, we must place ourselves in a waiting attitude; we must say with the church of old, " I will wait upon the Lord that hideth his face, and I will look for him."

3. Our Lord appeared to these disciples *at a time when they were talking together of him.*

All we read here is, that they " were assembled" together, but we turn to St. Luke, and he tells us how they were employed. The two disciples had come hastening to them from Emmaus with the news of what they had seen there; but before they could utter a word, the others in their eagerness address them. " The Lord is risen indeed," they cry, " and hath appeared to Simon." Then the two from Emmaus speak; " they told what things were done in the way, and how he was known of them in breaking of bread. And as they thus spake," adds the evangelist, " Jesus himself stood in the midst of them;" " as they thus spake"—not, as they thus prayed together or sought him together, but "as they thus spake" together. What an honour was here put on Christian conversation and Christian communion! Here is a company of men, brought together by their common love for the Lord Jesus, and under the influence of this love making him the one subject of their discourse, and though perhaps they no more thought of seeing him than we think of seeing him now, he works a miracle; he comes through closed and barred up doors and stands among them. And something like this had occurred just before to two of these men. "They talked together," we are told, in their way to Emmaus, "of all those things which had happened" at Jerusalem. "And it came to pass that while they communed together and reasoned, Jesus himself drew near and went with them." They were speaking together of him at the very moment when he came to their side.

And our own experience corresponds with this. When have our hearts been warmed in social converse? When have we left one another with refreshed and cheerful spirits, glad to have seen one another and longing to see one another again? Has it not been when, forgetting a vexing world and its vexing concerns, we have spoken together of our blessed Master? We have thought of him, and he has thought of us and come and made one of us. O how much have we often lost by thinking and talking of other things! "Where two or three are gathered together in my name," he says, "there am I in the midst." His presence with us at such times is only what he has promised; and it is a promise he delights to perform.

II. Let us pass on now to *the salutation our Lord gives these disciples when he comes to them.* "He saith unto them, Peace be unto you."

This was a common salutation among the Jews, but it was not common with our Lord; we never find him using it before. And yet he uses it here twice; and when a week afterwards he appears among these disciples again, he uses it again. He seems after his resurrection to have made it his ordinary salutation. We may regard it therefore as,

1. *An indication of the peace that reigned now within his own soul.*

We are generally most ready to speak of that, of which our hearts are full. With distracted minds, we are not likely to speak of peace, unless it be to deplore our want of it. Our Lord, before his crucifixion, could have known little of peace. To say nothing of his disquieting outward circumstances, there was the cross before him, and the burden of our sins ever upon him. We accordingly find him often speaking, not repiningly, but yet sorrowfully, like one with an oppressed and suffering heart. A little before his death indeed, in his parting address to his disciples, a calm seems to come over him; but it is easy to see that it is no deep, settled calm; it is only the lull that is the preparation for the coming storm. But now the storm is over; it is all finished; our Lord's sufferings and work are done, and there is a quietness in his demeanour, a settled quietness, that bespeaks a heavy load taken off his mind. Peace seems to rule over and fill his soul. Therefore he says, " Peace be unto you." He speaks out of the abundance of his own peaceful heart. " I am quiet now, and I wish you to know it, and be quiet too."

2. And we may regard this salutation as *an assurance of his forgiveness*.

Since these men last parted with him, grievous indeed had their conduct been. He told them they would abandon him when his sufferings began, and though they said they would not, they all did abandon him. They let him go to his cross a deserted man, and one of them openly and angrily disowned him. And after his death, they acted in the same way. Rather than encounter any risque, they suffered others to take him down from his cross, and allowed women and strangers to lay him in his grave. All this they must have remembered, and remembered with compunction and shame; and our Lord, as he comes amongst them, seems to feel that they were remembering it. No allusion does he make to it; not one upbraiding word escapes his lips; but the first thing he does among them, is to set their minds at rest concerning it. The very first sentence he utters is one that, without even glancing at their offence, assures them of his forgiveness. And he does this before they can open their lips; before any one of them can have time to say, " Our injured Master, forgive us." When he appeared to Mary in the garden, he appeared to one who had adhered to him and honoured him to the very utmost. Not one word does he say to Mary of peace. He meets her feelings better by simply uttering her name. But when he appears for the first time to these cowardly, deserting, and conscience-stricken disciples, he says to them and says it at once, " Peace be unto you."

And you understand this, brethren—you who, like these men, have sinned against this Saviour, and, like them, found his forgiveness. You have felt it to be a most free, and ready, and kind forgiveness. You have not had to wring it from him. He was more ready to give, than you to ask it. It was a forgiveness he delighted in giving. " I will arise and go to my father," said the prodigal, but his father would not wait for this. " When he was yet a great way off," his father went to him; yea, " ran" to him; and before he could cry, " I have sinned," was on his neck kissing him. None but a father can tell how a father can forgive; and yet just so the Lord Jesus forgives; and it is his forgiving so, so readily and tenderly and delightedly, that sometimes cuts the pardoned sinner to the heart, melts his very soul within him, and makes him the most contrite and self-abased of all living men. We may know a great deal of remorse and shame, brethren, without knowing any thing of the pardoning love of Christ, but we shall never know much of real contrition, of true godly sorrow, till we do know what this love is, till we have felt its power, till we have learned to hope that it has embraced and pardoned us. " Then thou shalt remember thy ways and be ashamed," says God to Israel, " and never open thy mouth any more because of thy shame"—when? " when I am pacified toward thee for all that thou hast done."

3. This salutation must be regarded also as *an intimation of our Lord's power to communicate the peace it speaks of*.

Observe the action which accompanied it; " And when he had so said, he shewed unto them his hands and his side." St. John does not tell us why he did this, but St. Luke gives us one reason for it—it was to convince them that he was indeed their Lord, their lately crucified but now risen Lord. But without straining this scripture, we may say that he himself must have looked farther than this. Why take this means to convince his poor, wondering disciples? Why so readily and naturally shew to them his wounded hands and side? His own feelings doubtless prompted him to do so. The wounds which he shewed them, were uppermost in his own mind, and he wished them to be uppermost in theirs. They were associated in his mind with the peace he desired for them. He knew that he had made peace for them through the blood of his cross, and when he tells them of peace, he opens his hands, he uncovers his side, and thus silently but most touchingly tells them of his blood. It is as though he had said, "I am not speaking to you of any thing which is not mine to give. Peace for you has cost me this. Look here and see that the chastisement of your peace has been really on me: I have purchased it for you with these wounds. O feel assured then as you look on them, that I have done so, and bear these wounds in your mind. I shall soon take them up with me into heaven. I shall go there as a Lamb that has been slain, with these marks of suffering and death on me. I shall shew this hand and this side to my Father on his throne, and as I shew them, I shall implore, nay, I shall claim, peace for you. I have paid the price of it; here are the proofs; and you shall have it. Peace, peace be unto you." And peace these men had.

III. Look at *the effect of this appearance and this salutation of their Lord on them.* It was more than peace, it was gladness. " Then were the disciples glad, when they saw the Lord."

How often, brethren, one passage of scripture becomes a fulfilment of another, even when not set forth as such, nor apparently intended as such! Here is a fulfilment and a striking fulfilment of one of those promises our dying Lord made to these disciples in his parting address to them. " Ye shall be sorrowful," he said, "sorrowful after I am gone, but your sorrow shall be turned into joy. I will see you again, and your heart shall rejoice." And now look at them. He has seen them again, and where is their sorrow now? It is indeed turned into joy, and a joy of the highest kind. One of them compared it many years after to life from the dead. " Blessed," says Peter, " be the God and Father of our Lord Jesus Christ, which, according to his abundant mercy, hath begotten us again unto a lively hope by the resurrection of Jesus Christ from the dead." And it was a joy that lasted these men through their whole lives. " No man shall take it from you," said Christ in his promise to them, and no man ever did take it from them. It would be too much to say that after this moment, these disciples never had one sad or disquieted hour; but men could not sadden nor disquiet their hours. They rejoiced in the midst of the bitterest afflictions the world could heap on them. If they were thrown into prisons, they sang there; and if they were led to death, they went to it triumphing. They lived and they died rejoicing.

And observe too in what an emphatic manner the evangelist seems to connect their joy with the sight of their Master; "Then were the disciples glad, when they saw the Lord," as though they could not be glad till they had seen him.

You remember Mary Magdalene in the garden. Nothing but the actual sight of him there comforted her. An angel appeared to her and told her he was risen, she saw his empty sepulchre, but it was all nothing to her; she wept on till she saw Christ. And now turn to St. Mark's narrative of what followed. Mary goes from the garden to the disciples, as the Lord had bidden her. When she comes to them, she finds them in just the same state in which she herself had been—absorbed in sorrow; "they mourned and wept." "I can drive that sorrow away," she perhaps said within her joyful heart as she stood among them. "I have that to tell which will soon dry up all these tears. The Lord is risen," she cried, "I have seen him." "Mary Magdalene came and told the disciples that she had seen the Lord." But of what use is it? St. Mark says, "They believed her not." She was no better comforter to them, than angels had been to her. Not one word do we read of their joy till Jesus himself came and stood in the midst of them. "Then were the disciples glad, when they saw the Lord."

Now there is such a thing still as a sight of this risen Saviour. And by this we do not mean any thing visionary or mystical. All that we mean, is such an inward, mental perception of the Lord Jesus, as may well be called, as it is called in scripture, a seeing of him. St. Paul tells the Galatians who could never have beheld his face in the flesh, that "before their eyes Jesus Christ had been evidently set forth, crucified among them." He considers the gospel which he had so faithfully preached in their city, as an exhibition or revelation there of his crucified Lord. To see Christ then is to understand this gospel, to receive the testimony it gives us of Christ and heartily believe it. It is faith giving a reality and a substance to those unseen things of which the gospel speaks; bringing Christ before the mind with a vividness which enables the mind to discern, lay hold of, and grasp him. So Moses is said to have "seen him that is invisible;" and so Paul himself is said to have had Christ "revealed in him."

You know the indistinctness, brethren, with which Christ, and his gospel, and all that concerns him, are looked at by you naturally. They seem far off from you; you find great difficulty in bringing them before your mind at all. Now the faith I am speaking of gives them clearness, distinctness, power. The person of Christ, the love of Christ, the cross of Christ, the resurrection of Christ, the glory of Christ, all are brought near to the soul by it, within reach of the soul, the soul realizes them; it feels their influence, and wonders as it feels it; and then the next moment it wonders that it never felt it before, that it could have been so long within sight of such over-powering realities, and yet never been moved by them, never even seen them. How differently now are the holy scriptures read, and sermons listened to, and sacraments attended! They are mirrors into which the soul looks that it may see its Lord, and is disappointed and grieved if its eyes are holden, that it cannot see him in them. And it looks for him in them chiefly as its crucified Lord; and is never so happy as when he shews it, as it were, in them his hands and his side.

Brethren, have you ever thus seen the Lord? Till you have thus seen him, you will never be happy men; you will never know any thing of real gladness of heart. Your religion, if you have any, will be the same cold, comfortless, powerless thing, it ever has been. It will want that which was the joy and brightness of these men's lives, and which, believe me, is the joy and brightness of many a happy life now. The gospel is said to bring peace to the soul; it takes its name from the glad tidings it proclaims; we profess to believe and embrace it; but how little do we know of peace! how many aching, disquieted, mournful hearts do these walls contain! One may say, "I am sorrowful," and another may say, "I am cast down," but were we to speak out, the greater part of us would say, we are sorrowful and cast down. There is but one remedy for us all. The peace we want and the joy we want, are not to be found where hundreds of us are looking for them, in the pleasures and pursuits of an empty world; no, nor in the empty religion of that world, a religion of form, and ceremony, and pretence: they are in a crucified and risen Saviour, and are to be made ours by a spiritual sight of him; such a perception of him by faith as draws us to him, and constrains us to cast ourselves on him, confide in him, cleave to him, love and serve him. "Then came Jesus and stood in the midst, and saith unto them, Peace be unto you. Then were the disciples glad, when they saw the Lord." O let us pray that he may come and manifest himself thus to us; that by his enlightening Spirit our eyes may be opened, and we too may see him. Shall I say, peace will follow this and gladness follow it? Yes, brethren, a peace that you will feel to be the peace of Christ, and a gladness that you cannot mistake. It is a gladness that comes down from the throne of a happy Saviour, and is nothing less than a portion and an earnest of his joy.

SERMON VII.

CHRIST PROCLAIMING HIS FINISHED WORK.

St. John xix. 30.

" He said, It is finished."

We all feel that any attempt of ours to enter fully into the mind of the Lord Jesus must be vain. It would be like attempting to penetrate with our feeble vision the depths of the sea. But we feel also that it is good for us to look as far as we can look, into his holy mind. It often brings the soul into a happy nearness to him. He himself seems well pleased with our poor efforts to understand him, manifesting himself, and laying himself open to us, surprising us sometimes with the unexpected discoveries he makes to us of himself and his glory.

The text presents him to us at a moment when his thoughts and feelings seem farther than ever out of our reach. It is his dying moment, and we might well shrink from venturing one glance into his mind now; but he himself gives utterance here to some of his feelings, and though he is described as doing this in one short sentence only, yet that sentence is like an invitation to us to look within him; it is a partial disclosure to us of what is passing in his heart. In the original it consists of one word only, and it bears the character of an exclamation. It is more than the statement of a fact; it is the language of emotion; there is our Lord's heart in it; it is expressive of the emotions of his heart in the contemplation of the fact it states.

We may consider it in three points of view— first, as connected with our dying Lord himself only; then, as addressed by him to his Father; and then, as intended by him for us.

I. Looking at it *in connection with himself only*, we may notice,

1. *The wonderful composure* it indicates.

Dying men have often spoken composedly, but this has generally been when they have been dying in what we may call a calm, with no intense bodily suffering to distract them, and all quiet within their souls. But the blessed Jesus is dying here in a storm. His bodily frame is sinking with agony, and as for his soul, none but himself can form an idea of the waves and the billows that are going over it. Yet where are his thoughts? Absorbed in the storm that is overwhelming him? No; he is described in the verses preceding the text, as calmly reviewing the predictions of all his prophets concerning him, and finding one of them yet unfulfilled, providing for the fulfilment of it. David had foretold that in his thirst they should give him vinegar to drink. He says therefore to the men around his cross, " I thirst;" and then, we read, " when he had received the vinegar, he said, It is finished; and he bowed his head and gave up the ghost."

What an honour then is here put on holy scripture! Our Lord, in the unutterable anguish of his dying moments, is not only thinking of it, but will not end that anguish till, as far as in him lies, he has accomplished it all. But how wonderful the self-possession, the calmness of soul, which could enable him to think of it at such a time, and of such a seeming trifle in it!

And this mental composure appears yet more wonderful, when we contrast it with the agitation he manifested only a few hours before in the apprehension of his sufferings. What was he in the garden of Gethsemane? a troubled, affrighted, trembling man; but now, when all that he dreaded is actually come upon him, what is he? As much master of his own mind, as though he had not a pang or a sorrow; as calm and collected, as when sitting, with Mary at his feet, at Bethany, or leaning on his beloved disciple's bosom at his supper.

We sometimes conceive of the Lord Jesus as almost overcome on the cross, as having just strength enough to bear him up under what was laid on him there. He could not perhaps have had more laid on him, but he bore it all as one who could have borne far more. It did not distract, it did not agitate, it seemed scarcely to oppress him. One of the most wonderful things attending his sufferings, is the amazing power of suffering he discovered under them. And where did this power come from? We can hardly call it his own. His human body was as weak as ours, and his human soul perhaps but little stronger. Gethsemane shews us this. His strength came to him from above. It was imparted to him from his Father. It was the strength of omnipotence flowing from the omnipotent Godhead into his feeble manhood. And for what end? We may say, to enable him to bear the weight of misery now laid on him, but we must not stop there. It was for this end also, that his Father might shew forth in him the boundless power of his strengthening grace. At the very moment that he is making him a spectacle of misery to his universe, he is shewing that universe how he can uphold and sustain the soul that trusts in him. His supporting arm is as strong as his afflicting arm, and there is his afflicted, dying Son bearing witness to its strength. He says to us as he points him out to us, not only, "Behold my Shepherd whom my sword hath smitten;" but, "Behold my Servant whom I uphold. I have put my Spirit upon him. He shall not fail nor be discouraged."

And this also must be remembered—the strength he communicated to the Lord Jesus has never been withdrawn from him. He possesses it now, no longer indeed to sustain his own soul, but that he may impart it to us, that we, in our troubles, may sustain ours. He calls it his grace, his strength, and he delights in sending it forth from him to the weak and suffering. It is nothing then, brethren, to believe him able to hold us up under any sufferings we may be enduring. He could hold us up were those sufferings increased a hundred-fold. And this is nothing. He who bore and bore with calmness the misery of the cross, could bear up a whole miserable world would that world but cast itself on him, and even then not feel its weight; even then have power to sustain, and comfort as he sustained, millions and millions more.

2. The language in the text is most certainly the language of *joy* also, and a joy flowing from many sources.

Here is, first, *great suffering over.* The strength given to our Lord on the cross, did not render him insensible of the burden he bore there. This is not the nature of divine grace. It enables the soul to endure suffering, but it adds to, rather than diminishes, its sensibility under it. Our Lord's misery throughout his whole life was as great perhaps, as though he had been the weakest of the sons of men, and at this time it was extreme; no misery ever equalled it. He felt himself bearing singly and alone the wrath of an almighty God against the sins of a whole world. But the moment is at last come when that wrath is exhausted. The travail of his soul, all his earthly anguish, he sees accomplished, and, " Finished," he cries; he utters a shout of joy as he comes to the termination of his destined sorrows. His joy is like that you may have witnessed, brethren, when the long tried Christian has been told on the bed of sickness that the hour of his release is come. It is the natural joy that human nature feels, to escape from pain and sorrow and be at rest.

And here is also *a great evil removed.* Think of the end our Lord's sufferings were to answer. They were to expiate, and expiate once for ever, the transgressions of his people. The blood of beasts had been flowing for ages at Jerusalem to accomplish this. Thousands upon thousands of sacrifices had been offered to effect it. But they had not effected it. All they had done was to proclaim to the world, that the world's great Governor was offended with its transgressions, and still demanded in his awful majesty a nobler victim. When therefore the blessed Jesus sees this end at last accomplished, and accomplished by himself; when he looks up and sees the divine justice satisfied, and more than satisfied, glorified by his blood; when he beholds the sins of his people, which, like some dark cloud, had interposed between them and his Father, all passing away, and that people, so dear to him, for ever safe, we cannot wonder that even in a dying moment joy springs up in him, and a joy that must have utterance. It is like the joy a father feels, whose children are gone into captivity, and who, after years of toil, has just completed and paid down the sum that is to ransom them; or like the joy of another father who has plunged into a raging sea to save his child, and after long buffeting with its tremendous waves, stands again on the shore with that child safe. " Finished " the Redeemer cries. " I have ransomed my chosen; I have saved them that they should not go down to the pit."

And here is *a great work accomplished*. Our Lord had not only to expiate sin for his people, he had to work out for them a complete righteousness; a righteousness which, by an act of grace, is to be imputed to them and accounted as theirs, and in which they are to appear at the last before the bar of God. This is called in scripture a " bringing in" of righteousness, an introducing of it where it was not before. And in order to this, it was necessary for him to obey under the most trying circumstances possible his Father's law, and to make his obedience to it faultless and perfect; as he himself expresses it, "to fulfil all righteousness." Now as we think of the purity of his nature, we are ready to say, this was an easy work to him; but when we think of the weakness of that nature he had taken on him and of the temptations which assailed him in it, we feel that we know not what it was. But whether arduous or easy, the work is at last done. We can imagine him at this moment retracing his whole life, looking through it all to see if a single sin, a single spot or stain, had marred his obedience in it; and then as he discovers none, but sees every where, in every thought, word, and action, an entire, perfect conformity to the divine law, we can imagine him hailing with delight unutterable his finished work; looking on his past obedience, I will not say as a father would look on beautiful robes that he has prepared to put on his ransomed children when they again come home, but rather as his own Father looked on this splendid universe, when, on the completion of it, " he saw every thing in it that he had made, and, behold, it was very good."

3. But we may discover *triumph* also in this exclamation.

We know but little of what passed during his abode on earth, between our Lord and the powers of darkness. It is certain however that in every way in which they could assail him, assail him they did. He " was in all points tempted like as we are," his apostle says; and he " suffered being tempted ;" the temptations he endured were painful to him. On the cross, there is reason to believe they were fiercer than ever, and more painful. We must not dare to think of him as shaken or exhausted there by them, but we may think of him as become at last " weary to bear them."

Picture to yourselves a general maintaining an important post against a numerous and powerful foe. He cannot move to drive away his foe, but there, where he has been stationed, he is obliged to remain and sustain all his reiterated attacks. And these are renewed so often and so fiercely, that they become at last exceedingly trying to him. " I can never be beaten," he says. " My troops will never yield. I am sure of that. But O that this harassing conflict were over! O that the hour were come, when I might put forth my strength, and by one blow crush that enemy."

The hour does come, he strikes the blow; and as he sees his astonished foes fleeing before him, scattered like stubble before the whirlwind's blast, with what a mixture of joy and triumph can we imagine him shouting, " It is over; it is done; I have finished it." There again, brethren, is a picture of the Lord Jesus as he is described in this text. For thirty years he had suffered these polluted spirits to come about him and harass him with their vile assaults; but their time is now over; his warfare with them is accomplished; in another moment he is to give them their death-blow; and anticipating this blow, like a warrior aiming a stroke that he knows will be decisive, " It is ended," he says, and exults in his victory. He knew that by his own death he should destroy " him that had the power of death," Satan and his hosts, and in the moment that he dies, he says, " I have destroyed him; he has got his wound." Hence scripture compares his cross to a victor's chariot, surrounded by captive enemies and laden with their spoils. " Having spoiled principalities and powers," Paul says, " he made a shew of them openly, triumphing over them in it." His meaning is, he not only achieved his victory over Satan on his cross, but proclaimed it there, and proclaimed it with joy and triumph.

Thus far then we have considered our Lord as speaking in this text simply to himself.

II. We may now view him as *addressing his Father in it.* In this light, the exclamation before us takes the character of a faithful servant's language, claiming from a faithful master his well earned recompence.

The blessed Jesus is often spoken of in scripture as his Father's servant. He seemed to take pleasure in speaking so of himself. " I came down from heaven," he says, " not to do mine own will, but the will of him that sent me." And again; " My meat is to do the will of him that sent me, and to finish his work." Now besides the covenant between his Father and his people, there was, from the beginning, another covenant between his Father and himself. Scripture indeed, though it often alludes to this, tells us but little of it, yet enough to let us know that lofty promises were given by Jehovah to his Son, promises of honour and reward to be bestowed on him at the completion of his work on earth. He is represented as entering on his work here in reliance on these promises, resting on them throughout it, and looking forward with desire and hope to the happiness they secured to him. " For the joy that was set before him, he endured the cross, despising the shame." Now then when his appointed work is done, when every prophecy concerning him is accomplished, every sin of his people atoned for, the righteousness of the law fulfilled, the last battle with the powers of evil fought, and the final victory over them won, all the glorious purposes for which he left the heavens, performed, and performed in the highest and most glorious manner, the words, " It is finished," take a new sense from his lips. We see him looking up to his Father as he utters them, with an appeal to his Father's faithfulness and munificence. He speaks, we may say again, as a servant would speak, who has borne the burden and heat of a trying day, and comes at the close of it claiming his reward. His resurrection, his ascension, his heavenly exaltation and joy, the diffusion and triumphs of his gospel, the salvation of his church, the establishment of his universal and everlasting kingdom, all enter his thoughts, and in one word he reminds his Father that they must be his, for he has paid the price of them. The day before he seems to have anticipated this hour, and the feelings we are ascribing to him in it. " I have glorified thee on the earth," he says. " I have finished the work which thou gavest me to do. And now, O Father, glorify thou me." And St. Luke describes him as committing himself when dying into his Father's hands, as though in the full confidence that his Father would raise him up, and glorify him, and give him all his covenanted reward.

Do we degrade the exalted Jesus, brethren, by language of this kind? God forbid. We are speaking of him to-day in his human character, as the suffering Son of man; and language like this dignifies rather than degrades him. It shews his deep humility as man, his willing subjection of his manhood to the Godhead, his jealousy for the divine honour. As man he triumphs, and as man he now reigns in glory, but lest we should imagine that he raised himself to that glory by his power as man, he speaks to us, as it were, from his throne and says, "My Father brought me here. I sit here and reign through the power of the everlasting Godhead. You see in me only the glorified Son of man, but I am more than man and more than angel; I am God over all blessed for ever."

III. But there is a third party concerned in this text, and this third party is *ourselves*.

Had the dying Saviour breathed forth this exclamation in secret, then it might have concerned himself and his Father only; but he spake it aloud; he uttered it in man's hearing; his Holy Spirit has recorded it in his word. We may be sure therefore that he intended it for man; that we ourselves who have it now before us, may regard it as addressed from the cross to us, as much so as though we were now standing at the foot of that cross, and beheld him turning to us as he utters it. And what does it say to us?

1. It speaks to us the language of *joyful congratulation*.

Angels came down from heaven to bid the earth rejoice, when this Saviour began his work on it; he seems to have uttered this cry to congratulate his church again now he has completed it. "Finished" he says, as though he beheld his people all surrounding him, gazing on him in his closing struggle, and anxious for the result. "The work is completed," he tells them; "your salvation is done." And we shall never look on his death aright, or celebrate it in our sacraments aright, or much rejoice in it, till we can see in it an accomplished, a finished salvation. "Has he left nothing then," it may be asked, "for himself to do?" He has left much for himself to do, and, blessed be his name! he is now doing it—he has to prepare his people for the heaven he has purchased for them. "And has he left nothing for us to do?" I answer again Yes, but what is it? Only to seek, accept, hope for, and enjoy, the salvation he has completed; only to give ourselves up to him to be led to that salvation, and to be prepared in any way he pleases for the enjoyment of it. A finished salvation—what we mean by this is, that all is finished and done, which is necessary to procure salvation for us. The blood of Jesus Christ so cleanses from all sin, that there is not a single stain left for our tears to wash out; his sufferings so atone for all sin, that no sufferings of ours are at all needed to atone for it; his righteousness is so complete, that no righteousness, not one good work, of ours is at all necessary for our justification and eternal justification before the living God. " We are accounted righteous before God, only for the merit of our Lord and Saviour Jesus Christ." Look at that sun which he has planted in the heavens above us. In one moment it shone forth in all its lustre. Man has never added one ray to its brightness, and never been vain enough to attempt it. His salvation cost him more, but from the moment he pronounced this word " Finished" over it, it has been as complete as infinite grace and power can make it. It is not a feast half spread, to which we ourselves are to bring and contribute something; it is a feast at which all things have long been ready, and all we starving sinners have to do, is to sit down and partake of its abundant provisions. " By one offering," says the apostle, " he has perfected," and perfected " for ever, all them that are sanctified;" and in the perfection of this offering, he calls upon them in this dying cry to rejoice. He congratulates them upon the completion and perfection of it, and bids them, amid the many misgivings of their hearts, confide in it, and be at peace.

2. And he speaks in it too the language of *nvitation.*

I may be addressing some who feel that they

are sinners, and who are at last, after a whole life of thoughtlessness, anxiously desirous of being saved from their sins. They know that as their Lord died, so must they, and they long, before they die, to find, if they can, pardon and salvation. Now, brethren, there are those who will tell you that the pardon you want, is something lying far away from you, and is only to be attained by painful and long continued efforts of your own, by tears, and penances, and a multitude of rites and ordinances. The heart sickens as we hear the language that begins again to be uttered and approved around us. We feel the dishonour it does to our dying Master, and we mourn over the injury it is doing to our fellow-sinners, deluding to their ruin the young and thoughtless, to whom the evil of sin appears a trifle, and perplexing and mocking the really contrite, who feel sin to be no trifle. In opposition to all such language, let me beseech you to turn to this text, and try to get the sentence it contains fixed and rivetted in your hearts. Short as it is, there is enough in it to guard you from many errors, and to bring to your souls many consolations.

What is your soul's desire? " I want pardon," you say, " the forgiveness of a multitude of sins, that make me shudder as I think of them." " It is finished," this sentence says. " There is a pardon purchased, a pardon ready, a pardon, as it were, written out for you, and all you have to do, is to go to this bleeding, atoning Saviour and say, " Lord, give it me. Do thou who hast purchased it for a world of sinners, make it mine." And do you want a righteousness such as you have never seen on earth, and despair of ever seeing there, a perfect righteousness in which you may stand with humble fearlessness before a holy God ? " It is finished," this dying Saviour says again. "I have wrought it out for you, and there it is. You may have it of me, and have it for the simple asking. It is unto all and upon all them that believe." Or is it the grace of a Holy Spirit, that you want, to teach you, to comfort you, to strengthen you, to sanctify and guide you ? Again the same voice says, "It is finished. I have purchased here for you the fulness of the Spirit, and they that seek it of me, shall find it. All is finished here, that your souls can desire or think of, and your safety lies, not in your own works or doings, but in your believing this, and seeking your all in me." It is not easy for a sinner to bring his proud soul to this; it is not easy for vain man to make the Lord his Saviour every thing and himself nothing; but let him once by God's grace be brought to this, and there is nothing lying between him and immediate pardon. The forgiveness of his multiplied transgressions is within his reach; he has only to put forth the hand of faith and take it. The man who entered these doors with a burden of sin upon him enough to sink him he knew not whither, and with his heart oppressed almost beyond endurance with fear and sorrow beneath this burden—that man may lift up at this very moment an imploring, believing cry to this mighty Saviour, and leave these doors, if not a happy, yet a pardoned man, with not a sin in God's holy book against him, but with a finished salvation his own. And between such a man and the full enjoyment of this finished salvation, there lies but little—at the most, a few short years of trial and conflict. Our Lord seems in this text to speak again to him. "You, like me," he says, " have a work to do. My Father has appointed many things for you also to accomplish and suffer. But think of me. My great work is now ended. I can say of all my Father gave me to do or suffer, I have finished it. There is nothing now before me but recompence, glory, and joy. And if you are like me, intent only on doing and suffering the will of God, what will there soon be before you? Am I the only one in my church, who has ever reached the end of his labour and sorrow? O no. Multitudes of my people are already " come out of their great tribulation," never to see tribulation more. They too have said, " It is finished," and you have only to endure a little longer, and your joyful lips shall say the same. You too shall see yourselves where I am now—at the very end of all pain and anguish, and within a step of everlasting rest and joy."

SERMON VIII.

THE CHRISTIAN TAKING UP HIS CROSS.

St. Mark x. 21.

"Come, take up the cross, and follow me."

EVERY real Christian thinks much of his Lord's cross. He must think much of it, for it is the foundation of his best hopes, the one great source of his richest comforts and joys. But there is another cross, of which he is sometimes apt to lose sight, and that is his own; a cross appointed for himself, and one from which there is no escape. He must take it up and carry it along with him, if he would ever follow his blessed Master to heaven.

This is the cross, of which our Lord speaks in the text. The command he gives in it, was addressed to a Jewish ruler, but there was nothing peculiar in his case to call for it. Our Lord addresses the same command to every one who would really be his disciple. "If any man will come after me," he says, "let him deny himself, and take up his cross daily, and follow me." And it is a touching circumstance, brethren, that even while thinking of his own cross, he so often remembered ours. The thought of his own seems generally to have reminded him of ours. Thus in the passage immediately preceding these very words, "The Son of man," he says, "must suffer many things, and be rejected of the elders, and chief priests, and scribes, and be slain;" and then, instead of indulging in a mournful contemplation of his future sufferings, they appear to pass out of his mind; ours take their place. He turns round to his dear disciples and says to them, "You too must suffer, and so must every one who belongs to me. I call you to suffering. If any man will come after me, let him deny himself and take up his cross."

We have three points to consider—first, the Christian's cross—what it is; then, his taking of it up—what it means; and then, the command our Lord gives him to take it up.

I. *The Christian's cross*—what is it?

It is plainly something painful and humiliating.

The ideas of shame and suffering are at once brought into the mind by the word. No death inflicted by the Romans was so agonizing as crucifixion. Their word "excruciating," expressive of the utmost torture and anguish, was taken from it. And no death was so ignominious. It was inflicted on none but the very lowest class of criminals, slaves and foreigners; the meanest Roman citizen, however guilty, was above it. Hence shame and the cross are joined together by the apostle. Speaking of our Lord, he says, he " endured the cross, despising the shame."

The Christian's cross then is that portion of pain and humiliation, shame and suffering, which the wisdom of God may allot to him in the way to heaven. It does not include simply the sacrifices or losses he must undergo for Christ; it means chiefly the positive afflictions he may be called on to bear for him. The word expresses not so much what he has to lay down, as what he has to take up. This is clear from the text. "What shall I do," said this ruler to Christ, "that I may inherit eternal life?" "Sell whatsoever thou hast," answered Christ, "and give to the poor," and that, we are ready to say, is to be this man's cross; but no, says our Lord, his cross is yet to come. "Then, when thou hast done this, here is something more for thee to do—come, take up the cross, and follow me." "But this was said," you may answer, " in Jewish days." The command is just as binding on us in these Christian days. The world is very little altered, and the will of God concerning his people, is not altered at all. Just as he appointed a cross for his Son at Jerusalem, so has he appointed one for every follower of his Son in England, and we should have it, though England and the whole world were turned almost into a paradise.

It comes on us in different forms. One of us has the world's hatred or contempt to bear; his cross is of the world's making. Another who escapes this, has a cross in his own house, sickness there, or poverty, or worse—an ungodly child, a selfish, unfeeling husband or wife, a hard parent or master, or, it may be, loneliness, the want within his habitation of any relative or friend whatsoever. A third may have a cross in himself; in his body—a weak, suffering frame; or in his mind—a sensitive, unhealthy, self-disquieting spirit; or in his worldly affairs—entanglements, hindrances; or in his station in society—a load of arduous duties which he cannot throw off and knows not how to fulfil. One man's cross may be visible—all around him can see it : another man's may be secret—it may be a thorn rankling in his side, which few know of but himself. And our crosses may be changed. What is my neighbour's to-day may be mine to-morrow, and I may be as free to-morrow from that which is bowing me to the earth to-day, as an eagle in the skies. And our crosses may come on us at different stages of our Christian pilgrimage. This follower of the Lamb may have his laid on him as soon as he sets his foot on the way to heaven, while another may go on long, may arrive almost within sight of heaven, before he is made fully aware that there is a cross ordained for him. Many and many a man has said, " How wonderfully have I escaped the afflictions of God's children !" and has found himself, almost while saying so, plunged suddenly into the lowest depths of sorrow.

II. But we are *to take up our cross.* What is meant by this ?

1. *There are some things it seems to forbid.*

We are not to make crosses for ourselves; not to draw sufferings upon ourselves by our own rashness and folly, as the enthusiast does, and not to inflict sufferings on ourselves, as the devotee and superstitious man does, as the pharisees of old did with their austerities, as many of the poor heathen do now with their self-tortures, and the Roman catholics with their penances. This is to invade God's province. It is to take God's work into our own hands. He will order our afflictions for us. He will lay down crosses enough in our path. All he requires of us, is to take up those he lays down, and just as he lays them down; not to aggravate them, or look about for more.

And as we are not to make crosses for ourselves, so we are not to choose, or wish to choose, what crosses the Lord shall make for us. Every one must take up what Christ calls elsewhere " his own cross," the peculiar cross prepared for him, that which his God has assigned him and put down before him. We often want other men's crosses, just as we want other men's comforts. We are ready to think that almost any afflictions would be better for us, than our own. If we are poor, " Give us sickness," we say, " we could bear that;" and if we are sick, " O for poverty," we cry, " or any trouble, rather than this disabling, withering thing!" The man with a lingering disease, thinks how glad he should be to exchange it for a sharper disorder that would soon be over; while another man, smarting under an acute, violent disease, cries out that he would gladly suffer longer, so that he did not suffer so much. But this is all a delusion. It comes from a wish to get rid of the cross altogether. And were it not so, it would still be wrong. We know not ourselves, nor our own evils or dangers; we must not therefore attempt to judge what kind of discipline we require in order to save us from them. We are like sick men who understand neither the nature of their disease nor the proper remedy for it. We must let the great physician prescribe for us just what he pleases. It would be folly in us to wish to choose our own medicine.

Besides, we shall one day discover that the Lord generally lays on his servants that very cross, from which they would most wish to be exempt. When he strikes, he strikes commonly where the blow will be most felt, in the tenderest part, the part we are most unwilling to have touched or even breathed on. Thus the man of strong affections is wounded in his affections; he sees his children and friends die around him, or they are alienated from him, or become sources of anguish to him; while another man of a colder heart scarcely loses a child or a friend, but his property goes, or his health fails him, or his worldly consequence and reputation are impaired. To say therefore to the Lord, "Any blow but this; change this cross;" would be to ask him to deal otherwise with us than he deals with his servants, or to change his ordinary method, his long established and most wise and gracious method of dealing with them.

And the text forbids too any thing like a stepping out of the way to avoid our cross. A man is frequently brought into such circumstances as tempt him to say, " From how much difficulty, or loss, or suffering, would a very little sin now save me!" And then perhaps, instead of making straight paths for his feet, taking up the cross that lies before him and going fearlessly on in the way of God's commands, he turns a little aside from it, under the idea that he shall thus avoid the impending difficulty or suffering, leave the cross behind him, and getting into the path again a little farther on, go on in it as well as ever. But this is choosing sin rather than affliction, and it never answers. God can meet us with crosses in sinful ways as well as in righteous ways; and he will meet us with them, and with heavier crosses too than we have turned from. Thousands with tears of anguish would tell us this. They would tell us too that though it is easy to get out of God's path, it is not always easy to get into it again. There are quicksands of sin and sorrow on each side of the road, and he who steps aside ever so little, may sink he knows not whither. "As for such," says the psalmist, " that turn aside unto crooked ways, the Lord shall lead them forth with the workers of iniquity"—lead them forth with them to judgment; as severely and visibly punish them. Be prepared, brethren, to have often to choose between sin and suffering in your way to heaven; and be prepared, in Christ's strength, to choose any suffering, the heaviest cross God can lay on you, the most painful and humiliating extremities to which the world can drive you, rather than the least sin.

2. We have thus seen what this taking up of the cross forbids : let us now see *what it enjoins.*

Christ speaks here of our cross just as he often spake of his own. That was appointed and prepared for him by his Father; his Father laid it on him; and yet nothing is more common with him than to speak of it as a cross he had taken up and placed on himself. " I lay down my life," he says, and " lay it down of myself." The truth is, that though it was the everlasting Jehovah who appointed him and sent him to be the great propitiation for our sins, though all his bitter sufferings were ordained for him by his Father, yet he met them, he underwent them, as though the Father had nothing to do with them, as though he had chosen them all for himself. " The Lord," he says, " hath opened mine ear, and I was not rebellious, neither turned away back. I gave my back to the smiters, and my cheeks to them that plucked off the hair; I hid not my face from shame and spitting." " He is brought," says the prophet, " as a lamb to the slaughter," but he might have said more; he was rather like a lamb that of its own free accord leaves the happy fold, and goes itself to the slaughter. He did indeed love us, and did indeed give himself for us.

Now transfer this to ourselves. The Lord has ordained crosses for us. " They are coming on you," says Christ " You must soon bear them, as

I am now going to bear mine. You may tell me that when my Father lays them on you, you will bear them; but I want more than this of you. I want you to take them up, to submit voluntarily to them, as though they were your own choice; nay cheerfully, as though you had rather have them than have them not. I want you to go through this world of suffering, not like men who have a burden on them that they would, if they could, throw off, but like men who rejoice in any burden, in any suffering, so that they may but follow and be with me."

To take up the cross is to welcome tribulation when God sends it, not to shrink from it; to kneel down, like the meek camel, to receive our burden, not, like the resisting ox, to have the yoke forced on us: and then when the burden is on us, it is to carry it quietly, not complainingly; rejoicing that we are counted worthy to bear it, not seeking for opportunities to throw it off.

And we are to carry it patiently. Our Lord calls on us in another place, to take up our cross "daily." Not that every day is to bring us some new cross, but is there an old cross on us? Then every day we are to welcome it again, to take it up again; to bear, to endure it, not to grow weary of it. And if there is no cross on us, then we are to live in the daily expectation of one, to remember that, as Christ's disciples, we are called and appointed to suffering, and to be prepared for suffering. We are to be like seamen who in the calm are expecting the storm; or rather, as one of our old divines says, like " the willing porter standing in the street waiting for his burden."

III. Look now at *the command our Lord gives us to do this.* " Come, take up the cross, and follow me."

We might think at first that he gave this young man this command for the sake of trying him, just as he before commanded him to sell whatsoever he had and give to the poor; but we find him giving the same command on other occasions, and in the plainest, strongest, and most general terms. " If any man will come after me, " let him deny himself, take up his cross daily, and follow me." He speaks in these words as one going somewhere, on his way through this world to some other place, and this place was his own kingdom, his own heaven. " Now," he says, " if you will indeed go where I am going, if you will enter after me the heaven I am on my way to, you must first follow me in the road which leads to it; and you cannot take one step in this road, without being prepared to do as I am doing; you must be ready to stoop down and take up your cross." And he uses elsewhere yet stronger language than this. "Whosoever doth not bear his cross and come after me, cannot be my disciple'—" not my disciple even; not only is heaven out of his reach, but I will not own him as one who is setting out with me in the way to heaven." "He is not worthy of me," he says again. "If he pretends to be one of mine, he does but disparage me; he deals unworthily by me. It is not for my honour to have any one calling himself by my name, who is not prepared to go through suffering, and any suffering, for my sake." And he applies this to every man without exception; "Whosoever doth not bear his cross, cannot be my disciple." "He saith to them all, If any man will come after me, let him deny himself, and take up his cross." Every one must do this. No matter how timid any man may be, shrinking from the cross; or how weak, unable, as he thinks, to bear the cross; or how amiable or even holy, not requiring, as he supposes, any cross; or how favourable his situation and circumstances in the world, living among those who love him and his Saviour too well to lay a cross on him; still he must do it, he must take up his cross. "This is the universal law of my kingdom," he says, "and not a man on the earth can belong to my kingdom on any other terms."

But we must be careful not to fall into a mistake here. There is a notion that suffering can expiate sin, and this notion has prevailed in every age of the world, and in almost every part of it. It existed among the heathen of old, and it exists in fearful power among some of the heathen now. Those cruel Brahminical practices which make us shudder as we hear of them, have their origin in it. It found its way, with other heathen notions, at a very early period into the Christian church. It is now a universal tenet of the church of Rome, and within the last few years, attempts have been made to introduce and inculcate it in our own church. Were I to express my own feelings, I should say a more revolting notion does not exist; but feelings are nothing in such a matter as this. Is the tenet scriptural? Is it to be found in the word of God? I answer, No; it is most unscriptural; there is not the least authority for it in the word of God; and while that blessed book does not sanction it, did ten thousand other books, covered with the dust of ages, assert or vindicate it, I would still say, it is revolting, heathenish, and false.

When therefore we turn to this command of Christ, and call on you in his name to take up your cross daily and bear it, we must tell you that you are not to take it up as something that can expiate your many and perhaps great transgressions. All the suffering you could possibly endure, lengthened out to your dying hour, could not expiate the guilt of the least transgression you have committed And if it could, it would not be needed. The suffering of the great Son of God has already done this work, and completely done it. " He has finished transgression," the scripture says, " and made an end of sin." Almighty God, when, of his tender mercy, he did give his only Son, Jesus Christ, to suffer death upon the cross for our redemption, did not give us one who could only half redeem us. He made on that cross, our church says, " by his one oblation of himself once offered, a full, perfect, and sufficient sacrifice, oblation, and satisfaction, for the sins of the whole world." God, in his wisdom, has made our cross needful, not to atone for sin, but to conform us to him who has atoned for it; not to restore us to his favour, but to bring us into a state of mind to enjoy his favour; not to give us a right to heaven, or to confirm or strengthen our right to it, but to subdue us, and purify us, and make us meet for heaven. The Captain of our salvation was made perfect through sufferings, perfect as the author of that salvation; we are to be made perfect by them as the receivers of it. Our Master's cross has opened the kingdom of heaven for us wide as it can be opened; our own cross is to prepare us to be numbered with his saints there in glory everlasting.

And now, brethren, let me ask, is there a cross on you? or if not, are you looking for one? Are you waiting for one? Are you willing, when God lays one down before you, to take it up and carry it? Questions like these must make us serious. How few, how very few, in any congregation come up to the picture drawn, and drawn by Christ himself, of a real Christian! A self-denying, suffering man; a man bearing a cross, and bearing it voluntarily, submissively, cheerfully, patiently; a Christian like Christ, crucified with him, a partaker of his sufferings, made conformable to his death, and content to be so, yea, anxious to be so—O what a different man to thousands, to millions, of the men who call themselves Christians! Do your consciences tell you that he is different to you? Then ask yourselves how and why this is. May it not be, that to this hour, though born in a Christian land and bearing a Christian name, you may have continued ignorant of the real character of Christianity, and destitute of the thing itself? May it not be, that a life of ease and thoughtlessness, or a life of hurry and distraction, may have deluded you, and gone a great way towards ruining you? May not this be true?—and O if it be, may a merciful God by his Spirit enable you to see it! that you have never followed Christ at all; that you have been going on all your years, with the men around you, in a road altogether different from the road he walked in; that you must stop, and remember yourselves, and get by God's grace into an entirely new path, or else find yourselves at the last, not in the kingdom Christ is gone to, but in one as much unlike it as misery is unlike joy, or the darkness of hell unlike the brightness of heaven?

But there is a cross on some of you. Let me ask you, who put it there? You will answer, " God ;" but could you say that, in the sense of this text, you have taken it up, and, were it to be removed off you, would at God's bidding take it up again? Are you willing bearers of the cross, cheerful and joyful bearers of it? O let us strive, brethren, to rise up to that loftiness of character, to which our Master calls us. We admire him as he suffers. We can see his glory and greatness in his sufferings. " Be like me," he says. " Do not stand still and tremble at the burden my Father lays before you, or lie down in despair beside it; take it up, as I took up my fearful burden, and gloriously bear it. It is heavy, I know, but what is it compared with mine? An atom to a mountain. I heed not its weight. Were it a thousandfold heavier than any burden any child of man ever bore, I could give you strength to carry it. When that cross was prepared for you, grace to prepare you for that cross was given to me, and here it is. I have it waiting for you, and you may have it for the simple asking."

And look forward, brethren. The cross that is on you, cannot take you to heaven, but what will you say when at the last you lay it down at the gate of heaven? " O how much do I owe, under God, to that painful thing! It taught me my own weakness, it brought me acquainted with my Redeemer's all-sufficiency and strength; it weaned me from the poor world I am now leaving, it lifted up my affections to that glorious world I am now entering; it made the sin I once loved, bitter and hateful to me, it made the holiness I once despised, the desire and delight of my heart; it emptied me of self that I might be filled with God. Thankful indeed am I that I am at last coming out of my tribulation, but I am thankful too, and ever shall be so, that I have been in it. I bless my Saviour now for taking my cross off me, but I have blessed him a thousand times, and will bless him a thousand more, that he put it on me."

SERMON IX.

THE HOLINESS OF GOD.

Psalm xxx. 4.

"Sing unto the Lord, O ye saints of his, and give thanks at the remembrance of his holiness."

This sentence, with a slight variation, occurs twice in the book of Psalms. You will find it at the conclusion of the ninety-seventh psalm, as well as here. It may not at first appear so, but it is in reality one of the most elevated sentences holy scripture contains. Here is a sinful creature adoring the Lord, not for his mercy, but for his holiness, and calling on other sinful creatures to do the same. This is a noble spectacle, brethren, a wonderful spectacle. It makes us feel at once that the grace of God in a sinner's heart is indeed a transforming and a lofty thing. May every one of you have it in your heart, and experience its power!

We find in the text two subjects for our consideration—the holiness of God, and the psalmist's call to us to sing unto him and give thanks unto him for it.

I. Holiness, as we generally use the word, signifies purity, a freedom from sin and pollution. But this is never found alone: wherever it exists in any mind, there always exists with it much positive righteousness. By *the holiness of God* therefore we must understand the entire absence from him of all evil, and, together with this, the presence within him of all good. We shall get perhaps the clearest view we can get of this perfection of his nature, by comparing it with the holiness of some of his creatures.

He calls his saints on the earth holy, and they are so in comparison with their fellow-men; but, as they themselves well know, their holiness is imperfect and mixed. There is still much that is unholy within them, indeed far more than there is of any thing else. Some humility, for instance, they may have, but they have more pride; some faith, but more unbelief; some heavenly-mindedness, but more of that mind which " cleaveth to the dust;" some love for God and man, but more love often for hateful self. In God however there is no mixture of this kind. He is *perfectly holy*. His nature is so pure, that it is purity itself, purity without alloy, or spot, or stain. Through every moment of his eternal existence, his mind has been as free from evil as light is from darkness. " God is light," says St. John, " and in him is no darkness at all."

And think of the angels above us. These too he calls holy, and they are really so; in them there is no mixture; but then their holiness is limited. Free they may be from all evil, but the good which is in them, has a measure and a bound. It is doubtless highly exalted in its character, rising above all our conceptions of it, just as their happiness rises above our conceptions; for ages too it may have been continually increasing, and will go on for ever increasing, and that is the glory of it; but its capability of increase shews its imperfection. The holiness of Jehovah, on the contrary, is above all increase. Its glory is, that it is so great, it can never be greater. It is unbounded, infinite holiness. Looking at him among his angels, we must say, he is *pre-eminently, transcendently holy*. As their power is weakness itself compared with his omnipotence, and their knowledge ignorance itself compared with his omniscience, so their highest purity is impurity compared with his holiness. Hence the scripture says, " The heavens are not clean in his sight," and "his angels he charges with folly." And if we turn away from his angels, and look at him far above them, alone in his loftiness, we must say he is *infinitely holy*; no holiness can rise higher than his, or go beyond it.

The creature's holiness again is a derived holiness. It is something that has been given him. He himself was not the author of it. "What hast thou," the apostle asks of his fellow-Christians, "that thou didst not receive?" and we might go into heaven, and ask the same question with the same propriety there. All the holiness which exists in all the universe, is a borrowed holiness. It has its origin in God. From him all holy desires, all good counsels, and all just works, do proceed. Even the holiness of Christ's human nature was not his own. Like his strength, it was imparted to him: his Father gave it him. But God goes no where for his holiness. He is indebted to no one for it. He is *independently holy*. The creature's holiness is at the best but the fulness of a cistern; the water that fills it, has been poured into it: the holiness of God is the fulness of a spring; its source is in himself alone. He gives of the good that is in him, to all who will receive from him; he himself receives from none. Think of a fountain overflowing on all sides, and sending forth its waters incessantly year after year, and age after age; filling cisterns innumerable with them, and lake after lake; fertilizing, adorning, and gladdening regions far away from it, and which but for it must be desolate. Then ask where the waters of this fountain come from, what supplies its abundant, exuberant, and eternal out-pouring; and be told that there is nothing to supply it, it has no hidden ocean or even stream to draw from; all it sends forth comes in some mysterious way from itself, and ever has done so;—then, brethren, you will have a picture, and but a faint one, of that immense, that infinite, that self-existent fulness of holiness, which dwells in the living God.

And beyond this we need not go. God is perfectly holy—that lifts him up far indeed above us; he is transcendently holy—that exalts him above angels; he is infinitely holy—that raises him where our thoughts attempt in vain to follow him; he is independently holy—that gives to his holiness a glorious magnificence. " There is none holy as the Lord," said the adoring Hannah, but hers was an earthly song, she had a distant view only of the holiness she was adoring: what do they say who are within sight of Jehovah, singing at the footstool of his throne? " Thou only art holy." There is none holy but the Lord. All other holiness is a shadow in comparison with thine.

And now arises the practical question, what effect ought this wonderful holiness to have on us?

II. *The psalmist calls upon us to sing unto the*

Lord, and give thanks at the remembrance of it. He does not indeed extend this command to us all. It is a high command to give even to the saints of the Lord. All ought to do what it enjoins, but he addresses it exclusively to these, because these only are at all likely to obey it, and because he feels that these above all others are under the strongest obligations to obey it.

If we look closely into his words, we shall see that they imply,

1. *A happy confidence in the Lord's mercy.*

This is not at once evident in the text, but learned men tell us that the word here translated " saints," signifies literally those who have received mercy. The use of it therefore here is a sufficient proof that David has the divine mercy now in his mind. And if we look at the psalm, we see at once that it was certainly written under a deep sense of mercy. The author of it had just received some signal instance of the Lord's goodness towards him, and it had much affected him, filling him, not only with thankfulness, but with enlarged thoughts of the Lord's goodness, and strengthening his faith in it.

And these are the happy seasons, brethren, in which the Christian's soul most frequently rises up to the feelings this scripture calls for. No man can ever sing unto the Lord for his holiness, or really thank him for it, till he is enabled to take a firm standing on the Lord's mercy. His holiness, looked at alone, is appalling to us. Instead of adoring him on account of it, we almost wish to divest him of it. We can scarcely bear to hear of it: we do all we can to blind our eyes to it and forget it. This proceeds from a latent consciousness within us, that we are sinful creatures, and that being such, all is not right and cannot be right between us and a holy God. But let the soul once discover something of the boundless extent of the divine mercy in Christ Jesus, let it once get a firm hold of that mercy, or rather let it once feel itself resting on it, and feel that mercy itself as a rock underneath it, the soul can then look upwards and contemplate, if not fearlessly, yet without any painful fear, the divine holiness. It can contemplate its God then in any character he may wear, in any of his glorious perfections he may manifest to it. "His mercy is mine," it says, "his great, unchangeable, everlasting mercy; and let him appear before me even as a consuming fire, let him have his way in the whirlwind and in the storm, and let the clouds be the dust of his feet, let him lift up his terrible arm and make nations and worlds tremble at the stroke of it, I can look on him, I can adore him, for I know I am safe." Embraced by this mercy, the man feels in the fiercest storm of the divine indignation, as Noah felt with a deluged world around him in his ark. "Here has the Lord shut me in, and here, come what will, I will fear no evil. The Lord may be dreadful, but the Lord is good, a strong hold in the day of trouble, and my soul shall trust in him."

And this is the reason that some men never shrink from any part of the testimony of scripture concerning God. Their conceptions of the mercy he has revealed to sinners through his dear Son, are so high, and their trust in it so firm, that they feel they have no need to shrink. With this amazing mercy as theirs, they can allow him to be the holy, the just, the sovereign, the awful God his word sometimes represents him.

2. Another feeling contained in the text is *a delightful admiration of God's holiness.*

"Sing unto the Lord, O ye saints of his," the psalmist cries. In the ninety-seventh psalm he says, "Rejoice in the Lord." The remembrance of his holiness is to give birth to joy within us, and a joy that will constrain us to sing aloud with admiration and delight.

And this carries us on, you perceive, a step farther. We have seen that a sinner, trusting in the divine mercy, can bear to contemplate the divine holiness; we have now to see that he ought to delight in contemplating it.

That God himself delights in his own holiness, we are sure. His own language proves it. Of all his attributes, he affixes this the oftenest to his name, speaking once in scripture of his "almighty name," occasionally of his "great name," but more than twenty times of his "holy name." Nearly fifty times he calls himself, as though he gloried in the title, "the Holy One." When too, in condescension to our infirmities, he describes himself as swearing to us, this is the attribute he singles out to rest his oath on. And an expression of St. Paul's places this circumstance in a strong light. "Since he could swear by no greater," he says, "he sware by himself." He goes as high as he can go, he takes the very loftiest object he can take, to swear by, even himself; and when he goes to himself, he takes his holiness, as though he felt that to rise above all his other attributes, to be the summit and glory of them all. "Once," he says, "have I sworn by my holiness, that I will not lie unto David."

And if we turn from God himself, and enquire in what light this attribute is regarded by such of his creatures as can best appreciate excellence, the result is the same. They all fasten their adoring minds on it; they are the loudest in its praise. The redeemed in heaven may sing more of redeeming love, for they have just received the salvation it gives them, its full tide of bliss and joy is just flowing into their happy hearts; but the most frequent song of those who have been the longest in heaven, and are best acquainted perhaps with the glories of him who is reigning there, is not a song of his love or mercy; to him cherubim and seraphim continually do cry, " Holy, holy, holy, Lord God of hosts." What can exalt his holiness more? In that very world where all his perfections shine with the brightest splendour, where the marvellous riches of his grace and love are unfolded as they are unfolded no where else, these rejoicing spirits often pass by his love and grace, and take his holiness for their praise, as though to them it were the most conspicuous and the brightest of all his glories.

Now what David requires of us here, is to look on this perfection of Jehovah, as Jehovah himself and those around him look on it. He wants us to get a perception of its excellency and beauty, and to delight ourselves in the contemplation of it. That which God delights in most, he would have us delight in; and that which angels and archangels high in the heavens are praising, he would have us praise in this our low earthly habitation. And he speaks elsewhere the same language. "The Lord is great in Zion," he says, " and he is high above all the people;" and then he looks upwards to this high God, and says, " Let them praise thy great and terrible name," and why? On account of its majesty and greatness? No; " for it is holy."

And beautifully has our communion service caught this feeling. "With angels and archangels," it says, "and with all the company of heaven, we laud and magnify thy glorious name; evermore praising thee, and saying, Holy, holy, holy, Lord God of hosts;" and then it speaks again of his glory, as though identifying it with his holiness; "Heaven and earth are full of thy glory. Glory be to thee, O Lord most High." And the same feeling is expressed a second time in it. Addressing Christ, it says, "Thou only art holy; thou only art the Lord; thou only, O Christ, with the Holy Ghost, art most high in the glory of God the Father."

Happy they who can understand such language and really join in it! It is a good thing to admire God for his mercy, but it is a higher thing to admire him for his purity. This indeed proves that we are made partakers of his Spirit and his nature; that we have begun to view things as he views them, and to feel as he feels; that our judgment and taste are at last coming into a blessed conformity with his. An admiration of holiness, especially such holiness as the Lord our God's, is not natural to us. If we have it, it has come from above. God himself has given it to us, and, next to himself, he could give us nothing higher. He plainly tells us by it that he is preparing us for the holy world he lives in, and for his own presence and joy in it.

But the psalmist goes farther yet.

3. We may discover in his words *a grateful sense of his obligations to the divine holiness.* " Give thanks," he says, " at the remembrance of it."

And our communion service echoes this language also. " It is very meet, right, and our bounden duty, that we should at all times and in all places give thanks unto thee, O Lord, holy Father." And, in another place, it makes the divine glory, in which this holiness bears so high a part, an express ground of thanksgiving, and of the loftiest thanksgiving; " We praise thee, we bless thee, we worship thee, we glorify thee, we give thanks to thee, for thy great glory, O Lord God, heavenly King."

But how strange a thought—I, a sinful creature, to give thanks to my God for the holiness that seems my enemy, the most opposed of all things in God to me! Admire it I may, and take pleasure in admiring it, but how shall I ever thank him for it? and why should I do so?

The very delight the contemplation of this holiness gives, is one reason why we should thank him at the remembrance of it. Is it nothing to a traveller in a dreary waste, to have one scene of surpassing beauty and magnificence ever within his sight? And in a world like this, where we see so much evil to pain us, and so much infirmity even in the best of men to disappoint and grieve us, is it nothing to have one object of perfect beauty for the mind to rest on? one Being to turn to, in whom we can feel sure, know him long and intimately as we may, we shall never discover imperfection or alloy? find nothing to grieve, but more and more to gratify and delight us?

And this attribute of Jehovah throws a new radiance over all his other attributes. It makes them at once more glorious in themselves, and, at the same time, more suitable, safer objects for our trust and dependence. What would his wisdom be without his holiness? It would be, like the wisdom of an ungodly world, mere policy and craft. What would his power be without it? He might oppress us to-morrow. Or his sovereignty? It would be partiality and caprice; it might be tyranny. Or his love? It would be like a bad man's love, it would be no honour to us, we could never trust it, we might as well be without it. Or his word and promise? There would be nothing to keep him stedfast to it; it might fail us in an hour. An unholy God! Who could adore, who could love, who could confide in him? If then we owe any thing to Jehovah's wisdom, or power, or sovereignty, or love, or truth, we owe as much to his holiness. This rules over all his perfections, and makes them not only such as we can admire, but such as we can hope in.

The connection too of the divine holiness with our own, must fill a thoughtful man's heart with thankfulness for it.

When we really take the Lord for our God, he makes himself over to us; that is, he gives us an interest in all his perfections, encouraging us to look on them as sources of good to us and of happiness. We may draw, as it were, upon them, and enrich our own empty souls from their glorious fulness. If we are weak, we may look to his omnipotence for strength, and if we feel ourselves ignorant, we may turn to his wisdom for knowledge and instruction. Now the desire, the great crowning desire of all the true saints of God, is to be holy, perfectly holy; and in this holiness of Jehovah they can find much to encourage them. They see in it not only the source of all the holiness they have at present attained, but a fountain from which they may draw, and freely draw, the perfect holiness they long for. "Little indeed is there of good in this evil heart of mine," such a man says, "but the little that is there, my God gave me. It is an emanation from his holiness. I must thank him therefore for his holiness. Amid the dark pollutions of my heart, I owe to it all there that is not dark and polluted. And I can look up to it with hope for the future. I see in it an assurance that he will preserve, and in the end perfect, the holiness he has given me. If there is any thing within me that he delights in, it must be this; this work of his own Spirit, this reflection of his own image; and will he ever suffer this work to be brought to nothing, and this image to be obliterated? His holiness and his love both tell me, no. He will complete in me the work his holy heart delights in, he will go on brightening his image there, till at the last the desire of my soul and of his soul too shall be given me—I shall wake up in his perfect likeness; my holy God will present me faultless before the presence of his glory with exceeding joy; I shall stand and stand for ever without fault before his throne. And shall I not give thanks unto him for his holiness? I praise him for the love that gave me a Saviour; O let me praise him too for the holiness which wrought with this love, and so saves as to purify me; a holiness that, while his abounding mercy takes me to heaven, covers me with a robe of righteousness, which makes me meet for heaven; that, while his grace calls me to the marriage-supper of the Lamb, puts on me the wedding-garment which fits me for that supper, beautifying me with salvation, glorifying me with the glory of my God, and giving me a nature that can partake of his joy!"

Before we end, we must all look for a moment at that word "remembrance" in the text. The psalmist, you observe, takes it for granted that all the saints of the Lord have a remembrance of his holiness. If then there are any of us who live in forgetfulness of it, what are we? God's chief glory, we, the professed worshippers of God, I do not say never praise him for, never give thanks unto him for, but never think of, never see! What should we say of that poor Persian who, while worshipping or professing to worship the rising sun, never thinks of its brightness, never sees its brightness, as he worships it? There is a blindness of the mind, brethren, as well as of the body; a blindness of the heart; and you will never worship the living God aright, till you have implored him to enlighten your minds, and to shine into your hearts; to give you there " the light of the knowledge of his glory in the face of Jesus Christ." If you ever really know God, one of the first things you will learn of him, will be, that there is a holiness about him men are naturally as blind to, as a dead man in his grave is to the sun's light.

" But we do remember his holiness," others of you may say, " yet with no delight, no praise, or thanksgiving. On the contrary, it lays us down in conscious vileness before him, it fills our hearts with fear, it makes us shudder at the thought of our own uncleanness;" and the inference you draw is, that you are not the saints of God, and know nothing aright of his holiness. But think of Job, think of Isaiah. They both felt at the sight of the divine holiness as you feel now. They both trembled at it; and there is not a man on the earth nor a man in heaven rejoicing in it this day, who has not often trembled at it. Here is no proof in any thing you feel, that you are not God's servants, or that you are not contemplating aright God's holiness. Here is rather a proof that God has really manifested his holiness to you, and that you are coming under its powerful influence. David is taking here a partial view only of it. He is looking at it in some of its last and highest effects. He is calling on those who know themselves to be the saints of the Lord, who, like himself, are fully assured of the Lord's mercy towards them, to rise above their early trembling and fears, to shew to the world how high a confidence in God's mercy can lift up a sinner's mind and a sinner's praise. What you have to dread is a losing sight of this holiness, a forgetfulness of it; feeling, thinking, and living once again as though it were an ideal thing. And what you want is a closer acquaintance with the Lord's mercy; a more enlarged knowledge of the freeness and abundance of that grace he has revealed to a world of sinners in his gospel; a more simple, full, and stedfast reliance on it. There your rejoicing in his holiness must begin; it must be preceded by a rejoicing in his mercy. Then will you begin to feel that you can sing with angels of his holiness, when you have learnt to sing with redeemed sinners of his redeeming love.

And are there any here, whose feelings at this moment harmonize with the psalmist's language in this text? I will not call on you, brethren, to cherish these feelings. You yourselves well know their sweetness and blessedness. But you do not as yet know all the blessedness which the contemplation of the divine holiness can impart. We see it here at a distance. We see but the reflection and shadow of it. We become acquainted with it only by description, or, at the best, as a man becomes acquainted with the ocean by looking on the rivers and lakes into which its swelling tide sends its waters. And our own vision is imperfect here. We see but little even of that measure of the divine holiness, which is within our sight; and of that little we do not perceive half the glory and excellence. But an hour is coming, when we shall see our "King in his beauty," and see him near, and have powers given us, that will enable us to take in, not all his beauty, but more and more of it continually; our own natures becoming holier, and our perceptions of holiness greater, and our delight in holiness higher; and all this for ever. How joyfully then shall we fall in with the songs of heaven, not only praising in our songs the love that has redeemed us, but adoring in them, with admiring and burning hearts, the holiness that transports us! "Glorious in holiness," are words which even now we can partially understand; but we shall understand them indeed, when with pure hearts we shall behold in heaven a pure God.

O let us think of this blessedness. Let us long for it; and while longing for it, long and follow after that holiness which will prepare us for it. Our highest feelings are good for nothing, if they do not lead us to this. Our admiration of the divine holiness is all delusive, if it is not accompanied with this. There is a transforming power in this holiness. It gradually assimilates to itself all who look on it. "We all," says St. Paul, "with open face beholding as in a glass the glory of the Lord, are changed into the same image from glory to glory, even as by the Spirit of the Lord." "Be ye holy, for I am holy," is the Lord's command to us, and this is one way whereby he enables us to obey it—he reveals to us his holiness, and teaches us to admire, love, and remember it.

SERMON X.

THE FAITHFUL SAYING.

1 Timothy i. 15.

"This is a faithful saying, and worthy of all acceptation, that Christ Jesus came into the world to save sinners, of whom I am chief."

These words are almost as familiar to us, as any holy scripture contains. They are introduced, with a slight omission, into our communion service, and into exactly that part of it where they are most likely to strike and affect us, immediately after we have approached almighty God as sinners and implored his mercy.

We must consider, first, the truth stated in them; next, the description the apostle gives us of it; and then, the view he takes of himself while contemplating it.

I. "Christ Jesus came into the world to save sinners." This is *the truth the apostle states*; and how many sorrowful hearts have these few words of his comforted! Many a bitter tear have they dried, and many a blessed tear also have they caused to flow, tears of abounding thankfulness, and love, and joy.

1. They remind us that *Christ Jesus was somewhere in existence before he was seen here.*

He "came into the world." This is not the ordinary way in which the scripture speaks of any one's birth, but it is the frequent way in which it speaks of our Lord's first appearance on the earth. He himself often uses the expression. "I am come a light into the world." "I came to call sinners to repentance." "The Son of man is come to seek and to save that which was lost." We might think nothing of such language were it used once or twice only, but the frequent and habitual use of it compels us to see that there is more meant by it than a birth; he who employs it, must have in his mind a coming here from some other place. Think of a new planet or star just created in our system and shining forth. We should never say, it is come here; we should say this of a planet or star that had travelled into our system from some distant region. And it was from a region distant indeed that Christ came here, from a heavenly one; and the place he held in that region, was the most distant and the highest. He was not an angel in heaven; he was the everlasting God. He came from the very summit, the lofty throne, of heaven to save us. This Christ Jesus was none other than Jehovah himself, condescending to enter into, and dwell and manifest himself in, our mortal flesh, a body of dust. Here begins the mystery of our salvation, and unless we look at it in this high beginning of it, going farther back than the manger and the cross, even to God's own throne, we shall never see its glory or feel its power. Our eyes will never weep, nor our hearts overflow, as we are told that "Christ Jesus came into the world to save sinners."

2. We are reminded also here that *there are lost sinners in our world, whom it was needful for Christ to come into our world to save.*

Every man that breathes in our world, is a sinner. Were the atmosphere of it impregnated with sin, there would not be one sinner more in it than there is now. "All we, like sheep, have gone astray." "All have sinned." "All the world is become guilty before God."

And every sinner every where is necessarily a lost sinner. This is the nature of sin, it ruins whomsoever it touches; ruins him fatally and irrecoverably; in scripture language, it destroys him. To sin is to fall; and not merely to fall down on the ground whereon a man is walking, it is to fall from an elevation, and one higher than we can see the summit of, and to dash ourselves well nigh to pieces in the gulph we sink into. We lie there disabled and mangled, with no more power to ascend that elevation again, than we have to scale the heavens.

'And on this property of sin, the ruinous nature of it, is grounded partly the necessity of Christ's interposition in our behalf. We say that his coming from his throne to save us, shews the greatness of his love to us, and so it does; but it shews as plainly the greatness of our misery. He would not have taken a step like this, so strange and wonderful, had not our situation required it. There were creatures nearer to us ready and willing to help us. We are willing to help one another. Who in this congregation would not rush at any time to save an infant from the flames, or a blind man from a precipice? and would not all the angels of God have rejoiced to come down to our world to save us, the creatures of God, from destruction? Could they have accomplished it, one word from Jehovah would have emptied heaven of them all for our deliverance. With what joy did they sing over Bethlehem when a Saviour was born to us! They would have made the whole creation ring with their songs, could they themselves have become our saviours. But our ruin was beyond their recovery. "I looked," says Christ, "and there was none to help, and I wondered that there was none to uphold; therefore mine own arm brought salvation." He speaks as though he interposed in our behalf, when none else could; as though he were obliged to interpose, and interpose as he did, or sinners not be saved.

It is easy, brethren, to use language on this subject, which ought never to be used; bold language, from which an humble and reverent mind shrinks; but still it seems true that our misery required the great remedy which has been provided for it. We argue from the providing of the remedy, that the remedy was needed. The living God came into the world to save sinners, because, through the greatness of our fall, we sinners could not be saved, consistently with the honour of his moral government, unless he did come. Love brought him down, but it was love that was obliged to stoop thus low to attain its object.

3. And when Christ came into the world to save sinners, *he came determined to save them.* He knew he could do so, otherwise he would not have come. We go hither and thither to accomplish objects, but never without some hope of accomplishing them. We do not go to the frozen regions of the north, to gather there the flowers and fruits of sunny climes. We never

think of going into vaults and charnel houses to raise the dead. Nor would our blessed Lord have come into the world for our salvation, had he not felt as he came, that he could work out salvation for us. The scriptures describe him as putting on his strength when he came, coming in his zeal, and might, and even fury—language shewing at once the greatness of the work he saw before him, and, at the same time, his determination to accomplish it. Yes, brethren, as surely as he has come into our world to save sinners, sinners in our world shall be saved by him; not all sinners—the text does not say that. All might be saved. It is no small salvation, that Christ Jesus has wrought out; it is no narrow entrance into heaven, that he has opened. All may go in; not a man on the earth is excluded; but some on the earth, he is determined shall go in, he is determined to have some of us as the monuments of his mercy, and the trophies of his love, and the objects of his delight, and the witnesses of his glory. He " came into the world to save sinners," for the express purpose of saving them, and sinners he will save.

What a source of consolation is this to the ministers of his gospel! We often preach to you, brethren, with much heaviness of heart. " Of what use is it," we say. " What comes of it?

Who hath believed our report, and to whom is the arm of the Lord revealed?" But " Be still," answers this mighty Saviour to us; " be still, and know that I am God. My word shall not return unto me void. It shall accomplish that which I please, and even from your unworthy lips, it shall prosper in the thing whereto I sent it. You think and preach of my love, but you forget my omnipotence; you forget that my power is as great as my love. I can save whom I will, and many will I save. No small company can fill the tables I have spread in heaven, and if they could fill them, they could not satisfy the love and mercy of my heart; they could not fill up my joy. I can and I will bring many sons unto glory. Every room in my Father's house, wide and lofty as that house is, shall have its joyful inhabitants. My wedding, when it comes, shall be abundantly furnished with guests. O happy hour for me, when all that my Father hath given me, shall at last have come to me; and of all that have come, not one shall be able to stand up and say that I have cast him out!"

II. Let us go on now to our second point—*the description St. Paul gives us here of the truth he states.* He calls it a " saying," " a faithful saying," and one " worthy of all acceptation."

1. It is *a saying*. And who says it? God himself, Christ himself. He might have come into our world, and never have told us that he had come here, or why he had come. This great truth, like many others and some probably which concern ourselves, might have lain buried in the secrecy of his own mind; but he publishes it abroad. Before he entered our world, he told us he was coming. Thousands of years before, it was a journey he often talked of. And when he did come, he proclaimed himself come. He said unto the cities of Judah, " Behold your God."

And it is not God or Christ only, who says this. The prophets declared it before it took place; the glorious company of the apostles said it afterwards; the noble army of martyrs died rather than not say it; the holy church throughout all the world has in every age acknowledged it; and as for the church above, it says this oftener perhaps than it says any thing else, and loves to say it better. Heaven often resounds with this saying and other sayings like it. Were we there, the first words we should probably hear from those who rejoice there, would not be, " O how happy are we," but the words we have so often heard in God's house on earth, " Christ Jesus came into the world to save sinners." If any of you die with these words in your hearts, they will soon be in your hearts and on your lips again. This is not a saying for you in your sin and misery only; it will be an everlasting saying for you in your future holiness and joy.

2. And this is *a faithful saying*, a true one. It is not only said, but it ought to be said, for it is true as truth itself. The apostle speaks in the text as though he were bearing his own personal testimony to its truth. "I know it to be true," he seems to say. "I am sure it is true. I have the best evidence possible, not only that Christ Jesus, my Lord, has come into our world, but that he has come here on the errand he says he came on, to save sinners." And if we ask how the apostle became so certain of this, the answer is ready—he felt that the Lord Jesus Christ had saved him. He had what St. John calls a testimony or witness of this truth within himself. He knew it, just as we know at this moment that our hearts are beating, and our pulses going, and that we are living and breathing men. He had experience of the fact.

And valuable as are the many outward testimonies we have to the truth of the gospel, and convincing as they are to a sound, unbiassed judgment, they are all nothing in comparison with this. I am not speaking of any thing mystical or enthusiastic, of any mere impulse or impression. What I mean is a consciousness within the soul, of a great change wrought in the soul by the power of Christ through the Spirit; a turning of the soul from sin to righteousness, from self to God, from the world to heaven; the softening of a man's hard heart by the love of Christ—a heart that nothing else ever could soften; the subduing of a man's proud heart by the grace of Christ—a heart which nothing else ever could subdue; the quieting of a man's discontented, restless heart by the peace of Christ—a heart which nothing before ever could quiet; the setting free of his earth-bound affections, and winning them over to the love and service of God;—this is what I mean, and he who has experienced this, has a better evidence of the gospel's truth and the gospel's power, than all the books and all the learning in the world could furnish. The miracles of our Lord, were they repeated again and could we witness them, would not be superior to this. They would not be equal to this. We should still each of us say, " My own converted soul is the greatest miracle of all. It is to me the best proof still, that my Saviour can really save." This is like saying, " I know that physician can heal, for he has healed me. They say the sun can warm, and I want not to read systems of philosophy to convince me of it; I have felt the sun warm and gladden me."

3. This saying too, we are told, is *worthy of all acceptation.* The words will admit of two interpretations.

It is, first, as our communion service renders the passage, " worthy to be received of all men." Few sayings are so. Many things which we hear, are worth no man's attention. They are either false or trifling; they are better not listened to. And others have only a limited interest. They may be worthy of one man's notice, but not another man's, for they do not concern him. This saying however concerns every man, and concerns him deeply. It concerns you, brethren, it concerns me; it concerns your children, and it concerns mine. Are we in the world and sinners in it? That is enough —no tongue can tell how worthy this saying is of our acceptance. We are sinners in different degrees, but this matters not; the least gulty amongst us cannot be saved without Christ, the most guilty may be saved by him—this saying concerns us all alike. O how eagerly will some of us listen to some things! the news of the day perhaps, the scandal of our neighbourhood, and the trifling occurrences that fill up the trifling lives of our fellow-men!—things, it may be, in which we have little more interest, than the inhabitants of some distant planet; but this saying, to which sometimes we have scarcely an ear to give, involves in it the highest interests of us all. Our happiness, our safety, through everlasting ages depends on it and on the reception we give it. Some of you may pity the man who is always thinking of it, but as for you who reject or neglect it, God and angels too pity you.

This saying is worthy also of the utmost reception we can give it, the most entire and cordial acceptance. Some things that we hear, are worth putting into our memories, but not into our hearts; they are dry matters of fact. But here is something worthy of our memories and hearts also; worthy of being attended to, worthy of being remembered, worthy of being thought on and studied, worthy of being delighted in, worthy of being laid hold of by our whole heart and mind—in this sense, "worthy of all acceptation." "Grasp this truth," the apostle means to say, "with all the powers you have, give it all the thought and affection you can give it—it is no more than it deserves; you will never make too much of it, no, nor enough. It is worthy of more acceptation than it will ever receive."

A feeble or cold reception of this saying, is no reception at all of it. It must be embraced by the understanding, as though the understanding had found something worth the embracing and worth the holding. And the heart must go along with the understanding. It must feel that it has enough in this saying to delight and fill it. The gospel is " good tidings," " good tidings of great joy." The angels said so when they proclaimed it, and so has every man said and felt, who has ever really received it. The regarding of it as so much authentic history merely, the contemplating of it as so much beautiful truth only, the giving to it of nothing more than the cold homage of an admiring intellect—this is not the " all acceptation" of which the apostle speaks. This is in fact no more than many an ungodly man has given it; it is little more than the devils who believe and tremble, are constrained to give it. Where the gospel saves the soul, the heart first opens itself to receive it, and when it is in the heart, the heart feels it to be its treasure and its joy.

III. Let us notice now *the view which the apostle takes of himself while contemplating this truth.* Of the sinners, he says, whom Christ Jesus came into the world to save, " I am chief."

Was he then really the chief of sinners? Perhaps not. In a preceding verse, he tells us that he had been " a blasphemer, and a persecutor, and injurious," but he was all this " ignorantly, through unbelief;" he did not know what he was doing; nay, I verily thought, he says in another place, " that I ought to do many things contrary to Jesus of Nazareth." It was all a mistake. And nothing else but this could be laid to his charge. His life was irreproachable. Touching the righteousness which is in the law," he declares he was "blameless." And yet, brethren, look here—this very Paul, this erring but yet zealous and apparently blameless man, says, " Of sinners I am chief." And what has led him to say this? The reception of this faithful saying has led him to say it. He never said it nor any thing like it, till he became a believer in Jesus Christ.

This is one of the many blessed but strange fruits of a cordial acceptance of the gospel—it lays a man down. And it is the only thing that can lay a man down. We never see much of our own sinfulness, till we look at our sinfulness and Christ together; till we begin to view it in the light which Christ's incarnation, and Christ's humiliation, and Christ's death, and Christ's continual intercession throw on it. We see the magnitude of the evil in the magnitude of the remedy provided for it, and in that only. The living God uniting himself to man; " the high and holy One that inhabiteth eternity," dwelling and dwelling for years in a world like this; the God who is so high, that he is said to humble himself even when he bends down to look on the things in his own lofty heavens, yet coming down among, and actually becoming one of, the things of earth—were this all God has done to save us, there is enough here to make us feel—what? that he is a God of stupendous goodness, of the most wonderful mercy? that we owe him more praise, more thankfulness, love, and service, than we can ever pay him? Yes, and to make us feel still more strongly that sunk and lost indeed must we have been, to render such wonders of grace needful for our deliverance. It is a mistake to suppose that the man who hopes only in Christ for salvation, makes light of sin; he is the only man in the world, who does not make light of it. And the more we see of the riches of God's mercy towards us in Christ Jesus, the more shall we see of our own guiltiness. The clearer and more affecting our views are of the one, the deeper and more abasing will be our sense of the other.

And this will account for the strange language of the apostle. He saw perhaps more than any other man ever saw on earth, of "the length, and breadth, and depth, and height," of the love of Christ; and that led him to see within himself more iniquity and evil. It made him, with his noble intellect, and high attainments, and unexampled labours and honours, one of the very humblest of the sons of men. Hence he speaks of himself, not perhaps as he really was, but as he appeared to himself to be, "less than the least of all saints," the very chief of sinners. And in the verse following the text, he goes farther. He represents himself as a spectacle of mercy; as having obtained mercy of the Lord, not from the Lord's compassion to himself, but in compassion to all other sinners, that they might see in him, the greatest of sinners, how much guilt the Lord can pardon and what enormous transgressors he can save.

Happy is the man who thinks and feels thus! Is there a man among us who feels thus? God grant that so you may feel for ever. It is Christian feeling. It is a proof that the gospel of Jesus Christ has not only reached your ears, but entered your mind and heart. You will carry that feeling with you to your Master's feet in heaven. When there, you will think yourself one of the greatest wonders there. You will say, " I was the very last to be looked for here. The chief of sinners was I. And now what am I? Happy as the happiest, high almost as the highest, a wonder to myself, a wonder to my fellow-sinners around me, a wonder to angels, and, I could almost think, a wonder to my God. It is true, true indeed, that Christ Jesus went into the world to save sinners, for here am I saved and blest."

O for something of this spirit among us now! a lowly, self-abasing spirit! It is one of the best preparations we can have for a heaven of glory.

It is one too of the sweetest feelings we can carry about with us in our way to that heaven. The more we have of it, the dearer will the Lord our Saviour become to us, the more joyful his house, the more delightful his table. Like that poor sinner who stood at his feet behind him weeping, we may feel unworthy to look on him, even when ready, as she was, to give him all that we have; but he will look on us, and sometimes he will let us see that he looks on us, and then, brethren, we shall feel indeed that in his favour is life, and in his presence joy, the richest and sweetest joy, the joy of salvation.

SERMON XI.

THE OFFERINGS OF CAIN AND ABEL.

Genesis iv. 3, 4, 5.

"It came to pass that Cain brought of the fruit of the ground an offering unto the Lord; and Abel, he also brought of the firstlings of his flock and of the fat thereof. And the Lord had respect unto Abel and to his offering, but unto Cain and to his offering he had not respect."

We are a company of sinful men gathered together here to worship the living God. This chapter brings before us, not perhaps the first congregation of men that ever assembled for this purpose, but the first of which we have any record. It consisted of two persons only, and yet, small as it was, it had, like this congregation and almost every other which has assembled since, a mixture in it, the good and the bad, the false worshipper and the true, a child of God's holy kingdom and a child of the wicked one.

To make our view of it instructive to us, let us notice, first, the resemblance between these two worshippers; secondly, the difference between them; and, thirdly, the consequences to which this difference led. And may he in whose holy presence we now are, take this scripture into his mighty hands and apply it to our minds and hearts!

I. *The resemblance* between Cain and Abel at this time, was outwardly very close.

1. *They both worshipped the same God.*

Great as was the mischief Satan had wrought in our world, he had not as yet introduced open, visible idolatry into it. God had been disobeyed here, but not disowned. Cain comes before "the Lord," the only living and true God, and so also does Abel; and they come together before him, worshipping, as we should now say, in the same church, at the same altar, as well as the same God.

2. And *they both bring an offering with them when they come.* There is a consciousness in the minds of both of them, that they are under obligations to the God they worship, and a willingness to acknowledge these obligations, and a readiness to render back to him of the blessings he has given them. Mere words do not satisfy them. Prayers

and praises do not content them. Here is an honouring of the Lord " with their substance and with the first fruits of all their increase."

3. And *there is a desire also in each that himself and his worship should find acceptance with God.*

That Cain had this desire, seems clear; he is disappointed and angry when God rejects him: and that Abel too had it, there can be no doubt; the Lord would not otherwise have had respect unto him. And who, it may be asked, has not this desire? If we shut our eyes, and blot out of our memories all we have seen and felt, we should say, every man has it. We should never think of a congregation of men in God's house, but as so many creatures looking most anxiously up to him who made them, for favour and acceptance. Our imaginations would paint them as a company of children with eyes fixed on their father's countenance, watching every movement of it for some expression of his regard. But what is the fact? The instant we ask the question, our picture vanishes. Men will come into God's house by thousands, and leave it again, utterly unconcerned about his favour, never once praying as they come that they may find grace in his sight, and never asking as they go away, Has the Lord accepted us? We often say, how different is the real world from all the ideal worlds our fancy has created! and never do we say this with more truth, than when we look at this real world in reference to its God.

Thus far then these two worshippers are alike —they come together before the same God, each bringing with him an offering, and each desiring to have himself and his offering accepted. Is there a man here who thinks all is well with his soul because he comes into God's house as his people come, and sits before him as his people sit? Let him see on what a miserable foundation his confidence rests. Here is Cain worshipping as well as Abel. Here is one of the very worst of men side by side in God's presence with one of the best, and bearing a close resemblance to him. And could we look on all the inhabitants of the earth as a heart-searching God looks on them, where at this moment should we find the most sinful of them? Not perhaps in heathen lands doing service to idols, not profaning this sacred day in places of business or pleasure in our own land, but in our churches, bowing down there in seeming devotion to the living Lord, or listening, as you are listening now, to the gospel of Jesus Christ. Millions in our world are far off from God, but among the farthest are some of those who seem the nearest. What said our Lord to "the chief priests and elders of the people" among the Jews in his days, the very men whom the Jews would have pointed to as the holiest and best of their nation? "The publicans and the harlots go into the kingdom of God before you."

II. Let us look now at *the difference* between these worshippers. And we discover this,

1. *In their different offerings.*

On the first view all here too on both sides appears right. They each bring exactly that offering which seems to accord well with their particular occupations. "Cain was a tiller of the ground;" "he brought of the fruit of the ground an offering unto the Lord." "Abel was a keeper of sheep;" "he brought of the firstlings of his flock." But the Lord himself tells us, there is much that is wrong here. He sees a wide difference between these two offerings. One of them is worthless in his sight, and worse than worthless; the other is pleasant to him, he values it. Four thousand years afterwards he remembers it and commends it. "Abel," the scripture says, "offered unto God a more excellent sacrifice than Cain." Wherein then lay the superior excellence of it?

It would be idle to speak of any value these offerings might have in themselves. In the sight of the great Lord of heaven and earth, they could have none. And if we say that Cain was willing to put God off with any thing, that he offered him that only which was near at hand and cost him nothing, while Abel gave him of his best, we should be saying more than the history warrants. Cain would have found it as easy perhaps to have brought a lamb as fruits or corn Here doubtless lay the difference — one of these worshippers draws nigh unto God as a creature of God, acknowledging his goodness; the other as a sinner against him, supplicating his mercy: the one comes before him as though he were a holy angel in a holy world, with a sacrifice of thanksgiving only; the other, as though he had deeply offended him, a guilty inhabitant of a guilty world, with a sacrifice of propitiation. Cain's fruits of the ground might testify of the gratitude of his heart, but they testified at the same time of its self-righteousness and pride; Abel's firstlings of his flock testified of the contrition, the abasement, the deep humility of his.

And this same difference distinguishes still every true worshipper of God on the face of the earth from every false one. If you are truly worshipping him, brethren, it is in your real character, as sinners, and as sinners whose transgressions have outraged his majesty and must be atoned for. Your worship is not so much that of a creature adoring his Creator, though it partakes of this character, as it is that of a guilty, miserable sinner, seeking, imploring, and casting himself on, a mighty Saviour. Our church service, every time we enter these doors, reminds us of this. The first thing it tells us of here, is our sinfulness, and the first thing it bids us do, is to fall down on our knees and with an humble heart and voice confess it. Almost every prayer it puts into our lips, like this bleeding sacrifice of Abel, recognizes our sinfulness; it is either a prayer for mercy, or if it is a prayer for any thing else, we are to ask for it in another's name, as though unworthy to ask it in our own. And when it calls us to the supper of the Lord, it still keeps our guilty character in our sight. There again it makes us acknowledge and bewail our manifold sins and wickedness; and would we find comfort there, it is as sinners we are to find it. The comfortable words it bids us listen to, are all words of comfort for the sinful, and as it puts into our hands the emblems of a dying Saviour's love, it is a love, it says, which gave his body and his blood for our transgressions. And when we are called from the church below to the church above, we shall go even there as men who once were sinners. No sin will cleave to us, we shall be pure as the angels or purer, pure as the sanctifying Spirit of a holy God can make us, but our highest joy there will be a sinner's joy, our praise there a sinner's praise; even in heaven our worship will still have this mark on it—it will be a sinner's worship, a worship in which none but a redeemed and happy sinner can fully join.

But look again to these men.

2. They differed *in the principle which actuated them in their worship.*

St. Paul tells us that it was " by faith Abel offered unto God a more excellent sacrifice than Cain." Not that Cain was altogether without faith. Had he been so, he certainly would not have been found worshipping here at this time. " He that cometh to God," the same apostle says, " must believe that he is, and that he is a rewarder of them that diligently seek him." Cain believed in God's existence, and superintending providence, and goodness, as truly and fully perhaps as many of us, and was as ready perhaps as his righteous brother to acknowledge them. But Abel believed in more than this. There was a faith in his heart, of which Cain was entirely destitute, and of which every man is destitute but the renewed and heaven-taught sinner.

We are no where told what it was that Abel believed when he made this offering, but all faith has respect to something said, some testimony; and his offering itself plainly intimates to us the testimony he believed. We infer from the Lord's acceptance of it, that he had commanded such sacrifices to be presented to him, for never has he left corrupt man to offer him what he pleases; no worship has ever been acceptable to him, but such as he himself has prescribed. And when he prescribed this, he doubtless connected with it some gracious promise explaining, in some measure, his object in enjoining it, and the benefit fallen man was to look for through it. Now up to this time but one promise can we find that he had ever given to sinners; and that is his glorious promise of a Saviour. Here then beyond doubt the faith of Abel rested. This was the divine testimony his faith embraced. In obedience to God's command, he brought of the firstlings of his flock and laid them bleeding on God's altar, and then connecting them with that Saviour God had promised to sinners, he gave credit to his promise, he hoped in his mercy, and, though a sinner, he looked to a coming Saviour for pardon and salvation.

His brother Cain, on the other hand, put all this aside. His faith did not lay hold of it, and consequently his worship had no reference to it. "The fruits of the ground," he thought, "will do as well for God as bleeding victims—why should they not?" He reasoned when he should have believed, and because he did so, he disobeyed. He kept back from God the sacrifice God had enjoined; he presented unto God an offering which had unbelief and disobedience plainly stamped on it, an offering which God abhorred. The consequence was, all the faith he possessed was reckoned as no faith at all. It rejected God's promise of forgiveness and mercy through a future Saviour, and in rejecting that, it dishonoured God; it came short of his forgiveness and mercy; it left Cain to perish.

A crowd of thoughts, brethren, come into our minds here. We see the Saviour our own guilty souls are trusting in, as a Saviour in ages long since gone, as the "Lamb slain from the foundation of the world," the very Saviour Abel, and Enoch, and Noah, trusted in; and we feel our confidence in him firmer and our hope in him brighter, while we look at him as their confidence and hope. We are like seamen sheltered in a secure haven from the beating storm, and discovering while in it that it sheltered, thousands of years before, the very first seamen that ever braved the deep, that it has sheltered since many whose names and memories have long been honoured by us, that our fathers, our brethren, our friends, and kindred, have all been in it, and not one of them all sustained in it harm or loss.

In him too we seem united to the early saints, one with them in Christ Jesus, sharing together the same great mercies, and linked together by the same love to the same Lord. The communion of saints passes from our creed into our hearts, and is at once understood there and enjoyed.

But that which strikes a thoughtful mind the most here, is the importance of a true faith in

Christ, and, with it, the folly of lightly esteeming such a faith. Men will sometimes tell us that we make too much of this heavenly grace, and they think perhaps in their hearts that God himself makes too much of it in his word; they would lift up outward things, rites and ceremonies, fastings and penances, above it; but we see here what it involves and how much depends on it—a knowledge of our true character in God's sight, a right state of heart before him, penitence, humility, obedience, all true and acceptable worship of him; and seeing this, we feel that we have never yet made enough of it. Instead of discovering that we have been carrying a common pebble about with us, and thinking it a jewel, we find that our jewel is of far higher worth than we ever thought it. Our prayer is, "Lord, teach us to prize more this precious faith. Lord, strengthen and increase it."

3. In one point more these men differed—*in the reception they and their offerings met with from God.* "The Lord," we read, "had respect unto Abel and to his offering, but unto Cain and to his offering he had not respect."

In both cases here, the persons are first mentioned. The Lord accepts Abel first and then his offering, he rejects Cain first and then his gifts. This shews us that we ourselves must be approved of God, before any services of ours can be pleasing to him. It is not with him as with our fellowmen—the gifts we bring him will not cause him to look favourably on us; it is the favour which, through his abounding goodness, he bears to us, that will lead him to look favourably on our gifts. "The sacrifice of the wicked," scripture says, "is an abomination to the Lord," not worthless only, but offensive, loathsome; and what a blow it gives as it says this to those who are living in pride and ungodliness, and yet think their prayers, and sacraments, and almsgivings, will help them! "but," adds the same scripture, "the prayer of the upright is his delight;" it may seem less than the others offer him, a prayer instead of a sacrifice, but he accepts it, and not only accepts it, it gives him pleasure as he accepts it; it is "his delight." How difficult is it to believe this! We mourn over our prayers and praises, Christian brethren. We often leave this house of God thinking that we must have insulted and offended God by the cold, heartless, polluted worship we have offered him here. Instead of looking on it with satisfaction and pride, it humbles us to the dust; we go home and, casting ourselves down before the Lord, beseech him to pardon it and to pardon us. But has he made us "accepted in the Beloved?" Then is our poor worship accepted also. Coming from those he loves, it is, like Noah's sacrifice, as sweet odours, pleasant to him; just as the veriest trifle from the hand of a beloved child, is dear to a father's heart.

In what way it pleased God to testify his approbation of Abel's offering, the history does not tell us. It is generally supposed to have been by fire from heaven, as in the case afterwards of Aaron's first sacrifice in the tabernacle, and Solomon's in the temple, and Elijah's on mount Carmel. It must have been in some visible manner, for it is clear that Cain, as well as Abel, perceived and understood it.

III. We come now to *the consequences which followed this act of worship.*

1. See them in *Cain.*

Here again imagination would mislead us. We might expect to behold this man falling down to the earth, humbled and ashamed at God's rejection of him; taking up Job's language, and saying unto God, " Thou hast rejected, but do not condemn me. Shew me wherefore thou contendest with me." But it is not easy to beat down to the earth proud, self-righteous man; and give him up to his pride or any other bad feeling, he will act in a way that will confound all our imaginations. Not sorrow or shame, envy takes possession of Cain's mind, anger and hatred follow it; and though God comes and mercifully expostulates with him, this man, but lately so devout and grateful in appearance before God's altar, ends with defying God, lifting up his arm, and becoming his brother's murderer. The mind almost sickens as we endeavour to fathom the malignity of his crime. It seems to have been the will of God to set him forth to us as an awful proof of the depth of that depravity into which man was already sunk; as a proof too of what evil tempers can do with fallen man, of what man can be and can do when man indulges his own selfish feelings. There is no setting of any bounds, he seems to say, to a disappointed, envious, malignant man. And for what end does he shew us this? To make us fear and shun our fellow-men? No; to lead us to bless him who hour by hour so wonderfully restrains their evil hearts, and to implore him every hour we live to restrain our own. Is there any one wrong feeling now at work in our minds? envy, or jealousy, or malice, or revenge? "See here," God seems to say, "what that feeling, if not checked, can do with you. It can make you a monster of iniquity, a scourge to others, a torment and terror to yourselves." We often say that one sin leads to many. As certainly does one evil temper lead to many. There is no telling where it will stop.

It seems also to have been the will of God to let his people see thus early what they have to expect in this fallen world. "Cain slew his brother," says St. John; "and wherefore," he asks, "slew he him?" Here is no injury done him, no provocation given him; Abel has not robbed him of the divine favour, or of any thing else; and yet Cain, his fellow-worshipper, his brother, slew him: and wherefore? The apostle gives the answer, "because his own works were evil and his brother's righteous." He traces his hatred of Abel to Abel's holiness, and then, naturally enough, he turns round to his holy and persecuted fellow-Christians and says, "Marvel not, my brethren, if the world hate you." It is a mournful honour to receive, one that we must not seek, but the very highest honour the world can put on us, is the world's hatred for such a cause as this.

2. Look now at *Abel.*

He has been humbly and faithfully worshipping the Lord his God, and what does he get from it? First hatred and then death—hatred, observe, from a fellow-worshipper, death from a brother's hand.

This however is not God's usual way of dealing with his servants. He exposes them indeed to the world's malice, and allows many of them deeply to feel it; but, after a time, he generally comes in and delivers them from it, letting the world see that it must oppress them no longer, and perhaps turning for a while the world's hatred into kindness and respect. " When a man's ways please the Lord," he sometimes, not always, " maketh even his enemies to be at peace with him." There were times when he suffered no man to do his Israel wrong ; " yea, he reproved kings for their sakes," saying, " Touch not mine anointed, and do my prophets no harm." But in other cases he seems to stand aloof, abandoning his church and people, in a great measure, to the world's violence, and giving them up as a prey to it.

The men themselves generally bear this well. " Let comforts go," they say, " let friends go, let character go, let all we once held dear go, yea, let life itself go. If we lose them in our blessed Master's service, they are well lost." But this tries sometimes exceedingly their godly brethren who are looking on. " I could bear all that myself," such a man says, " but it makes my soul indignant to see that honest brother, that meek, unoffending Christian, that noble-minded servant of the Lord, so unjustly treated, and by a world that is not worthy of them." But look here, brethren. Did you ever know a righteous man treated worse than righteous Abel was treated by wicked Cain ? Had you seen him struck down by that unworthy arm, would you not have felt indignant then ? and would you not have mourned over him, more than you have ever mourned over an ill used Christian yet? But was there cause for mourning over him? Follow him upwards. Cain slew him, and he became—what? The first of human kind, that ever entered God's holy kingdom; the first pardoned sinner that ever stood there in God's holy presence; the first trophy in heaven of redeeming love; the captain of that noble army of martyrs who are the highest and brightest in its courts. What joy must there have been in heaven, when this liberated man was first beheld there! Never again perhaps was there joy so great, till the man Christ Jesus left the earth and went there, and never will be again till the last saved sinner takes his station before the throne, and he who sits on it, says, "I am satisfied. The number of my elect is accomplished. My work is done." O brethren, pity the persecutor if you will, help the persecuted if you can, but if not, quietly leave him to a faithful God. He can recompense, and often recompenses the most, when he seems the most to forsake. Stephen's shining countenance plainly told what was going on within his heart, when he stood before the infuriated Jewish council; and when he looked up and saw the heavens opening and his own glorious Saviour there, little did Stephen care for the men who were rushing on him, or the stones that were destroying him. As little does the servant of Christ care now for the ill usage of this poor world, when he can look up and say, "That Saviour and that heaven are mine."

3. But there is yet a third party to whom our thoughts must for a moment turn. What parent can read this history and not think of *the wretched parents of these two men?*

"In the day that thou eatest thereof, thou shalt surely die," said God to Adam before he touched the forbidden tree, and after he had taken and eaten of it, he said to him again, "Dust thou art, and unto dust shalt thou return." But year after year passes, and Adam is not turned to dust. Death comes not near either him or his fellow-sinner. We can easily conceive that they might begin to think it never would come. God showered down perhaps so many mercies on them in their degradation, that they half forgot his threatening, and imagined that he too had forgotten it. But the blow comes at last; and in how unexpected a manner! It falls not on them, but on their child, and perhaps their holiest and best loved child; and it comes not directly from God's hand, it comes from man's hand; their child lies dead before them struck dead by another child. And at what a strange time did this thing happen! Did they see these brothers going forth to present their offerings to the Lord, their hearts must have rejoiced to see them. "The blessing of the Lord upon them," they must have said, " will follow this." But little do we know the turn any thing will take in our families. We look for good, but evil comes unto us; we wait for light, but there comes darkness. These very offerings bring about the death of Abel and the crime of Cain. Scarcely had they been presented, when these parents have before them one son dead and another worse than dead. The perplexity, the wonder, the terror, the self-reproach, the anguish of their souls, we can hardly think of. But let us see, as we look at them gazing in trembling silence at Abel's corpse, the dreadful evil of sin, the certainty that it will at last find us out. Let us learn that God's justice is as great and sure as God's mercy; that his threatenings are never forgotten; that the longer the execution of them is delayed, the more terrible, sudden, and confounding, will it come at last. None but a sincere believer in Christ Jesus, can tell how a scene like this makes him cling, as it were, to his bleeding Lord. He feels that he must have a refuge from his sins, and from Jehovah's awful displeasure against his sins; and he blesses God that in his incarnate Son, he can find it. The blood of Abel carries his thoughts to the blood of Christ. He does not turn away from the one, he listens to the solemn things it tells him; but he thinks at the same time of the better things the other tells him, and while he too, with Adam, could tremble over the murdered

Abel, he feels that in the crucified Jesus he can rejoice. He can revere God's justice there without any harrowing fear of it; he can repose in his mercy, because he knows that it is a mercy his justice sanctions, yea, a mercy in which it glories, triumphs, and delights.

And here, brethren, we must end; yet not till I have again reminded you, that this congregation is made up of exactly the same men as that early congregation at which we have now been looking. There are two classes of men here, and, in God's sight, two only. The believing, righteous Abel, with his bleeding sacrifice, is a pattern of the one; the proud, ungodly Cain, with his empty offerings, is a picture of the other. Circumstances have softened down a little, have glossed over, the difference between these two, so that we ourselves may scarcely see it, but it is clear enough to a heart-searching God. He can tell whether you and I are of Abel's class or of Cain's class, as easily as we can now tell whether it is day or night.

We are going to his table, just as these two men went six thousand years ago to his altar. In what spirit are we going there? That will tell us perhaps to which of these two classes we belong. Are we taking a self-sufficient, captious, half-sceptical mind there? Or are we taking there a self-righteous spirit, imagining that we are about to propitiate God by our presence and offerings, feeling as though we were going to do some great thing, thinking more of our prayers and worship than of our Saviour and our sins? I will not say, brethren, to what class we belong. But are we going there as sinners who feel unworthy to go there, and yet love a dying Saviour so well, that where "his precious blood-shedding" is commemorated or even spoken of, there they delight to be? Shall we carry there with us a self-accusing, self-loathing, a broken, contrite heart, and yet a heart that can burn with joy there if it meets its Lord? Then I will say to what class we belong. It is that to which the living God has the same respect as he had to Abel, and concerning which he has said, "They shall be mine in that day when I make up my jewels."

SERMON XII.

THE MARRIAGE SUPPER OF THE LAMB.

REVELATION XIX. 9.

"Blessed are they which are called unto the marriage supper of the Lamb."

We are again invited to an earthly supper of the Lamb. This text speaks of a heavenly one. Some indeed explain it differently. They consider it as descriptive of that abundance of spiritual blessings, which will be poured out on the church in its millennial glory. And this perhaps really is its primary meaning; but it certainly calls for a higher application. It is more true of a scene which will one day take place in heaven, than of the brightest scene the most glowing imagination ever painted any where else.

We may divide it into four parts—the Lamb,

the marriage supper of the Lamb, those who are called to this supper, and their blessedness.

I. It brings before us *the Lamb;* and we know at once who this is; but it is remarkable that, with one exception and that occurring in this evangelist's own gospel, this is the only part of the inspired writings, in which our Lord is ever called by this name. Isaiah compares him to a lamb; "He is brought as a lamb to the slaughter;" so does St. Peter; "Ye were redeemed with the precious blood of Christ as of a lamb without blemish and without spot;" but St. John applies this term to him as a name. Nearly thirty times in this book he calls him the Lamb, as though he scarcely knew him by any other title. Now this could not have happened by accident. There is a meaning in it, and it is not difficult perhaps to see what it is—the Lord Jesus would have us look up to him in heaven as the same Jesus who died for us on the cross. This book describes his glory in heaven as no other part of holy scripture describes it; it speaks continually of his throne and his greatness, of his majesty and splendour; and lest this should put his manhood and his cross out of our minds, he keeps telling us in this book that he is a Lamb on his throne, the Son of man still in the midst of his greatness, delighting to feel himself such and delighting to be thought such. High he would have us regard him, higher in the heavens than our thoughts can follow him, reigning there as the Lord God omnipotent, clothed with majesty, glory, and power; but still all kindness, all gentleness and grace to us; our merciful High Priest in the heavens, our once wounded and bruised and crucified Saviour on the throne of God.

II. Next comes in the text *the marriage supper of the Lamb.*

Here, you observe, is a complete change of metaphor. Our Lord puts off the character of a Lamb, and takes on him that of a Bridegroom; or rather he takes this character on him without putting off the other. We are to regard him as a Lamb and a Bridegroom at the same time, that is, we are to look on him in his once crucified but now glorified humanity as a Bridegroom.

"The marriage supper" of the Lamb represents him as having just accomplished his nuptials, and about to make on the occasion, according to eastern customs, a joyous feast. It brings before us the hour when the great Redeemer's work shall indeed be finished, when all his people he shall have saved, called them from their graves, gathered them around him, brought them to the heaven he has prepared for them, and about to enter with them into the fulness of its joy. A wonderful hour, brethren. The mind labours in vain to comprehend its glory and blessedness, and we feel thankful for a metaphor like this, which gives some distinctness to our thoughts concerning it.

1. It describes it as *a long looked for and much desired hour.*

The blessed Saviour himself desires it. None but himself can tell how ardently his soul is even now looking forward to it. It is the hour that will bring him the consummation of all his wishes, the full reward of all his labour and sufferings.

And his church desires it. Before he came the first time into our world, it longed for him to come. Patriarchs and prophets age after age looked for his coming as the greatest thing on this side heaven they could look for. And after he had come and was gone, the church took up again the same position. "We want him again," it said. Scarcely had he disappeared, when its language was, "Come, Lord Jesus, come quickly." It has been ever since a waiting church; a church looking for and longing for the appearance of its Lord; a betrothed bride anticipating the coming of her Bridegroom to take her home.

2. And this hour when it comes, will be an hour of *great love and affection.*

No earthly affection is equal to that of a redeemed sinner for his Saviour. There may not at times seem much warmth in it, but when it is real, there is as much strength and depth in it perhaps, as man's nature, in its present state and circumstances, is capable of. But still it is an imperfect love, very much broken in upon by the love of other things, and damped by the cares of life, its business and troubles. It is an unseen object too that we love, and we find it difficult to realize any thing we have never seen. And even in our best moments, we often feel as though we only half loved our Lord. Our love for him seems a desire, an effort, to love him, rather than love itself. Our souls, we say, are straitened within us, as though they had not power enough to love him. We long for a better and higher nature, that we may love him more. At this marriage supper we shall have what we long for. We shall see our Lord, and see him in a form in which we shall know him; and shall have souls within us, that will for the first time feel large enough to love him, and these souls shall be filled to overflowing with admiration of and delight in him. There will be nothing to distract, nothing to straiten, nothing to impede, our love. Man scarcely knows his own power of affection now; we shall wonder at our power of affection when we are face to face with Christ in his kingdom.

And his own feelings there will correspond with

ours. We dare not say that he will love us more than he loves us now, but he will indulge his love for us more, he will manifest it more, we shall see more of it, we shall understand it better; it will appear to us as though he loved us more. He will lay open his whole heart and soul to us, with all its feelings, and secrets, and purposes, and allow us to know them, as far at least as we can understand them and it will conduce to our happiness to know them. The love of this hour will be the perfection of love. This marriage feast will be the feast, the triumph, of love—the exalted Saviour shewing to the whole universe that he *loves us to the utmost bound love can go*, and we loving him with a fervor, a gratitude, an adoration, a delight, that are new even in heaven.

3. This scene will be also a scene of *abounding joy*.

The affection that reigns in it, would of itself make it so. "Let me only be with my Lord," the Christian says, "and I ask no more. That, without any thing else, will make me happy, and happy to the full." And the language of scripture corresponds with this. "In God's presence," it tells us, "is the fulness of joy," and of heaven it says that "the glory of God doth lighten it, and the Lamb is the light," the glory and bliss, "thereof." But though the presence of God and Christ is the one chief source of happi-

P

ness in heaven, we shall doubtless find there other sources of additional happiness. The text speaks of it as a supper, a feast, a marriage supper, a splendid and joyous feast. The heavenly Bridegroom provides for his guests all that can gratify and delight them, and all too that can shew his love for them and his munificence. The provisions made by him for our enjoyment, will astonish us. Conceive of a beggar taken for the first time to a splendid monarch's table, and this at a season of unusual splendour and rejoicing. How would he wonder at the magnificence he would see around him, and the profusion of things prepared for his gratification; some altogether new to him, and others in an abundance and excellence he had never thought of! So will it be with us in heaven. We shall find it a feast and a monarch's feast. It will have delights for us, of which we have now no conception, and the pleasures we anticipate in it, will be far higher and more abundant than our highest expectations have ever gone. We shall have a provision made for us, that will befit, not our rank and condition, but the rank and condition, the greatness, the magnificence, the love, of a glorious God.

As for the joy of the great Saviour himself at this hour, we may speak of it, but this is all we can do; we cannot understand it. The work of thousands of years completed; the people he loved and died for, all saved; all around him, not one missing; and not a stain or a blemish among them all; all holy, all happy, and an eternity of happiness with them before him—we may try to comprehend his joy in this hour, but we might as well try with one glance of our feeble vision to take in the ocean. Scripture speaks of this " day of his espousals," as " the day of the gladness of his heart." It describes him as presenting his church to himself in this day " with exceeding joy." " As the bridegroom rejoiceth over the bride," says one prophet, " so shall thy God rejoice over thee." " He will rejoice over thee with joy," says another; " he will rest in his love; he will joy over thee with singing." He " taketh pleasure" in his people now, he says, now in their state of degradation, and imperfection, and distance; but what is his pleasure in them now to his pleasure then! In one word scripture sets forth the greatness of it. It shall " satisfy" him, it says, meet all his desires, fill up all that amazing capacity of happiness, which exists in his mighty soul.

And the holy angels too are to share in the joy of this scene. They are described in this chapter as saying one to another, " Let us be glad and rejoice, for the marriage of the Lamb is come," and the utterance they give to their joy, is compared to the loudest and sublimest sounds with which we are acquainted—a shouting multitude, resounding waters, and rolling thunders, and this multitude " great," these waters " many," and these thunderings " mighty." Even now they rejoice, we are told, " over one sinner that repenteth," rejoice when his salvation is begun ; how will they rejoice over millions of sinners when their salvation is completed, and these sinners are before them, sharing their joy and responding to their songs !

Heaven is a happy world now, brethren, but this marriage supper of the Lamb will add wonderfully to its happiness. It will be a feast, a festival, in it ; a joyous day above all others even in that joyous world.

Without straining then the metaphor before us, we may consider it as setting forth the first meeting of Christ and his church in heaven as a long looked for and much desired meeting, a scene of great affection and of abounding joy.

III. Let us turn now to *those invited or called to it.*

All feasts are made for certain guests. They are not open to any one who chooses to come to them ; they are for those only whom the maker of the feast chooses to invite. So this marriage supper will not at last be thrown open to all of us. It is prepared for those only whom the great Bridegroom, in the day of his appearing, shall summon to attend it. And here our imaginations are ready to picture him as sitting on his throne, separating his redeemed from among the amazing throng before him, and saying to them, as he has promised to say, " Come, ye blessed." But we must not at once look so far forward as this.

It is a custom in the east for invitations to any great feast to be given a considerable time beforehand. Then on the day of the feast, servants are sent round to summon again those who have accepted these invitations. Thus in our Lord's parable of the wedding supper, the king is said to " send forth his servants to call them that were bidden," that had previously been bidden, "to the wedding." And this will help us to mark out more precisely the persons we have now before us.

1. They are *those who have been invited before to this supper.*

And here we are all included. The gospel which has been sent to us, is nothing else than a most gracious, free, urgent, pressing invitation to this supper, and an invitation addressed to us all, to one as much as to another. It proclaims heaven to be a feast for sinners, for sinners redeemed from among men, and the only qualification required to bring us within the call to it, is to be men and sinners. "Go ye into all the world," are the orders given by the magnificent Lord of it to his servants, " and preach the gospel," tell of my happy marriage and of my universal invitation to it, " to every creature."

But though we are all included in this first call to this supper, we are not all included in the number of those who will be called to it at last.

2. They are *those only who have before accepted the invitation to it.*

An eastern king or noble does not ordinarily send a second summons to his banquet to those who have either refused or slighted his first invitation. His servants, when the feast is ready, go round to those only who said they would come to it. And all of us who will be summoned hereafter by Christ to his marriage supper, are such as have embraced now Christ's gracious offers of admission to it. They are not all of us who have received the gospel invitation, they are those who have accepted, and thankfully and joyfully accepted, the gospel invitation; not those whom the gospel calls, but those who, in the language of our church, " have through grace obeyed the calling."

We often think it will be otherwise, brethren; that though we despise or neglect the gospel now, we shall yet when we die inherit with others its salvation; but it will not be otherwise; if we do not heartily embrace its offers before we die, we shall never see its salvation. Who are the men that Christ says shall never taste of his supper? The heathen, those that are far off, the outcasts whom his servants never approach and who never hear of his supper? No, the men who have been bidden to it; such men as are now within these walls, told continually of Christ's salvation, urged continually to accept it, and yet turning away from it, plunging into the world's pleasures and pursuits till they actually forget it. Christ calls now and you refuse; but if this goes on, the hour will come when you will call and Christ will refuse. His mercy may have followed you through many years, it may follow you down to the grave, calling after you, but at the grave it will have done with you, and done with you for ever; not another sound of mercy shall you hear again through a dark eternity.

3. But these guests are yet further distinguished—*they are ready and prepared for this supper.*

They whom our Lord, in the parable of the ten virgins, describes as going in with him to the marriage, are such as " were ready" to go in with him; and this chapter speaks of the bride, the Lamb's wife, as having " made herself ready." " Fine linen, clean and white," is her raiment, a bridal dress for a bridal hour.

And, in this figurative way, we are again taught the solemn truth, that no one of us is naturally fit for heaven, that every one of us must undergo in this life a preparation for heaven before we shall be called there. Take a miserable beggar from our streets—he is fitter in his polluted and wretched garments, with his low and perhaps depraved habits, for a king's table, than any of us in our natural condition for the heavenly table of our Lord. This every real Christian knows and feels; the wonder with him is, that any man who knows any thing of himself and his God, should ever doubt it.

This readiness for heaven is sometimes spoken of in scripture as God's work. " He hath clothed me with the garments of salvation," says the church; " he hath made us meet to be partakers of the inheritance of the saints in light." " To the bride it was granted," this chapter says, that she should be arrayed in fine linen. At other times, it is spoken of as our own work; " The bride hath made herself ready;" we are called on to " prepare to meet our God." The reason is, the wedding dress that we need, is a dress which God our Saviour has provided for us, just as a king in the east provides suitable garments for the guests he invites; but we ourselves must consent to wear this dress, must, through God's Spirit inclining and enabling us, take it up and put it on.

It consists partly in the spotless righteousness of the Lord Jesus made ours by faith—this gives us a title for admittance to this feast; and partly in heavenly dispositions and affections, a wedding spirit, the fine linen that is " the righteousness of the saints," holiness of heart, without which, if admitted to this feast, we could not enjoy it, we could not partake of it, we should soon be cast out of it. A worldly-minded, ungodly man in heaven, would be a miserable man in heaven. A prepared place for a prepared people, a holy place for a holy people—this, brethren, is the heaven of the Bible, and if you are looking for any other, you are looking for that which has no existence, a dream of your own imaginations, as shadowy as those illusions of the desert, which seem real to a man at a distance, but when he would approach them, are gone.

IV. We have now to look at *the happiness of these men.* " Blessed are they which are called to the marriage supper of the Lamb."

It is not an invitation to every feast, that will make a man happy. Some such invitations a man who loves his God, is obliged to decline; he cannot tell whom he may meet in them, he knows they will lead him from the God he loves, and send him away miserable. " Better," he says, " any house of mourning, than a house of such feasting as this." And even when he does accept one of them, and finds in it nothing to offend him, he cannot always enter into the enjoyment he sees around him; and if he does enter into it, it is only for a little while; the visit is soon over, and the pleasure is gone. But these men, called to the marriage supper of the Lamb, may go to it as fearlessly as a child goes to its mother's arms. "There shall in no wise enter into it any thing that defileth." Not a snare or a danger can await them there. Not a single being will they see there, who can do them harm or whom they would wish away.

As for the enjoyments of this feast, they are all their own. We have been speaking of these men, agreeably to the text, as mere guests at this supper, but this figure might be changed. They form collectively that church which is the Lamb's bride. They will find no one at this marriage supper more loved by the adored Bridegroom than themselves, no one whom he is more anxious to satisfy with his presence in it or with its provisions and delights. "Give me the very lowest place in heaven, let me eat only of the crumbs which fall there from my Master's table, partake of nothing more than the fragments of its joys, it will be enough for me," the Christian sometimes says; "I shall be content." But "No," Christ answers; "I have prepared this feast for you, and its highest places, its best and richest provisions, are all yours."

And with this abundance of delights before us, there will always be in us an appetite, a taste and relish, for them. Earthly festivities after a while weary, but not these. They refresh the soul while they gratify it, and prepare it for new pleasures, enlarging and strengthening it, and adding to its capacity for enjoyment and happiness. A soul ever desiring, and more and more desiring, and having all its desires met and gratified to the utmost—that is the happiness of the soul in the presence of its God. And it is a happiness which will last for ever. This marriage feast will never know interruption, will never come to an end. Our marriage feasts on earth are sometimes happy ones; but what mournful scenes often succeed them — the decay of affection, the withering of long cherished hopes and anticipations, the wreck of all our earthly happiness; or if not this, the turning sooner or later of the sounds of joy into sounds of sorrow, the festal board into a board of mourners, the bridal chamber into a chamber of death! Who has not found himself looking into the future as he has sat at such a feast, and with difficulty suppressed the tear or sigh? But look far as we will into the future at this heavenly feast, we can see not a cloud to darken it, we can see nothing in it but brighter and brighter delights. The Bridegroom's love and the Bridegroom's joy will never abate, nor will our love for him abate or our rejoicing in him. That fulness of joy which is in his presence, never can know diminution, and we shall never be out of his presence. The pleasures which are at his right hand, are pleasures for evermore, and we shall evermore be at his right hand to enjoy them.

And may we not now say, " Blessed are they which are called unto the marriage supper of the Lamb?" If we are among those who are really following the Lamb, " the called and chosen and faithful," may we not say too, " Blessed are we?" O brethren, how poor does our highest earthly happiness seem, when once we get a view of that which is before us! Sweet and dear as it is, how ashamed do we feel of making so much of it, of letting it have so much of our hearts and thoughts. It is a nothing, and we feel it a nothing, in comparison with the happiness we shall soon share. And unlike all other joy, we may anticipate this and long exceedingly for this, and yet it will not mar our present enjoyments. Our own homes will become pleasanter to us as we think of this heavenly home, our own meals more cheerful as we look forward to this heavenly meal; and the love and affection and endearments of home will not wither, they will brighten and increase, in the prospect of this heavenly love and affection. Let us try to make our homes more like the home we are going to, and our feasts in them, more like this last great feast, the marriage supper of the Lamb. As for the earthly suppers of this Lamb, this scripture tells us plainly what we should endeavour to make them, not memorials only of a scene of love and sorrow that is passed, but patterns and foretastes of a scene of love and gladness that is to come. We may eat bread with a joyful heart with him to-day at his table, and think ourselves blessed, but blessed indeed will he be who eats bread with him at his table in the kingdom of God.

SERMON XIII.

THE VIRGIN MARY'S JOY.

St. Luke i. 46, 47.

"And Mary said, My soul doth magnify the Lord, and my spirit hath rejoiced in God my Saviour."

These are happy words, brethren, and happy indeed must she have been, who uttered them. We have often felt this perhaps as we have heard them and responded to them in our public worship. But the joy they express, has a loftiness in it, which is in a great measure lost to us there. They come before us apart from the circumstances under which they were spoken, and there is a peculiarity in those circumstances, which gives to these words a new and almost surprising nobleness and force.

We will review then first the events in Mary's

life, which led to this burst of joy, and examine afterwards her joy itself.

I. 1. The first event to be noticed in her life, is *the high honour God unexpectedly puts on her.*

We find her, in an earlier part of this chapter, living at Nazareth, a city or town of Galilee. Little however is said of her rank or condition there. Young she must have been at this time, for she was betrothed, according to the custom of her country, to a man whom she had not yet married; and from his occupation and other circumstances, there is reason to conclude that, though a descendant of the royal David, her station in life was a very humble one. But suddenly comes down an angel from heaven to her, salutes her as the highly favoured of Jehovah, and announces to her that she is the destined mother of the world's Saviour.

We often tell you, brethren, that there may be many an unexpected affliction and sorrow awaiting you in the future; we may tell you now that there may be too in that future many unlooked for joys and honours awaiting you. These things, like all others, are in the hands of a sovereign God, and in his wise and holy sovereignty, he often pours them out abundantly where they are the least expected. He delights in noticing those whom others pass over, in putting honour on those whom the world despises, in lifting on high those who are thinking of nothing else but humbling themselves and lying low. Who could have anticipated his designs towards this Mary at Nazareth, or towards David among his sheepfolds at Bethlehem, or towards Peter and James and John in their fishing boats on the lake of Galilee? He may have designs if not as glorious, yet as gracious and unlooked for towards some of us. There may be thoughts of peace, thoughts of kindness and love, in his heart towards us, of which now we have not an idea, and shall not have till his intended mercies are made ours. " He hath regarded the lowliness of his handmaiden," says Mary, as though recognizing the pleasure he takes in exalting the humble, and surprising them with manifestations of his love.

2. We see next in Mary's life *the painful trial with which this high honour was accompanied.*

One moment's thought, brethren, will bring this to your minds. The angel appeared to her privately. None saw or heard him but herself. When she tells of his visit and message, who will believe her? and if she is not belived, what in a short time will be her situation? Her character ruined, the world scorning her, her friends mourning over her, and worse—her betrothed husband, the object perhaps of her warmest youthful affections, lost to her, loving her still but casting her off; nay, her very life endangered, for she will be charged with an offence which, by a Jewish law, is death. Dearly, some would say, will she pay for the honour intended her. But when does God bestow honour on any one without calling on him to pay something for it? We could not bear the divine mercies, were it not for the afflictions, the sorrows and mortifications, which generally accompany them. We are proud beings, proud even when God has put his humbling Spirit within us. It has beaten down our pride, but it has not slain it. The Lord has only to comfort us and exalt us a little, and it stirs itself up again, and, if let alone, would soon make a footstool of those very comforts and honours for itself to stand on. There is humiliation therefore, something lowering and abasing, generally connected with God's mercies towards us, something to counteract their self-exalting tendency. Mary is to be blessed above all women, but she is to become for a time little better than an outcast; and Paul who is to be honoured above all men, is to suffer more than they all. Besides his shipwrecks, and scourgings, and stonings, and imprisonments, he is to carry about to his dying day a thorn in his flesh " lest he should be exalted."

3. Observe next in Mary *her submissive ac-*

quiescence both in the honour and in the trial allotted her.

It is easy, we may say, to submit quietly to honours; but when these honours are great and unexpected, there is in some minds a strong disposition to shrink from them. Self comes into our thoughts. We compare them with our merits and deservings, and because we see clearly that they surpass these, we are ready to say, " Let us not have them." Thus Moses, when God himself appears to him at Horeb, and makes known to him that he has chosen him to be the deliverer of his people, begins to debate the matter with God, telling him he has made a mistake, and chosen a wrong instrument for the accomplishment of his purpose. " Who am I," he asks, " that I should go unto Pharaoh, and that I should bring forth the children of Israel out of Egypt?" Now there is some humility in all this, but more pride; some knowledge of our own unworthiness and nothingness, but more ignorance of the Lord's goodness, sovereignty, and greatness. Mary rises above it all. The angel delivers his message to her. For a moment she is confounded and perplexed. Encouraged however by the angel, she asks in the simplicity of her heart for an explanation; and no sooner does she get it, than she is quiet, willing and obedient. There is no bidding him pass her by and go elsewhere, no telling him of her unworthiness, no obtruding of herself or her own feelings in any way. " Behold the handmaid of the Lord," she says; " be it unto me according to thy word." And that is real humility, which leads us to regard ourselves as God's servants and property, to place ourselves entirely at God's disposal, to be willing to be any thing or do any thing he pleases.

But Mary was a thoughtful as well as an humble woman. It is more than probable therefore that all the consequences which must naturally follow the honour designed for her, rushed at this moment into her mind. The tone of her answer seems to intimate this. And a word from her, we are ready to say, would have averted these consequences. " Go," she might have said to the angel, " to my parents, or go to some of my neighbours and friends, or go to Joseph and tell him what is to happen to me. Save those kind hearts from sorrow, and me from shame." But not a word of the kind comes from her. She looks on honour and dishonour, evil report and good report, with the same calmness. " Come what will," she seems to say, " be it unto me according to thy word." Here is the spirit of her father Abraham already at work in this youthful daughter of his. He quietly went out at God's command, not knowing whither he went; and she meekly acquiesces in God's will concerning her, not knowing whither it may lead her.

We must now follow her to another scene. It would appear that the consequences we have spoken of, soon came upon her. Her interview with the angel was not credited. Her husband, a kind but yet a holy man, was minded, we are told, to put her away. Suspected and perhaps reproached, she rises up and " goes with haste," flies with her wounded spirit, to the house of Zacharias, an aged and godly kinsman some distance off. And there, on her arrival, takes place one of those touching and at the same time lofty scenes we in vain look for out of the Bible, except indeed in real life among the people of God. The old and honoured Elizabeth, the wife of Zacharias, receives her young relative, not as a fugitive driven to her for protection, but rather as an angel of God come to honour her. No kindness or sympathy does she offer her; it does not enter her thoughts that she can possibly need any: she breaks out the instant she sees her in a strain of high congratulation. " Blessed art thou among women," she cries, " and blessed is the fruit of thy womb." The next moment, this aged saint, a daughter of Aaron, the wife of a temple priest, seems filled with wonder at the condescension of this girl of Nazareth in coming to visit her. " Whence is this to me, that the mother of my Lord should come to me?" And now look at Mary. She will be on Elizabeth's neck, we should have said, or she will be at her feet. Overcome by all this, her anguished heart will be pouring out before her its long pent up feelings and sorrows. But not a word does she utter of anguish or sorrow; not the slightest allusion does she make to her troubles; she has a tongue for nothing but joy, adoration, and thankfulness. This young woman seems to catch at once the lofty spirit of her relative, and with a spirit as lofty or loftier, gives utterance to her feelings in that burst of praise we have now before us. " My soul doth magnify the Lord, and my spirit hath rejoiced in God my Saviour."

II. We must now look at her joy.

1. It is clear that it was a joy *accompanied with both affliction and submission.*

Her trial was not yet over. All was well here, for Zacharias and Elizabeth appear to have been supernaturally made acquainted with the truth concerning her; but no angel had as yet been sent to make it known to Joseph. At Nazareth, Mary's home, all was still dark as before. Yet Mary is happy; she magnifies the Lord and her spirit rejoices.

You hear of spiritual joy, brethren, and you sometimes wonder that you yourselves know so little of it; but what has your life been? For the greater part perhaps a smooth, unruffled one. Or if you have had trials, compared with those of this young Nazarene, they have been light; compared with those of some of your fellow-Christians around you, trifles. But what is the promised joy of the gospel? It is abounding joy in abounding tribulation. You must wait therefore for your tribulation to abound, before you are warranted to complain or wonder that your spiritual joy does not overflow. Mary perhaps was never so happy in her whole happy life at Nazareth, as she was here a fugitive at Elizabeth's door.

But are your trials severe? Then you have to learn that there is no abounding joy for you, till you are perfectly content to have them severe; till your minds are completely reconciled to them; till all murmuring, and rebellion, and impatient struggling to get rid of them, are come to an end. The soul often keeps up a long effort in affliction to make terms with its God. It must have this trouble removed and another a little lightened; this solace must be given it in its sorrow, and this or that gourd, so dear to it, spared, or if not spared, only withered a little, not smitten and destroyed; and then it will submit. But if the soul would find peace in affliction, it must submit at once; not attempt to capitulate with God, but surrender itself unconditionally to him, "submitting ourselves wholly to his holy will." Tribulation must work patience before it can work joy, or hope, or any thing pleasant. The Father of mercies will not comfort a contending, debating child, but he delights in pouring out his richest consolations on a quiet, submissive, passive one.

2. And this joy before us is *a deeply seated joy.* "My soul doth magnify the Lord; my spirit hath rejoiced."

This is common language in scripture. Isaiah, when he would express the intenseness of his longing after God, speaks of his "soul" as desiring him, and of his "spirit" as seeking him. David often tells us that his "soul" thirsts for and longs for him. So Mary speaks here of her soul and her spirit, in order to express, if she can, the strength and depth of that happiness she feels within her. It was no superficial, transient pleasure, excited in her by Elizabeth's words or kindness; it was a joy lodged deeply within her, filling her heart and soul; quickened and called into outward expression indeed by the sympathy she had experienced, but existing in perfect independence of that sympathy and of all outward things. It is evident that, young as she was, she had a mind and feelings of unusual strength. Her joy partook therefore of the character of her mind and feelings. It was a powerful joy. And there must be a depth, brethren, in our mental and spiritual character, before there can be much depth in our inward enjoyments. Light minds will have light joys. They are not spacious enough for the joy of the Holy Ghost to dwell largely in them. And let our minds be naturally as strong as they may, they must have been exercised unto godliness, have been spiritually exercised and spiritually strengthened and enlarged, before we can expect them to abound in spiritual consolations. A child must not wonder that it can take little or no share in the pleasures of a man. It must wait for a man's strength, and a man's experience, and then it shall have a man's enjoyments.

3. This joy again is *a sinner's joy in a sinner's God*. It is joy in a Saviour.

We have been looking at Mary hitherto as a blameless, godly, and highly distinguished woman. Such she certainly was. We are ready to go farther and say, though we have no warrant for saying so, that the holy God who had set her apart to be the virgin mother of his Son, had from her earliest childhood filled her with his Spirit, and given her a purity and excellence scarcely known before among the children of men. We will suppose that all the virtues which admiration or superstition have ascribed to her, were really hers. We then ask, what was Mary's estimate of herself? We have her before us singing with joy; on what does she ground her joy? Whence does this holy woman draw her overflowing happiness? We look at her words, and her holiness and excellence all vanish from our sight. We find her, like every other happy creature in the universe, deriving her happiness from an infinite God; and like every other happy sinner in the universe, happy in that God as the God of sinners. "My soul doth magnify the Lord," she says; "my spirit hath rejoiced in God my Saviour." She might mean by this language the eternal God in the heavens, or she might have in her thoughts that God become incarnate, the Lord Jesus, of whom she was soon to be the parent. In either case, the force of her words is the same. Holy as she was, she felt herself a sinner; and her highest joy was not in Elizabeth's kindness, though that must have been at this time a balm indeed to her; nor in the honour the Lord had put on her, though in that she exults; it was in this—that she had found for her guilty soul a mighty, a divine Saviour.

And was there any thing wonderful or peculiar in this? Nothing *peculiar*, for the saints of God in all ages have felt the same. "My heart shall be joyful in the Lord; it shall rejoice in his salvation;" had said her father David long before, and said it, not in disgrace and trouble as she was now saying it, but on his throne, among all the honours, and splendours, and mercies, God had showered on him. " I will greatly rejoice in the Lord," had said one prophet, " my soul shall be joyful in my God," and why? " for he hath clothed me with the garments of salvation." " And I too will rejoice in him," had said another and for the same reason—" I will joy in the God of my salvation." Mary's song here was no new song. It was merely the echoing of songs that had been singing almost from the first moment a Saviour had been promised to the world. And it is a song that will never be an old one. The church on earth is singing it constantly now, and so is the church in heaven, and will sing it long as that heaven shall last. The reason is, the Lord in all his dispensations with us deals with us as sinners. There is a peculiarity in his dispensations towards us. He will have a corresponding peculiarity therefore in our conduct and in our feelings towards him. The worship that he requires of us, is a sinner's worship; the praise we offer him, must be a sinner's praise; and the joy too we feel in him, will be a sinner's joy. It will resemble the joy angels have in him, but it will have a character of its own; it will go, when perfect, beyond the joy of angels in heaven, and rise higher. We shall not only have the divine goodness and holiness and greatness to delight in, as they have; but we shall have the divine mercy also, the pardoning mercy of a saving God. And this will be the sweetest to us of all. Among all the streams of happiness flowing to us from our God, the fountain of all happiness, this will be the most rejoiced in and the most abundant. Mary mentions in her song, and mentions with delight, the condescension, the power, the holiness, and faithfulness of Jehovah, but she mentions again and again his mercy. With this she begins, and with this she ends her song. If she had not told us so, we should have seen at once that her spirit is indeed rejoicing, rejoicing above all things, in God her Saviour.

Nor is this *wonderful*. Consider what salvation is. It is the restoration of a ruined soul. There is a soul within you and me, brethren, that must live for ever, and live for ever in feeling and consciousness; and a soul that has unknown powers of feeling, that is capable of being far happier than it has ever been yet, and far more miserable; inconceivably happy and unutterably miserable. And this soul is in a miserable and condemned condition. Sin has cut it off from its God, has brought on it his displeasure, and the moment it is dislodged from this mortal body in which mercy now keeps it, it is lost; it is gone into a world where there is no mercy, where it will be wretched, and wretched to its utmost capability of wretchedness, and this constantly and this for ever, wretched without intermission, without alleviation, and without end. We do not know what the powers of an immortal soul are, or we should tremble at the prospect before us; we do not know what the everlasting destruction of a soul is, or we should wonder no longer at a sinner's joy in the God who saves him from it. Salvation is not the taking of us from this world of labour and sorrow to a world of rest and peace, from earth to heaven. It is the taking of us from the very gates of hell to heaven. It is like the plucking of a brand out of the fire that is catching it, and placing it, not where it may be laid hold of and thrown into that fire again, but where no harm can ever happen to it—the placing of it in the paradise of God, and planting it there, and transforming it there into a noble and lofty tree, in which even God himself delights. The angels knew something of this when they sang with such rapturous joy of the birth of a Saviour for us; and the instant a sinful man feels any thing of this, he too begins to rejoice, as he rejoices in nothing else, in God's salvation. " He has given me many blessings," he says, " and I thank him for them; would that I could thank him for them more! but what are all the blessings he has given me? children, friends, property, health, peace of mind, honour in the church and in the world? I think of them sometimes, and perhaps too often and too much; but when I think of the salvation of this immortal soul of mine from a dreadful hell, I can scarcely think of them at all. I would not forget God as my Preserver, my Benefactor, my Comforter, the sole Author and Giver of all my blessings; but if I magnify him, my soul must magnify him the most, and if I rejoice in him, my spirit must rejoice in him the most, as God my Saviour."

4. And this also we must notice in this joy —it was *a joy that was the fruit and effect of faith.*

Almost all joy in God must be this. We do not see God. Something we have received from him to gladden us, but it is nothing compared with what he has promised us. It is as a Saviour that we must chiefly rejoice in him, and his salvation is a future thing, not one of us has received more than an earnest and foretaste of it. Faith therefore becomes a necessary pre-requisite to joy. It is the eye of the soul, which enables it to discern the beauty, and excellency, and glory, of its unseen God; and the reality, greatness, and certainty, of the salvation and blessings he has promised us.

We turn to Mary, and in her we see this faith exemplified. As we repeat her words in our service, we are ready to imagine that they must have come from her with the infant Jesus in her arms, that they were a young mother's first words of joy over her new-born babe. But that Jesus is as yet unborn. She is singing here a song of almost pure faith. She is placing God's promises before her mind, and in them she is exulting. Beautiful indeed was her faith when the angel first appeared to her. Sarah, her ancestor, laughed when a heavenly messenger told her of a far less wonderful thing; Zacharias, the pious and aged priest, hesitated, and doubted, and required a sign, when the angel of the Lord assured him that Elizabeth in her old age should bear him a son; but this holy virgin, when told of one of the most marvellous things the power of God ever accomplished, doubted not; one simple question answered, she regarded that marvellous thing as certain and sure. The old Elizabeth knew how to appreciate such faith as this. She commends her for it. "Blessed is she that believed, for there shall be a performance of those things which were told her from the Lord." And here, in the strength of the same faith, this noble-minded young woman is looking forward, and speaking of all these promised things as already performed. "From henceforth," she says, "all generations shall call me blessed. He that is mighty, hath magnified me. Remembering his mercy, he hath holpen his servant Israel, as he promised to our forefathers, Abraham and his seed for ever."

And here, brethren, lies the great secret of almost all a Christian's joy—he is living, not a life of sense, but a life of faith. Many of you look to what you have for comfort and happiness; he looks to what he is to have, to what God has promised him, to what the rolling years are to bring him ages and ages hence. He gets as much blessedness out of what he now possesses as you do, and more; but he knows that he should be acting a most unwise part, were he to rest his happiness on what he has. It is fleeting as the summer clouds or the winter sunshine. It is as unstable as the shifting sands on the shore of a boisterous sea. If he builds on it, it may slip from under him in an hour, and leave his happiness a ruin. And were it not so, much as his God may have given him, he well knows that he has not given him enough to make him happy; that it is not the intention of his God to make him happy here in present enjoyments. The fountain of his happiness is above. From above therefore he draws now his chief delights. "In thy presence," he says, "is the fulness of joy;" and when he wants his soul to be joyful, he sends his thoughts up into God's presence, and endeavours to anticipate and realize the joy that is there.

Would you, brethren, share his happiness? There is but one way for you to share it—you must seek to share first his faith. In God lies his happiness, the same God of whom you have been hearing ever since you were born, and have never perhaps once thought of yet with any feeling of pleasure. He is nothing to you, or, if any thing, a terror. What you want is something that will strip him of his terrors; bring him within your sight; reveal to you his goodness, excellence, and beauty; enable you to see him, not as a fearful object, but as an attractive one, as your soul's salvation, your soul's rest, your soul's blessedness, your exceeding joy. You want an eye that can pierce the heavens, and look on the great Jehovah in some measure as he is; as he is looked on at this moment by angels and archangels who behold him there. Now all this faith can do for you, a simple faith in the gospel of Jesus Christ. That gospel is a discovery to us of what God really is; it is a mirror which shews him to us. Faith looks into this mirror; it becomes acquainted in the gospel with its revealed God; and wondering at his grace and glory, wondering still more at its former insensibility and blindness, it seeks through Christ Jesus to have this glorious God for its own, to obtain an interest in his grace and love and all his perfections; and obtaining this, it is happy; it rejoices sometimes even on this side heaven with a joy that is " unspeakable and full of glory."

This is no delusion, brethren. It is not, as you may suppose, an ideal thing. It is a real thing. There are those now around you, who could tell you that it is a real thing. The joy of Mary's soul in God her Saviour, is a joy they can understand as well as you can understand a parent's joy in his children, or a friend's joy in his friend, or a thirsty man's joy in a fountain, or a weary traveller's joy in his home. It is a joy they have known and felt. O that you also, if only for one short minute, could know and feel it! It is a joy you would remember all your life long. It would at last convince you that there is a happiness felt and enjoyed in this dreary world, which would make the world wonder if it could see it, and make you happier than the happiest worldling on the earth's surface, could you obtain it. You may obtain it, brethren. It is as much within your reach, as it ever was within the reach of those who are now rejoicing the most in it. " The same Lord over all is rich unto all that call upon him." They called upon him, and now they are delighting in his riches; you also may call upon him, and in the end delight in them. Your prayer must be for a real and heart-felt belief in the gospel of his Son; and that one simple but mighty thing will discover to you, when you have obtained it, all the glories of his Godhead, and among them his wonderful power to save the most sinful, and bless and delight the most sorrowful soul.

SERMON XIV.

THE LORD'S SUPPER AN EMBLEM AND MEMORIAL.

St. Luke xxii. 19, 20.

" And he took bread, and gave thanks, and brake it, and gave unto them, saying, This is my body which is given for you; this do in remembrance of me. Likewise also the cup after supper, saying, This cup is the new testament in my blood which is shed for you."

Were a heathen stranger to come into this church, and observe us while celebrating here the supper of our Lord, it is probable that he would at first be startled by the scene before him. He would soon however come to the conclusion, that there must be more in this rite than meets his eye. Its apparently trifling character would of itself convince him, that no company of reasonable men would observe such a ceremony for its own sake, and that it must have in it some spiritual meaning, impenetrable indeed to him, but well understood by those engaged in it. Now suppose a man of this class to question us to-day on this subject, to ask us when returning from the table of the Lord, " What mean you by this service?" how should you answer him? It would not satisfy him to say, " This is an awful mystery which must not be enquired into." Such an answer would probably send the man's thoughts home to his own pagan land. " We have mysteries there," he might say, " and this is just what our priests tell us when we wish to understand them; but you call yours a reasonable religion; shew me then the reasonableness of this strange rite of it, that you have now been celebrating." The text before us furnishes us with an answer for him. Our Lord does more in it than institute his holy supper; while instituting, he explains it. Instead of wrapping it up in mystery, he at once unfolds to us its nature, its spiritual meaning and design. Let us look upwards for an humble, teachable spirit, while we carefully consider his words.

They present his supper to us in a two-fold character.

I. It is *an emblem*. By this we mean a sign or symbol; something visible representing something else that is invisible. Now all that we have visible here, is bread and wine. The question is then, what unseen things do these simple objects represent?

1. *The human nature of Christ;* his incarnation.

He took bread and said of it, " This is my body ;" and he took the cup also and said of that, " This is my blood." He calls it indeed " the new testament in his blood," but he means his blood itself on which the new testament or covenant is founded ; and agreeably to this, two of the other evangelists describe him as saying, " This is my blood of the new testament."

But why make his human nature of so much importance? Why does our Lord in instituting this solemn rite in his church, bring forward so prominently his mere humanity? No man who denies his Godhead, could answer this question. But bring in his divinity, and the question is answered in a moment. The human frame represented by that bread and wine, is a frame inhabited by the great Lord of all. It is a shrine, a dwelling place, for the everlasting Jehovah. The fulness of the Godhead, all the fulness of it, is there, and there continually, and there for ever. " It is my body," says the one only living and true God, and our Lord, in reminding us of that body in his supper, speaks like the only living and true God. His own thoughts are full of the wonderful act of condescension he has stooped to in becoming man, and he wishes to bring it into our thoughts and to fill them with it. He would have our minds continually fixed on that great mystery of godliness, an incarnate God, God manifest in our mortal flesh.

2. *The death of Christ* too is shadowed forth in this ordinance. We have more than bread before us in it, it is bread which has been broken; and more than wine, it is wine which has been poured forth. And it was the same in the original sacrament, and this, not from accident, but from design. Our Lord, we read here, " brake" the bread when he took it in his hands and compared it to himself; and so brake it, as to let his disciples see that he meant something by the act. They record the circumstance. It arrested their attention and dwelt in their memories. And mark the importance St. Paul attaches to it. In recording his Master's words, he slightly alters them, with the evident design of forcing this action of his on our notice, and explaining to us its import. " This is my body which is given for you," says Christ here, " but in the eleventh chapter of his first epistle to the Corinthians, the apostle makes him say, " This is my body which is broken for you." And immediately

afterwards he speaks yet more plainly; " As often as ye eat this bread," this broken bread, " and drink this cup, ye do shew forth," not the Lord's body only, but " the Lord's death till he come."

It follows then that we have in this sacrament a picture of the blessed Jesus as he hung on the cross; a representation of him, not as a man only, but as a man of sorrows and suffering. Here is presented to us a broken Saviour; a wounded, and bruised, and bleeding, and dying Saviour. His agony in the garden, the shame and insults, the mocking and scourging he endured in the judgment-hall, the piercing of his temples by the crown of thorns, the nailing of him to the cross, his anguish there of body and of soul, his last cry of misery, his dying groan, the flowing of his blood from his wounded side, and the laying down of his lifeless body in the grave —all these the sacred symbols set before us on his table are intended to represent. They are designed to bring all these things to our memories, to paint them to our imaginations, and most certainly to impress them on our hearts.

3. They are emblematical also of *the great end and design of our Lord's incarnation and death.*

" This is my body," he says, " which is given for you, and this cup is the new testament in my blood which is shed for you. You are the persons interested in my wonderful incarnation and death. They do not happen in the ordinary course of events. You see me a man like yourselves, and you may think that like yourselves I was born, and like you I shall die; but no. I was born as none ever before me was born, and I shall die as none ever before me has died. My birth and death are both of them new and strange things in God's universe. They are peculiar things intended for a peculiar purpose. No debt of nature shall I pay on my cross, no penalty for any sins of mine; I shall die there for you, a willing victim for your guilty souls."

This follows then, that we are to see on the table now spread for us, not only the body of Christ and the death of Christ, but the ends they were both to answer. We are to connect ourselves with them, to view them as the means infinite wisdom has ordained for our pardon and salvation. The bread and wine placed on that table are to remind us of " the exceeding great love of our Master and only Saviour, Jesus Christ, in dying for us, and the innumerable benefits which by his precious bloodshedding he hath obtained to us." We are to behold shadowed forth in them guilt expiated, incensed justice satisfied, mercy triumphant, the great Jehovah pacified towards the sinner, his grace reclaiming him, his love embracing him, his Spirit purifying and comforting him, his arm sustaining him, his kingdom opened to him, his joy entering into his soul, and his glory covering him.

And now what becomes of the seeming meanness, the low and trifling character, of this sacrament? Only look through its simple emblems to the objects they represent, and in one moment a majesty and grandeur overspread it. Now let the heathen stranger ask us what this service means, we have an answer for him. We behold in it, we say, the living God descending from on high and becoming man, and dying as man for our sakes. We see in it deliverance for us from a wretched hell, and an entrance opened for us into a happy heaven. There is an innumerable company of immortal beings before us, once degraded and lost, now rescued, glorified, and for ever blest. And then we will ask this heathen whether this is not a reasonable service, and whether we are not acting as reasonable men in observing and delighting in it.

II. Let us now go on to another view of this ordinance. It is a *memorial.* The text represents our Lord as making the bread and wine emblematical of himself for one special purpose, that they might perpetuate among us the memory of himself. "This do," he says, "in remembrance of me."

There is a resemblance then and a difference between this sacrament and the ancient Jewish ordinances—they were shadows of Christ before he came, keeping up the expectation of his coming; this sacrament is a shadow of him after he is gone, keeping up the remembrance of his coming, and of the blessings he obtained for us while among us.

But it is not himself simply considered, that our Lord calls on us here to remember; it is himself as these emblems set him forth, given and bleeding for us; it is himself in his humiliation, sufferings, and death. These things he would have borne in mind in his church, thought of, spoken of there; these things above all others; his manhood, more than his Godhead; his death, more than his resurrection, or ascension, or heavenly glory; his thirty three years of shame, and degradation, and misery, more than his whole eternity of honour and joy. "This do," he says, "in remembrance of me; of me, not as you expect to see me hereafter when I rend the heavens and come down in my majesty, amidst shouting angels and burning worlds, but of me as you behold me now; of me in your form and nature; of me, the companion of your wanderings, the partaker of your sufferings, the sharer of your griefs; of me the Son of man, the despised and rejected Nazarene; me in the manger, me in the judgment-hall, me on the cross, me in the grave."

And why this? Why the institution of an ordinance to bring things like these to our remembrance?

1. Partly perhaps on account of *the joy Christ himself feels in the recollection of them.*

He greatly loves us, brethren, and because of his love to us, he delights in any thing that communicates good to us. And that which brings the most good to us, affords the most delight to his soul. Hence before his appearance in our flesh, he was continually speaking in his word of his coming here; and when he came, he was as continually speaking of the sufferings and death he had to endure; he describes himself as "straitened," eager almost to impatience, till he had accomplished them; and all this because he knew that blessings unutterable would flow from them to his beloved church. And now they are past, the same feeling exists in him still. He sees them to be sources of blessings to his church, and he dwells on them again in his word as though the recollection of them were pleasant to his soul, and as though he wished his people to have them ever in their remembrance, that they might share in the pleasure they give him. They shall be remembered by his church in heaven, for there his own incarnate form shall every moment testify of them; and they shall be remembered by his church on earth, symbols of them shall be set up, a new and peculiar ordinance shall be instituted to shew them forth. Is it sweet to you, brethren, to think of sorrows that are past? It is sweet also to the Lord Jesus Christ. Is it sweet to you to think of the blessings you may have purchased for those you love, by your past labours and sufferings? It is still sweeter to him. His heart overflows with joy at the thought of his cross and passion, and he would have us think of them and sympathize with him in his joy.

2. *The remembrance of Christ's incarnation and death is of the utmost importance to us;* therefore also he may have established this memorial of them among us.

There are some things which equally benefit us, whether we think of them or not. The sun shines on us day by day, though we may never give him a thought; and the ocean supplies us with clouds and rain, even if we forget it exists. Not so however with our dying Lord. He must be thought of, or his dying love will be of little avail to us. It may keep us for a few short years, in common with all mankind, the objects of God's patience and kindness, but, at the end of those years, it will leave us to perish. The salvation of our immortal souls depends as much on our remembrance of our crucified Lord, as on that Lord himself. He himself tells us so. He compares himself to our food. "My flesh is meat indeed;" he says, "and my blood is drink indeed;" and just as that food must be eaten or it will not preserve our lives, so must he, by an habitual remembrance of him and a lively faith in him, be fed on by the soul, or the soul must sink. "He that eateth me," he says, "even he shall live by me." "Except ye eat the flesh of the Son of man and drink his blood, ye have no life in you."

And it is the same with our spiritual comfort, and strength, and growth. They all flow from the Redeemer's cross, and that cross must live in our memories and hearts, or they will languish. We shall be like men who have forgotten the fountain that refreshes them, and the food that nourishes them. "All our fresh springs" are in our crucified Lord, and therefore he brings himself frequently before us as our crucified Lord, that we may go to him as the great source of our mercies, and take of his blessings.

3. There is another reason to be given for the setting up of this memorial of our Lord's sufferings—it is *our liability to forget them.*

Every real Christian becomes sensible, almost

on his first turning to God, of their immense importance to him. They may be to other men matters of affecting contemplation, to angels in heaven subjects of wonder and adoration; but he feels them to be to him as his very life. His Saviour's cross is to him more than his tongue could tell—his refuge, his hope, his strength, his peace, his joy, his glory. To lose sight of it seems scarcely, in his case, within the limits of possibility. Talk to him of the time when it will half fade away from his remembrance, with a soul glowing with admiration, gratitude, and love, he will say he could as soon forget that he lives and breathes. A crucified Jesus is on the throne of his heart, and nothing, he thinks, even for an hour will ever remove him thence. But look at him when a few years have passed away. He has not forgotten his once loved Lord. No; he is still dearer to his soul than its dearest earthly joy, but the man has been buffeting with the troubles of life, been weighed down with its cares, harassed with many spiritual conflicts, often struggling with the corruptions of his own vile heart till that heart has been well nigh breaking with the misery of its warfare; and the consequence is, in his own sufferings he has half forgotten his Lord's. Theoretically he attaches as much importance to his cross as ever; it holds precisely the same place in his creed and in his judgment; but it does not hold the same place in his memory and feelings. He has been thinking of his trials more than of his sins, and in so doing, he has learnt to look on Christ as his sustaining Friend, more than his dying Redeemer. His presence in trouble, his power to uphold, his readiness to comfort, his tenderness in comforting, the amazing sweetness and strength of the consolation he imparts—these have somewhat eclipsed in the man's mind the glory of his atonement, and he needs once again to be laid low at the foot of the cross; he needs to be reminded that he is a sinner as well as a sufferer, and that all the comfort he can get from his Lord in his sufferings, is nothing compared with the deliverance he gives him from bitter sufferings to come. To some of you this may seem a purely ideal case, but others of you understand it well. You have again and again started with a mournful surprise at the distance to which you have found yourselves wandering from the fountain of a Saviour's blood, even when not sensibly wandering from that Saviour himself. Most wisely then as well as kindly has he who knows us well, ordained among us a standing memorial of his cross; of that which it is life to us to remember, death to us to forget. His glorious ascension, his lofty exaltation, his coming again in triumph, the joys and splendours of his future reign—all these he tells us of, all these he calls on us to bear in mind; but as for his humiliation and death, he will trust to no command, he brings symbols of them visibly before our eyes, sets up on high in his church a monument of them, and bids those who love him, gather round it and mark it. We are to eat of the bread he has ordered to be broken for us, and to drink of the cup he has commanded to be poured forth.

There are two or three practical conclusions to which we must now come.

1. If the Lord's supper is an emblem, then *as an emblem we must regard it.* "No," says the Romish church, "it is not an emblem, it is a reality." And if ever Satan obtained a triumph over the common sense of poor weak man, it is when he first brought him to believe an absurdity like this. Among all the follies and delusions of heathen lands, there is not one stranger nor one more pitiable.

"This is my body," says our Lord. A child could tell what he means—"It is a symbol of my body, a representation of it, something which is to remind you of it;" just as we often write the name of a man on the picture of him and, in pointing to it, call it by his name. "Not so," says this church; "it is our Lord's body itself;" and when we ask them how that can be; how any one can hold his own body in his hand, and break it in pieces, and give it to others that they may eat it, we are gravely told that we must not ask such questions, that at their command we must lay our understandings asleep, and believe any absurdities or any impossibilities they may tell us. We are often tempted to ask, brethren, which is greater, the craft or the folly of man? Let us learn not to despise or hate him for either, but to pity and feel for him more under both.

2. Is the Lord's supper an emblem? Then *as an emblem let us be satisfied with it.* Let us not make to ourselves other memorials and emblems.

It is an instance of great condescension in our Lord to stoop so low as this to our carnal nature, to give us one sensible image of himself and his sufferings. Could he have gone further, we may be sure from his love and pity to us, that he would have done so. But he knows the danger of interposing material things between God and his creatures. We soon learn to transfer to those material things the worship and reverence, the love and fear, which are due to him alone. And therefore he holds back. He gives us one symbol of himself, and there he stops. And there we must stop, brethren, or mischief to us will follow. Crucifixes, and crosses, and paintings, and images, seem very harmless things; nay, they help us in our devotions, some of us may say; but poor indeed must be those devotions which things like these can help, and if we knew whereof we are made, we should be afraid of their help; we should trample on them, rather than seek assistance from them. What does the Hindoo say while worshipping his deformed idol? " I worship not that idol. I am worshipping the great God it represents; and that figure before me lifts up my heart to him." But we well know what the fact is—the man is as much bowing down his body and soul to that thing of iron or clay, as though he had never heard of the living God. So with all those miserable representations that are found in some of what are called Christian churches. They are worse than childish and offensive; when they cease to offend, they become perilous. In introducing them, we are bringing symbols of our own into God's sanctuary, and he will not bear the pollution. He will give us up to those empty symbols. He will withdraw from us his spiritual presence, and with a Christian name and a Christian creed, scarcely a benighted heathen can be found on the face of the earth more superstitious or idolatrous than we.

3. Has our Lord appointed his holy supper

as a memorial of himself? *We must thankfully accept and celebrate it as a memorial of him.* And in order to this, we must renounce all false ideas of its design and character. The old superstitious notion that the sacrament is a sacrifice, that in some way or other it has the power of doing something to expiate sin, is not extinct among us. It may not be so common in protestant England as in papal Rome, but it is here. Many in our land are going to the table of the Lord, not for the purpose for which our Lord has bidden them go there, to remember there his great love to us, his incarnation and death, but for a purpose of their own—to quiet an accusing conscience, to get relief under inward uneasiness and self-reproach, to wipe off the sins of the last month's frivolity, or the last year's worldly-mindedness, or the transgressions and ungodliness of a whole life. But what folly, brethren, to look to a simple rite like this, a mere emblem of a sacrifice, to do that which nothing but that great sacrifice itself can accomplish! It is like turning, when starving, to a picture of food, and expecting it to satisfy us; or flying in a storm to the painted likeness of a house, and expecting it to shelter us. "Do this," says our Lord—for what end? "that your sins may be blotted out?" No; but would he not have said so could the doing of it have blotted out our sins? "Do this," he says, "in remembrance of me."

But we may err in another way. While some are making too much of this ordinance, we may make too little of it, regarding it as a mere form and attending on it we hardly know why. Our Lord represents it here as a reasonable service, as having a spiritual object in view, as intended to recal to our minds those great facts on which our everlasting happiness depends, his own abasement and crucifixion for the expiation of our sins. Now to lose sight of this, to go to it as though it had no meaning at all in it, not to see in it our humbled and suffering Lord, or, seeing him, to forget why he was humbled and why he suffered, to treat the sacrament as any thing less than a symbol and memorial of that without which you and I and every soul of man must perish everlastingly, what is this but to dishonour this holy sacrament, and to receive the same unworthily? It is stripping off from it its reasonable, spiritual character, and degrading it to an unmeaning ceremony. In that chapter of his first epistle to the Corinthians, to which we have already referred, St. Paul is speaking of an unworthy receiving of this rite, and to what does he trace this evil? To this one simple circumstance, a forgetting of the origin and design of it—" not discerning in it the Lord's body," not seeing a crucified Christ in the broken bread and poured out wine, not thinking of him as an atoning Saviour, losing sight of his cross. There are other ways of profaning this ordinance, but they all proceed from this. If we profane it not in this way, there is but little fear of our dishonouring it in any other. To remember the Lord's body, to set Christ before us as our dying Redeemer, to look on him as the salvation, the life and rest and happiness, of our souls, to live day by day with him in our thoughts and hearts; this, brethren, is the best safeguard from every evil and every sin. None need fear for us while we are doing this, and while doing this, we need not fear for ourselves. We may approach the table of the Lord this morning without one apprehension of being rejected there; nay, could we fly this moment to the heavens above us, we might sit down there in the kingdom of God, and God himself would pronounce us welcome and blessed.

SERMON XV.

THE SONG OF SIMEON.

St. Luke ii. 28, 29, 30.

"Then took he him up in his arms, and blessed God, and said, Lord, now lettest thou thy servant depart in peace according to thy word, for mine eyes have seen thy salvation."

Our church calls these words a song, and if words of joy make a song, this surely is one. May our own dying lips sing it! or rather, may the God of all grace put it into our hearts in our dying hour!

I. Let us notice *the occasion* of these words.

It is an affecting circumstance, that although our Lord came to abolish the whole ceremonial law, he himself submitted to it all. It was a law for the ignorant and sinful; he was neither, but being as a Jew born under it, he conformed to every rite it enjoined, as if he had been both. Eight days after his birth, his sinless flesh was circumcised; and forty days after it, we find him, not at Bethlehem or Nazareth, but far away, in the temple at Jerusalem, carried thither by his parents in obedience to another ordinance. The object of this visit to the temple was twofold.

It was, in the first instance, for Mary's purification. Every Jewish mother, after the birth of a child, was considered by the law as ceremonially unclean. For seven days she was to be regarded as altogether so, and then for thirty three days more, though some of the restraints laid on her were taken off, she was not allowed to " touch any hallowed thing nor to come into the sanctuary." At the expiration of this period, the law called on her to go to the door of the tabernacle or temple, and carry with her there a lamb and a young pigeon or dove, the one for a burnt-offering in testimony of her gratitude, the other for a sin-offering in acknowledgment of her guiltiness. In case however she was too poor to bring a lamb, she was permitted to substitute for it another pigeon or dove; and then, an atonement being made for her within the temple by the animal she had brought, its doors were open to her, she was restored to all her privileges and considered clean. Wonderfully, brethren, amidst all his mercies to us, does a holy God keep up the remembrance of our sinfulness, and command us also to keep it up. We cannot even shew our gratitude, lay a thank-offering upon his altar, without approaching his altar in the character of sinners. A grateful heart and a contrite heart must go together. He will not look at the one, unless at the same time, in conscious guilt and unworthiness, we offer him the other.

Now from a rite of this nature, we should have been well pleased to see the mother of our Lord exempt. The very idea of her contracting defilement, or even the appearance of defilement, connected with him, is strange and unwelcome to us. But the law commands, and the law must be obeyed. To Jerusalem, a distance of at least sixty miles, she goes, and there with the infant Jesus in her arms and her lowly offerings by her side, she humbles herself before the Lord at the temple door, confessing herself unclean.

Another object was accomplished by this visit.

To keep up the remembrance of his mercy in sparing the sons of the Israelites when those of the Egyptians were destroyed, it was the command of God, that in all succeeding generations, the first-born of Israel, both of man and beast, should be considered as his property. " Sanctify to me," he says, " all the first-born, it is mine." Accordingly the firstlings of all clean animals were set apart by the people as sacrifices, but permission was given them to redeem, as it were, from the Lord their first-born sons by paying a price for them. The child was to be brought to the temple as an acknowledgment of God's right to him, and then, after the appointed sum was paid and certain ceremonies gone through, he became free.

Now this chapter represents Mary as taking her holy child Jesus into the temple with her, to do for him after this custom of the law. Again we should have been ready to stop her. " There is no need of this," we should have said. " He is the Lord's already, and requires no presentation of him to the Lord by your hands, nor any redeeming of him from the Lord's service; he has sealed him as his own." But what answer would that Saviour himself have given us? The same that he gave afterwards at his baptism to the hesitating John; " You must suffer this. I am now one of yourselves, and I deem it no dishonour, it gratifies as well as becomes me, to be made in all things like unto you my brethren. Besides it is my Father's law that I am obeying, and my Father's law must be honoured. You may tell me that it is shadowy and soon to pass away, but were it within an hour of its passing away, I would fulfil it. In my own church hereafter I shall have rites and ordinances as shadowy as these, and I would have my people reverence these ordinances though they are shadows, even as I am now reverencing and obeying these."

And this is the ground on which we rest the honour that we pay to our Christian sacraments. They are no more in themselves than the long abolished ceremonies of the Jewish temple, but, like those ceremonies, they are of divine appointment, and, according to the example of our Saviour Christ, we will revere them. We will not worship them as the heathen worships his idol-god; nor trust in them for salvation, or pardon, or any thing else, as the pharisee of old trusted in his carnal ordinances; but we will take them from our Master's hands just as he gave them to us, afraid to make more of them and not wishing to make less, and in obedience to his authority, with humble and grateful hearts, we will observe them, looking for him in them as the pious Jew perhaps looked for him in the temple worship, and then deeming ourselves happy and blest, and then only, when we discover him in them and they bring him near us.

We may now place before us the scene connected with the text. We must conceive of Mary, her own purification over, as standing in the temple with the ministering priests before her and a company of other worshippers around her. And then we must imagine an aged man approaching, gazing for a moment at the heavenly babe in her arms, then taking it into his, and, with a look upwards, bursting forth in the hearing of them all into this happy song.

II. Let us consider *the happiness he expresses in it.*

We feel at once that it is happiness he expresses, not that overflowing of delight and joy which we see in Mary at Elizabeth's door, but a calm, subdued happiness; the happiness of one who has been long accustomed to strong emotions, and knows how to govern and restrain as well as indulge them. We are not told that Simeon was an old man, but it is probable from the narrative that he was so, and his happiness seems to be the happiness of old age, less lively and exuberant than that of youth, but as heart-felt and deep or deeper, and, like deep waters, quiet and serene. And this is one great beauty of the scriptures, as well as one of the many internal evidences of their truth—every thing in them is so agreeable to nature. Here is a young Christian before us in this page—she rejoices with all the exultation and glowing ardour of youth; we look to the next page, and there is an aged Christian, or, if not so, an experienced one, a man with a grave open before him—his joy in his God is as great, but he makes less of it, he manifests it less, he wants to go at once to his God that he may rejoice in him more.

But in what did Simeon's happiness consist?

1. *In praise for a blessing given.*

"He took him up in his arms, and"—what? gave utterance at once to the joy that thrilled within him? Yes, but not in what we should call the language of joy; "he blessed God:" the first indication he gives us of his delight, is blessing, praise. And Mary did the same in her song. "My soul doth magnify the Lord," she cried before she said one word of her rejoicing spirit. And Zacharias did the same in his; "Blessed be the Lord God of Israel." And the angels at Bethlehem did the same in theirs; "Glory to God in the highest." The shepherds too on their return after they had seen the babe, are described, not as rejoicing, but as "glorifying and praising God;" and here is the aged Anna at this very time in the temple, not telling those around her of the joy that was within her, but "giving thanks likewise unto the Lord."

When some of us have a mercy sent us, we must welcome it, we say; have a little time allowed us to feel that it is ours, to examine it and delight ourselves in it. Then comes late and slow the thought, that we owe this mercy to a gracious God, and must thank him for it. But this is because our joy in our mercies is not holy joy. Holy joy is like the joy of heaven—its natural language is praise, and its happiest language is praise. Praise is the overflowing, the running over, of its happiness; and it is the crowning, the perfecting, of its happiness. Blessings become sweeter to us, when they draw forth our praise. Who, when he has been praising God for a blessing, has not felt his heart lifted up at times above that blessing, almost forgetting it in the delight he has found in praising and adoring the God who has given it him? These saints and angels cannot rejoice even in a Saviour given, without first blessing his Father who sent him. They all begin with praise, as though their hearts were more full of it than of happiness or joy. They who are in heaven, understand this, and it is understood by some on earth. "Praise is pleasant," says David. "My mouth shall praise thee with joyful lips." Praise he often calls "a joyful noise;" he seems every where to identify it with joy.

"He blessed God," it is said; not Christ himself for his love in coming into our world, but God for giving him to us and sending him into our world. And, in accordance with this, he calls him in his song God's salvation, and a salvation which God has prepared.

And it is this looking on Christ as a Saviour provided for us by the everlasting Jehovah, that leads the soul to feel so thankful for him and rejoice so much in him. It is against the living God, that my sins have been committed. It is his law that condemns, and his displeasure that is threatening me. When therefore he himself appoints me a Saviour, I not only see and see with delight the love which is in his heart towards me, but I feel that the Saviour he has appointed me, is one I can confide in. He comes with his Father's full consent to save me; his Father is well pleased that he should save me; he has sent him down from his throne into this miserable world for the very purpose of saving me; there is the whole Godhead concurring with him while he is saving me. Trusting in him therefore for salvation, I am happy, for I know that I am trusting in one who really can save me.

2. *A hope realized* was another part of Simeon's happiness at this time.

Man, in his present state, is never perfectly happy, but he longs for perfect happiness, and, dissatisfied with the present, looks anxiously forward into the future that he may find it there. This brings hope into exercise, and much of the present happiness of man consists in the workings of hope; in anticipating good, and, when it comes, rejoicing in it as the good he had anticipated. Some of the happiest moments perhaps in our lives, are those in which we first put our hand on things we have long hoped for. Moments indeed they often are, or little better than moments. The things we have for years been longing for, turn out when we have them to be scarcely worth the having, and poor disappointed man has to look forward again to be perhaps again deceived and disappointed. But this does not materially alter the fact—man still goes to hope for his happiness, and from indulging and realizing hope, draws much of the happiness he enjoys.

The history represents Simeon to us at first as under the influence of hope. "It had been revealed unto him by the Holy Ghost, that he should not see death before he had seen the Lord's Christ." How long this revelation had been made to him, we are not told; it might have been many years before. We must regard him therefore while he stands in the temple with that blessed child in his arms, as one realizing a moment he had long looked for, as one receiving a blessing that had long been promised him, as one with the strongest desire of his heart, perhaps its only earthly desire, accomplished. The result is, he is satisfied; he asks for no more, he wants no more. Like a man who feels that the earth has no more to give him, that it has made him as happy as it can make him, he says,

"Let me leave it. Lord, now lettest thou thy servant depart in peace. I have waited for thy salvation, O Lord; and here it is. Mine eyes have seen it. Lord, set me free, that I may come up to thee and praise thee for it."

We who are fathers, can enter into old Jacob's feelings, when his long lost Joseph met him in Egypt, and "fell on his neck and lay on his neck weeping." "Now let me die," said that affectionate but weak old man, "since I have seen thy face." This was all nature, and Simeon here is just as natural, but he is a man of a loftier mind, or, if not so, he has a hope realized of a far loftier character, and he has therefore a loftier joy within him. We must be Christians and such Christians as he was, before we can fully enter into a joy like his. You have felt something like it, who have been bowed down for years with a sense of sin, and have at last seen God's salvation, looked on a mighty Saviour and been able for the first time to call him yours. Joyfully, you will tell us, would you in that moment have left the world and carried your happy hearts to heaven.

3. There was yet something more in this man's happiness—*delight in a glorious prospect opened to him.*

Let God give the real Christian what spiritual blessing he may, he immediately longs for more.

The blessing he has received, seems to bring into his view other blessings, and to kindle his desires for them. With him therefore hope realized is a new impulse given to hope. It stands, as it were, on the blessing given, and stretches itself forward to farther and higher things. And this was now Simeon's case. He seems to have had a two-fold prospect before him—one above in heaven and the other on the earth, and both glorious.

There is at last the new-born Saviour in his arms, and what does he say? " Let me keep him in them: let me stay in the world as long as he stays in it, and follow his blessed footsteps to the end?" No. " Let me die," he says, "and inherit his full salvation." His thoughts pass from that Saviour to the glory and happiness with which he would fill the realms of bliss above him, and he longs to be in those realms of bliss, that he may behold and enjoy that glory and happiness. But this is only for a moment. There is a sudden and beautiful turn in his thoughts and language.

Think of a dying man, and you immediately place before you a man with almost all his thoughts centred in himself and the change that is passing on him. If he is a real Christian, you expect every word he utters to be of the Lord who has loved him, or the heaven he has prepared for him, or the peace he is giving him. But look at this dying Simeon. Though he is thinking of the heaven he is going to, not a word does he say of it, nor of his personal interest in that Saviour he is beholding. He passes abruptly from himself and all that concerns himself; he rejoices in Christ as a Saviour for the whole world, the future glory of his own nation, and the future light and joy of all the nations of the earth. " Mine eyes," he says, " have seen thy salvation which thou hast prepared before the face of all people, a light to lighten the Gentiles and the glory of thy people Israel." There was Christian love at work at this time in this man's mind, triumphing over personal feeling, bringing into his mind the glorious promises delivered by God to his church through his prophets; love for the world he was leaving, delighting in the mercies that were coming on it; and love for that world's Saviour, exulting in his triumphs and glory.

And this, we may say, was his happiness. It consisted in praise for a great blessing received, joy in a long cherished hope realized, and delight in a glorious prospect opened to him. And it is obvious that his happiness, like Mary's, all sprang from faith. What had he before him to excite in him these feelings? A mighty God rending the heavens, and with a burst of glory coming down and proclaiming himself a Saviour? The heavens were as quiet above him as they are now above us. He had nothing before him but a young and lowly woman of Nazareth with a weak infant in her arms. But in some way that we know not, the Spirit had marked out that infant to him as " he that should redeem Israel," and poverty, meanness, and weakness, are all nothing to him; his faith raises him above them all; and as he holds that humble babe in his arms, his spirit rejoices in him as God his Saviour.

III. Let us now endeavour to draw from his happiness *some useful instruction for ourselves*. And in doing so, we must regard ourselves, brethren, as dying men. Simeon speaks here as a dying man. He probably went home from this happy scene in the temple, and soon laid himself down and died. We too must lie down and die. We have heard of death, we have thought of death, most of us have seen death, but ere long we ourselves must experience it. A few more of these swiftly rolling years, and there will not be one of us now within these walls in the land of the living; the darkness of the grave will have closed upon us all. As we sit here and look around us, it is difficult to believe this, but it is notwithstanding true, as true as that yesterday is gone. In what light then do we regard that great change which is coming on us? With what feelings are we looking forward to a dying hour? Not to look forward to it at all would be mournful folly. If there is a man here so thoughtless as this, his own conscience will tell him what he is. We need not say to him, " Thou fool;" there is a voice within him that is even now saying, " If there is one foolish being in the universe, it is I."

" We long to die," some of you may say; but let me ask you, brethren, why do you long to die? It may surprise you to be told so, but, with the exception of this prayer before us, scarcely any wish for death can be found in all the scriptures, which is not a sinful one. Job, Elijah, Jonah, all cried out, " Let me die," but they were some of the very worst words these men ever uttered. They were tired of God's dealings with them, weary of the discipline or the work he had allotted them, and they wanted to get away from them. The case may be the same with you. Bring your desire for death then, just as you would bring any other feeling, to the standard of God's word. Before you indulge it or even think it safe to indulge it, try it by this text. It tells you that if it is a holy desire, it is the desire, not of a wretched, but of a happy hour. It is the strongest when the soul's happiness is the greatest. It springs no more from the ills than from the joys of life. The world has in truth little to do with it. When your souls are above the world, looking down on all the vexing things in it as petty trifles or not looking on them at all, then say, if you will, " Lord, now lettest thou thy servant depart in peace;" but when harassed and worn by worldly things, beware of such language. Take rather Jeremiah's language, " It is good that a man should both hope and quietly wait for the salvation of the Lord;" or Job's language in a sober moment, " All the days of my appointed time will I wait till my change come." " We shrink from death," others of you may say. You hope that Christ's salvation will in the end be yours, but you have never been able to reconcile yourselves to the dying hour that is to make it yours. " Would it were over," you say. " For years we have been sighing for a willingness to die. We have sought it and prayed for it, but we have never felt it. Death seems to us as cold and dark a thing as ever, and as terrifying." Now you will admit at once, brethren, that this is a wrong state of mind, as well as an unhappy one; and you will be almost as ready to admit that there must be something wrong in you to produce it. This scripture perhaps will discover to you what this is. It tells you that Simeon's happiness in the prospect of death was happiness in a Saviour. No matter in what it consisted, it all rested on Christ or rather flowed from him. "Mine eyes have seen thy salvation," explains it all. And you must understand this and fully understand it, before you can participate in Simeon's peaceful feelings. Sin is the sting of death. It is guilt on the conscience, that makes death so terrible to man. To do away its terrors then, the soul must see its own great guilt done away with, its iniquities all forgiven and its sins covered: it must see the sufficiency, completeness, and glory, of the atonement Christ has made for its sins. And it must go farther, and get something like a sight of the satisfaction and delight which God feels in pardoning sin and in saving sinners through Christ. It must connect Christ with God, see him as God's salvation; and it must connect itself through Christ with God, regarding itself as mixed up with his lofty plans and purposes, as a soul which God in his amazing mercy has formed for himself, and set apart to be an everlasting monument to the glory of his grace. And then, brethren, how shall we look on death? Prospects will open before us, feelings will arise within us, so elevating, that we shall care no more for it, than the eagle cares for the fog or the cloud through which it is piercing to get to the sun. I am going to my Saviour, we shall say, and what matters to me the darkness, or roughness, or loneliness, of the road which leads me to him? Once with him, I shall never feel lonely again. I shall be in all the brightness of heaven, and the joy of heaven will be mine.

"This was once our language," some of you may answer, "but it is not so now; the fear of death has again fallen upon us." You perhaps, brethren, may have to learn from this scripture, that happiness in death is connected with a holy life. It gives us this man Simeon's previous character. He was "just and devout," it says, "waiting for the Consolation of Israel." Not that his just and devout life was the spring of his dying happiness, but had it not been for his devout life, he would never have experienced that happiness. A man who looks to a well spent life for peace in death, makes a sad mistake. He is worse than a foolish or deluded man, he is a proud, arrogant man. He may die in peace, for his pride of heart may hold him up to the last; but it is a peace that he will think of with wonder when he is dead; it is the last moment of peace he will ever know. But, on the other hand, what is that man doing, who is looking for happiness in death without a well spent, a holy, heavenly life? He is shutting his eyes to that order of things, which God has established; he is forgetting what God has told him in his word, and often shewn him in the world. Think of David. See what sin did in his once happy soul. "Though I walk through the valley of the shadow of death, I will fear no evil," was his song in his youth, but what did he say in his after life? Death seems really coming upon him, and does he, like this Simeon, fearlessly welcome it as it comes, and almost run to meet it. No; he shrinks from it. "O spare me," he cries, " spare me a little, that I may recover my strength. I am not fit to die." He had the same Saviour to rejoice in that holy Simeon had, or the blameless Paul had, and he did rejoice in him, but not as they did. Sin had mingled fear in his joy. They were as ready to die as a stranger is to go home, or a prisoner to go free. David, with the same Saviour for his own and the same salvation before him, hangs back. He feels as you feel now, when death approaches him. And what does all this tell us but that same thing over again, Sin is the sting of death? Have done with sin, brethren; have done with it in heart and life. Search it out, and, by the help of God, cast it away and cleanse yourselves from it. The clearest knowledge of the gospel, the most enlarged views of God's salvation, cannot stand against a worldly or undevout, much less a sinful life.

Honour the Holy Spirit as your Sanctifier, and he will in the end honour himself as your Comforter. He brought Simeon up to the temple that he might shew him Christ there and comfort him. Take him as your guide, and he will lead you where you shall be comforted; where you too shall say, " Lord, now let me depart, for mine eyes also have seen thy salvation."

SERMON XVI.

THE LORD'S SUPPER A SHEWING FORTH OF HIS DEATH.

1 CORINTHIANS XI. 26.

"As often as ye eat this bread and drink this cup, ye do shew the Lord's death till he come."

In the preceding verses of this chapter, the apostle has given us our Lord's own account of his holy supper. He ordained it, he says, to be an emblem and memorial of himself. But a memorial may answer two purposes—it may serve to remind us of something, and we may make use of it to remind others of that same thing. A dying friend, for instance, bequeaths me a portrait of himself. I may often look at it myself to quicken my own remembrance of him, and I may hang it up in my house or shew it occasionally to my family, in order that those around me may not forget him. So this sacrament answers a double purpose. "This do," says Christ, "in remembrance of me." Yes, we answer, blessed Lord, we will do it, and keep the memory of thee and thy dying love ever alive in our minds. But the fervent Paul puts on the words immediately a wider sense. " As often as ye eat this bread and drink this cup, ye do shew the Lord's death till he come; you exhibit it; you hold up to others a picture of it; you are as really preaching your Master and your Master's cross while celebrating that sacrament, as I am while going about the world proclaiming his gospel." Indeed in the thirteenth chapter of the Acts, the very word which is here translated " shew," is twice over translated " preach;" "They preached the word of God in the synagogues;" " Through this man is preached unto you the forgiveness of sins." And our Lord's words will bear this interpretation as well as that which we generally give to them. Our translators have accordingly rendered them in the margin, " This do for a remembrance of me," thus anticipating the apostle's application of them.

In taking this view then of the Lord's supper, our enquiry must be what it is connected with his death that we shew forth in it.

I. *The manner of his death*, its violence and painfulness.

We talk of the dying love of Christ, brethren, and the Lord grant that we may talk of it for ever! but it was more than dying, it was bleeding love. He did not die, he was slain, for us. And in the sacrament, it is not merely his cold, lifeless body that we have represented to us, it is his wounded, mangled body. "This is my body which is broken for you," he says, "broken to pieces, as I am now breaking this paschal cake."

And recollect what importance is attached to this circumstance elsewhere. Look back to the old testament church. The very first promise ever given it of a Saviour, spoke of him as a bruised Saviour: he was proclaimed such in paradise. Abel's firstlings of his flock, Noah's burnt-offerings after the flood, the paschal lamb and the various other sacrifices under the law, all represented him as a slain victim. The prophets too described him, one after another, in a similar way. "He was wounded and bruised," says one; he shall be "cut off," says another; a third calls on the sword of Jehovah to awake and smite him. We cannot read the old testament without being reminded continually in it of that title given him in the new, "The Lamb slain from the foundation of the world."

And if we look into heaven, it is the same. He appears there, and he is adored there, as one who has been slain. "Behold my hands and my feet," he said to his disciples after he was risen; and now in his glory the marks of his wounds are still on those hands and feet; and would he lose them? would his redeemed around him lose them? No, much of the beauty and brightness of his presence would seem gone.

Now come to the Christian church. Here in this sacrament is something in harmony with all this. Christ appears in it just as he appeared in his church of old, just as he appears in his church above, just as he most loves to appear, as our slain Lord. Then we rightly regard this ordinance, when we regard it as setting forth, not his death only, but his death on a cross; a death brought on him by violence, and violence inflicted by our hands. Man would not let the Lord of glory die. When he appeared on our earth, he would not suffer him quietly to leave it. He lifted up his own desperate arm against him, and cut him off from it. We proclaim man's great guilt, as well as Christ's great love, at his table. We say there one to another, See what we are, as well as, see what our blessed Master is.

II. We shew also in this sacrament *the efficacy of our Lord's death*, its sufficiency for the ends it was designed to accomplish.

His body, he tells us, was broken for us, and his blood shed for us. We are the persons who are to be benefited by his violent and painful death. The main benefits we are to derive from it, are explained in other parts of scripture to be the expiation of our sins, the removal from us of God's righteous displeasure, and a restoration to his life-giving favour and love. We sinners, miserable sinners, offending every hour, are to be placed by it in the situation of creatures who have never sinned, who have never once offended the living God; or rather in the situation of children whom that living God tenderly loves and delights in. Now the institution of this ordinance by Christ is a declaration by Christ that his death has really accomplished these ends; that he really has removed the divine displeasure from his people, perfectly removed it, and brought them within the full sunshine, the full light and glow, of the divine favour. He would not mock us, brethren. He would not call on us to celebrate continually a work which is not accomplished, or only half accomplished. This would be like a vaunting general ordering a column to be raised for a victory that was never won. The sacrament of his supper is a staking of Christ's honour as to the completeness of his mediatorial work, so far at least as the expiating of our guilt forms a part of it.

It is like a continual echo of his own dying cry, "It is finished." And our celebrating this sacrament becomes in consequence a repetition on our part of this cry, a declaration that we believe in the full sufficiency of his atonement. It is telling the world, not only that we feel ourselves to be sinners, but that we are sure there is pardon for us in Christ Jesus, a free and full redemption for us through his blood, even the forgiveness of sins. It is crowding round the monumental column; it is adding another and another stone to it—a plain indication that we think the victory won. "Ye do shew the Lord's death till he come"—its efficacy, your conviction of its efficacy, your persuasion that it is a sacrifice acceptable to God, and one in which you can confide. If you do not say it has taken away your sins, you say that you are sure it can take them away; that you wish for no other sacrifice; that you are willing to stake the pardon, the life and death of your guilty souls, heaven and hell, on this. And this, you remember, is exactly the language of our church in our sacramental service. Words are heaped on words there to express, as forcibly as words can express, the fulness of the Redeemer's propitiation. Speaking of his death on the cross, the service says, he "made there, by his one oblation of himself once offered, a full, perfect, and sufficient sacrifice, oblation, and satisfaction for the sins of the whole world."

What then must we think of that notion of the Romish church, that the sacrament itself is a sacrifice for sin; that the bread and wine themselves, when the priest has consecrated them, have the power to take away sin? I will not call this an absurdity, for it is not its absurdness, that is the worst of it—it is a mournful impicty. Instead of declaring the all-sufficiency of Christ's sufferings, it declares their insufficiency; it says that though he has bled and died to take away sin, sin is not taken away; something more must yet be done, and done continually, before God can be satisfied and the guilty soul go free. And there are men risen up in our own church, who are ready to say this same thing: yes, men in this protestant church of England, who are insinuating, if not plainly declaring, that the Lord's supper is itself a sacrifice, is regarded by God as a sacrifice, possesses some mysterious, unaccountable power to propitiate God and cleanse from transgression. Would that when we lost the forms of popery, we had thoroughly got rid of popery itself! It has left us in this country many a sad legacy, and this is one of them. I will not say, there is no scriptural authority for this notion, I will not say, it is opposed to many plain declarations of God's word and the whole spirit of the gospel, though this is most true; but I would ask, where are the Christian feelings of these men? This notion is revolting to every feeling of the soul, when the soul has once felt its own guiltiness, and has seen the glory of its Redeemer's cross. Once, brethren, get a sight of that cross and its glory, and every notion like this you will cast from you, as you would cast away a polluted veil that hides from you a sight you love. Without calling scripture or common sense to your aid, your own feelings will settle all such matters, and settle them in a moment. You will say, " Guilty as I am, and none guiltier than I, my Master's cross is more than enough for me. I am not offering in this sacrament any new sacrifice to my God, nor offering again an old one; I am refreshing my soul with the remembrance of one already made. I am declaring to all around that I deem none other needful. I am doing what all the redeemed in heaven, I am sure, are doing—rejoicing in one great sacrifice long ago offered, and feeling that in that I can never rejoice enough; wanting no other, and satisfied that if I did, no other could be found."

III. We shew in this sacrament *the necessity of a particular application of Christ's death to ourselves.*

To make this point clear, we must look back a little.

The Lord's supper, we say, is a memorial. It is, in its original design, a simple commemorative rite. What it commemorates is the death of Christ as a sacrifice for us sinners. This is doubtless the account of it any one would give us from a mere reading of our Lord's own words in instituting it. But this is not a complete account; or rather, it is a complete account involving in it more than at first appears. It is not simply the death of Christ that is shadowed forth in this ordinance, but several of those great benefits resulting to us from his death. The bread and wine, the bread broken and the wine poured out, are not only emblems of our Lord's sufferings; when received by us, they become emblems of those spiritual blessings, that spiritual life, and refreshment, and strength, we derive from his sufferings. They do not touch the soul. How can they? They are no better than material, lifeless things. A piece of wood or stone might as soon touch the soul. But though they cannot do this, they represent that which can do it. They signify, as our catechism says, "the strengthening and refreshing of our souls by the body and blood of Christ," as our bodies are strengthened and refreshed by the bread and wine.

Now this, we may say, has no mysticism in it; it is all plain. And this will make plain the point before us.

You must remember that we do not merely look at the sacred elements in the Lord's supper; we are not commanded to stand still and contemplate them, or bow down and worship them; we are to take them in our hands, to eat and drink them. So our Lord commanded. "Take, eat," he said, "this is my body;" and he took the cup and gave it to them, saying, "Drink ye all of this, for this is my blood." "As often as ye eat this bread," says St. Paul in the text, "and drink this cup, ye do shew the Lord's death." Without eating the bread, observe, without drinking the wine, we might shew the manner and efficacy of his death—the bread broken and the wine poured out would of themselves do the one, our gathering round the bread and wine would do the other; but this partaking, this communicating, shews something more—that we ourselves desire to participate in the benefits of Christ's death, that we feel we must participate in them, receiving them within our souls as we receive the bread and the wine within our bodies. This eating and drinking becomes in fact an emblem of that faith which applies the sacrifice of Christ to the soul; comes to Christ, embraces him, partakes of him, makes him and the soul one. In his own strong language, it "eats the flesh of the Son of man and it drinks his blood." We pray for this in our service; "O merciful Father, grant that we receiving these thy creatures of bread and wine, according to thy Son our Saviour Jesus Christ's holy institution, in remembrance of his death and passion, may be partakers of his most blessed body and blood." And our service declares that through faith we are partakers of them; "If with a true penitent heart and lively faith we receive that holy sacrament, we spiritually eat the flesh of Christ and drink his blood."

A company of sinners then, going together to the table of the Lord, is a company of sinners declaring aloud the importance and necessity of a personal interest in the Lord; some seeking that interest, some blessing God with joyful hearts that they possess it, but all feeling that they must possess it, or what is any sacrament, any sacrifice, yea, what is Christ himself, to them?

And thus we shew the Lord's death at his table—the manner of his death, the efficacy of his death, and the necessity in every case of a particular application of his death to ourselves. This is in truth, you perceive, preaching the gospel, or the chief part of the gospel. A blessed work! Some of you perhaps half envy us ministers who are allowed sabbath after sabbath to come before our fellow-men and proclaim a crucified Saviour to them, and there are moments when we ourselves feel that a greater honour or happiness could not be ours. Better, we are ready to say, to be speaking of Christ to sinners on earth, than to be singing of him among angels in heaven. But here, brethren, is a way in which you are often doing the self-same thing; you are preaching Christ at his holy sacrament, and the chief glory of Christ, his cross. You are doing more than comforting and warming your own hearts there, you are telling your fellow-sinners where to take their cold and comfortless hearts; you are saying to all the guilty and perishing around you, " Behold the Lamb of God, which taketh away the sin of the world." And this view of the Lord's supper suggests to us several useful remarks.

We learn from it that *a knowledge of the gospel itself is needful for a right understanding of this sacrament.* It is a picture of the gospel; an embodying of its great truths in outward, visible things. It differs from the ordinary mode of preaching the gospel in this—the one preaches it to the ear by words, the other to the eye by emblems and signs. If we understand the gospel, we find no difficulty in understanding this sacrament. It becomes almost at once simple and clear to us. And then in its turn it illustrates the gospel, enabling us to understand it better. Just as many of the ordinances in the ancient church both receive light from the gospel and reflect light back again on it, so this ordinance in our Christian church is both explained by the gospel and itself explains it. And it will generally be found that where the gospel is best understood, this sacred rite is the most highly esteemed and the most frequented. Less may be heard of it there than in other places, in words less may seem to be made of it, but it stands higher in the minds and hearts of men; and if we want a proof of its doing so, we have it in the greater number of those who of their own free accord, without entreaty or solicitation, attend it.

But we shall never understand this sacrament till we do understand the gospel. We shall be in the same situation with many of the ignorant Jews under the law—not seeing the spiritual import of the things before us, we shall not look beyond those things, we shall rest in them. They will not only be misunderstood by us, they will be abused. The shadows of " good things" will take the place in our minds of those " good things" themselves, " carnal ordinances" will be confounded with spiritual blessings, and the emblems of a dying Saviour will be more to us than that dying Saviour himself. Go through Roman catholic countries

—there is the crucifix, the cross of wood or stone, the elevated host, adored; the great Saviour himself practically despised, and his gospel scarcely heard of or known.

Here too we may see that *Christ's gospel must be highly valued and loved by us before we can rightly attend his holy supper.* He makes a poor preacher of the cross, who has no love for it, or who lightly esteems it. It is a sight of its glory and a happy experience in his own heart of its power, that sends a minister of it into the pulpit prepared to preach it. And the same things are needed for the right shewing forth of the Lord's death at the Lord's table. You want them as much there, as we ministers want them here; and no other things will supply the place of them. What should we be without them? We might be very thoughtful and painstaking for many days before we preached, but our laborious preparation would be worth nothing; it would be all thrown away, you would say, if we came before you without a real love within us for our Master and his cross. And just as worthless is the most serious preparation on your part for the table of the Lord, when it is not accompanied with this love. Ask yourselves, brethren, what feelings ought to fill our hearts as we stand up to preach a crucified Jesus to our fellow-sinners. Then look upwards, and beseech the God of all grace to put the same feelings into your hearts as you shew forth the crucifixion of that same Jesus at his table.

We may infer also from the text, that *the Lord's supper should be celebrated by us frequently.* Is it a shewing of his death? Then the more frequently his death is shewn forth in this world of sinners, the better. " As often as ye eat this bread," the apostle says—the expression implies that the sacramental bread was often eaten by the people he was addressing; and such we know to have been the case. Some think this sacrament was observed every day in the primitive church, others every sabbath; it is certain that it was very frequently observed. But we have no command on this subject. In the Jewish church, every thing was fixed and determined. The time for the performance of its rites was as much appointed as those rites themselves. Nothing was left to the people. But there is a liberty about the gospel. God deals with us under it as with his willing children, not as his unwilling servants or slaves. " I will trust you," he seems to say. " I will not bind you to weeks and days. There are my ordinances; the time for observing them I will leave to yourselves. If my love is within you, I know how you will act—you will come to my table, and gladly come, as often as you can. Your own feelings will not suffer you to turn away from it. This would be almost as strange as for one of my redeemed around me here in my glory, to turn away from my presence and throne."

And *this sacrament is to be celebrated perpetually.* It is to be a standing ordinance in the church; one that is never to be repealed, never to be forgotten. "As often as ye eat this bread and drink this cup, ye do shew the Lord's death till he come."

The church then, we may say, will not only last till Christ comes, but will last in nearly its present form and condition. That which now constitutes his chief glory in it, will constitute it to the end. His death shall be perpetually shewed forth in it; his death above every thing else. And the ordinance which has now for eighteen centuries shewn it forth, is to endure and shew it forth to the end. Not like circumcision or the Jewish sacrifices and feasts, the Lord's supper is never to pass away: it is to be celebrated till the heavens are opened and the Son of man is revealed. Then indeed there will be a change. This sacrament then will have done its work. We see now a picture only; a picture indeed that we love, for it is a picture of our Master drawn, as it were, by our Master's own hand; but when Christ comes, we shall see the original of that picture; not the faint resemblance, but the reality; not the dark shadow, but the bright substance, the living man, the living God. And what will that sight be to us? What will it do for us? What has it already done for some who once gathered round the table of the Lord with us in this church? We cannot tell. It is a happiness to sit with Christ at his table here; some of us know that it is, for we have felt the happiness of sitting with him here; but to eat and drink with him in his own kingdom, to sit down at the marriage supper of the Lamb in the Lamb's own palace—we know not what this is. Our sacraments are poor imitations of this, but still they are imitations of it. May you often feel them to be such. May you often find them within these walls pledges and foretastes of the feast of heaven.

SERMON XVII.

THE LORD'S SUPPER A FEAST AND A COMMUNION.

1 Corinthians x. 16, 17.

"The cup of blessing which we bless, is it not the communion of the blood of Christ? The bread which we break, is it not the communion of the body of Christ? For we, being many, are one bread and one body; for we are all partakers of that one bread."

The Lord's supper is a standing memorial in the church of the Lord's death. This was its original meaning and design. Accordingly, when we celebrate it, we both recal his death to our own minds, and we remind others of it. "As often as ye eat this bread and drink this cup," says the apostle in the next chapter, "ye do shew the Lord's death till he come." But it often happens that besides the one main purpose for which any thing is intended, it answers incidentally other purposes. And this is the case with this holy sacrament. It is more than a continual memorial of Christ's death, and much more. The words before us represent it to us in no fewer than four other distinct characters.

I. It is *a thanksgiving for our Lord's death;* more than a remembrance of it, a grateful remembrance of it; and more than a shewing of it forth, a thankful and joyful shewing forth of it.

"The cup of blessing," says the apostle, "which we bless." He does not mean, as we might at first suppose, a cup full of blessings; he alludes to a well known custom among the Jews in celebrating the passover. You must imagine the lamb slain and dressed, the evening come, and the guests assembled. The master of the house then took a piece of bread prepared for the occasion, one of the passover cakes, and blessed it, or rather blessed God for it; and, breaking it, distributed it among the persons present. The feast then went on. At the conclusion of it, he took a cup of wine and did likewise. He prayed over it, and thanked God for all his mercies over it, and then drinking of it, sent it round. Our Lord, you remember, did this when he kept his last passover with his disciples and instituted his sacrament, and the Jews have something like it in their service at the present day.

"Now," says the apostle, with his mind full of the general resemblance between the passover and the Lord's supper, "the cup of which we drink at our sacraments, is exactly like this paschal cup—it is a cup of blessing. We remember what we owe to the great God our Redeemer as we drink it, and we give thanks while drinking it for his great mercies. Our sacraments are thanksgivings; they are so many services of praise." And hence it is that the Greek church calls this ordinance "the eucharist," or the giving of thanks. "It is a sacrifice," says the Romish church; but "No," says St. Paul and the whole protestant church with him, "no sacrifice at all. It is a feast in remembrance of a great sacrifice that was offered, once for all, centuries ago; a feast of thanksgiving and joy." Our church indeed calls it, in one of our sacramental prayers, a sacrifice; but of what kind? "A sacrifice," it says, "of praise and thanksgiving." Three times over with a noble fearlessness the word is made use of in that prayer, but not once in the strict or Romish sense of it, to signify a propitiation. It every time denotes what this apostle uses it to denote in the last chapter of his epistle to the Hebrews—an offering, a grateful offering, a sacrifice of praise.

See here then, brethren, in what frame of mind we ought to attend this ordinance; most humbly doubtless, and sorrowfully also, with great mourning for sin, for it was our sin that brought on Christ all the sufferings we are commemorating. We pierced him. We drew forth the precious blood which the wine in that cup of blessing shadows forth. But great sorrow for sin must not shut out of our hearts great joy for our salvation from sin. We must not so mourn over the evil, as to forget the glorious deliverance vouchsafed us from that evil. A broken heart is a good thing at the Lord's table, but a thankful and rejoicing heart becomes us as well there. Think of heaven. It is a temple with a service going on in it, that is one never ending commemoration of redeeming love. It is a splendid monument erected by omnipotence to the glory of redeeming love. And with what does heaven overflow? Not with grief and mourning, but with joy and singing. Like heaven should our sacraments be, only with this difference—tears must now be mingled with our songs. The stains of sin are yet on us, the remains of sin are yet within us; and while they are there, we must feel in some measure like men who know they are there and who hate them. The Lord will soon take them away from us, and when they are gone, farewell to sorrow. With the same blessed hand in the same blessed moment, he will wipe away all stains from our souls and all tears from our eyes.

Beautifully indeed are these two feelings, sorrow and joy, blended in our communion service. We are taught there to mourn for sin as those whose hearts are breaking; we are to be " heartily sorry for our misdoings;" the remembrance of them is to be " grievous unto us, the burden of them intolerable;" and yet where can we find loftier praise than we find there? more glowing, exulting, soaring thanksgiving? " We praise thee, we bless thee, we worship thee, we glorify thee, we give thanks to thee for thy great glory, O Lord God, heavenly King." This is indeed to have the high praises of God in our mouths. May that God grant that as you approach his table this day, you may have them in your hearts!

II. The Lord's supper is *a symbol of our spiritual reception of Christ*. This will take us again over ground we are frequently passing, but the text leads us to it, and we must not turn away from it.

The scripture speaks of our accepting the gospel, of receiving into our understandings and hearts that faithful saying so worthy of all acceptation, that " Christ Jesus came into the world to save sinners." It speaks too of our receiving Christ himself. The meaning is in both cases the same. The words signify a laying hold of Christ as the soul's Saviour, an appropriating to ourselves by a lively faith in him the blessings of his salvation. To receive him is to receive as true God's testimony concerning him, and to act on it. It is for the guilty soul to turn itself to him, saying, "Lord, save me," and to commit itself as it says this into his hands, in all its guiltiness and wretchedness, to be saved by him. And without this reception of Christ, he is nothing to us; no more than a fountain is to a thirsty man who will not drink of it, or a lifeboat to a drowning man who will not get into it.

Now see the compassionate thoughtfulness of our Lord. The very ordinance which shadows forth to us his death, he takes care shall shadow forth also, not our need of his death, but more than that—our need of a personal, peculiar interest in his death. "These sinners," he says, "may forget themselves as they think of me." He commands us therefore not to forget ourselves; not to stand gazing on or contemplating the bread and wine in his supper, but to take them up, and eat and drink them. The apostle accordingly calls this ordinance "the communion of the blood of Christ," and "the communion of the body of Christ." By communion he means a taking together, a joint participation in. Just, he says, as the bread and the wine in the Lord's supper are emblematical of the body and blood of Christ, so is our receiving of that bread and wine emblematical of the spiritual reception of Christ into our hearts, or, as our service expresses it, "the feeding on him in our hearts by faith with thanksgiving." And faith does partake of Christ in this ordinance, and feed on him. It really receives him; it takes him into the soul with all that pertains to him—his blood to cleanse us, his righteousness to cover us, his Spirit to purify us, his wisdom to guide us, his power to keep us, his love to solace us, his peace to quiet us, his joy to elevate and delight us. "Take, eat; drink ye all of this," is an invitation to a spiritual communion and fellowship with the blessed Jesus. This eating and drinking is a symbol of an inward transaction going on secretly in the Christian's soul. Happy are you who understand by experience what it is!

But here comes in the Roman catholic, and with him men of the same mind among ourselves. "This is all we contend for," they tell us. "We say, to receive the sacrament from the hand of a duly authorized minister, is to receive Christ himself, pardon, and grace, and every blessing that Christ gives; and here is the testimony of an inspired apostle that, in saying this, we speak the truth. He tells us that participating in the bread and wine is really participating in Christ's body and blood." We answer, the catholic is perfectly consistent with himself in all this. His notion is, that the bread and wine are no longer bread and wine when the priest has consecrated them, but actually the Lord's body and blood. To receive them must therefore be to receive, not emblematically or figuratively, but really, Christ's body and blood. This is absurd enough, but there is nothing contradictory to itself in it; it is a consistent absurdity. But see the inconsistency of the other men, the men in our own protestant church. They rise up and tell us that the Roman catholics are wrong. "The bread and wine in the sacrament," they say and rightly say, " are not our Lord's flesh and blood, but only symbols, outward and visible signs, of them." And yet they tell us the next minute, that to receive these symbols is in all cases really to receive our Lord himself; that the benefits of his cross and passion do not become ours by any mental act, the exercise of faith in him, but by a bodily act, the eating and drinking of the symbols before us. They will not set out with the papist; they seem to be going quite another way; but all at once we see them side by side with him, and arriving at the same point.

O the follies into which men will fall when men talk of heavenly things! We say, where is their common sense? Alas! they will use it in things pertaining to this world, things that perish in the using; but bring the things that concern a never dying soul or an everlasting God before them, and their understandings, like their hearts, are torpid; they will not act, or, if they act, it is only to let us see that they are blinded and perverse.

As for St. Paul's language in this text, look for an explanation of it to the sixth chapter of St. John. Our Lord speaks repeatedly there of eating his flesh and drinking his blood; and does he mean any thing outward by this? The ignorant Jews thought at first that he did so, but the idea is absurd. You may say, he alluded to this very sacrament—this sacrament had not then been instituted or heard of. He meant a spiritual feeding on him; a laying hold of him, and a delightful laying hold of him, by the mind and the heart. And St. Paul means precisely the same thing here, only he couples with it here the outward, emblematical sign of it, eating the bread and drinking the wine at the supper of the Lord.

The whole comes to this, brethren—if you approach the table of the Lord this morning with nothing spiritual going on in your minds, you will no more partake of Christ this morning at his table, than you did yesterday at your own; but if you go there exercising, or trying to exercise, as sinners a lively faith in Christ as a Saviour; stirring up your souls to call on him, to get near to him, to make his grace and blessings your own; hungering and thirsting in your souls after him; you will then have communion with him at his table; you will participate of him there; you will receive from him there new life, and nourishment, and refreshment, and strength, not in any mystical way by the bread and wine you will take there, but by that drawing near of the Redeemer to you, that outpouring of the Redeemer's grace, with which your eating and drinking will be accompanied.

III. The supper of the Lord is also *an open avowal by us of our being the disciples of the Lord.* The connection in which these words stand, will make this clear. The apostle is speaking to the Corinthians, and Corinth, you are aware, was a heathen city. It was moreover a very luxurious and dissolute one. After offering sacrifices to their deities, it was a common practice among the people of it, to make a feast of those sacrifices. These feasts they held sometimes in their temples, and sometimes in their own houses; but in either case, they were generally scenes of riot and excess. Strange as it may appear, so much under the influence of early habits were some of them, that after embracing Christianity they continued to frequent and partake of these unhallowed feasts. St. Paul, in this chapter, reproves them for this practice. He shews it to be utterly inconsistent with a profession of the gospel; nay, to be a virtual renunciation of the gospel and a falling back into paganism. In the fourteenth verse he calls it idolatry, and speaking to them as to wise men, appealing to their common sense, he proceeds immediately to prove it to be such. His mode of doing so is by a reference to the holy sacrament. That, he says, is the Lord's feast. It implies a very close connection with him and a participation of him. It is " the communion of the blood," and " the communion of the body," of Christ. It involves in it consequently a profession of faith in him, an acknowledgment of him as our Lord and Saviour. " How then," he asks, " can you partake of that sacrament, and then go to the feasts of your old heathen deities?" or, as he calls them, " devils?" " Your going there is an act of communion with those deities; it is a practical declaration of your respect for and adherence to them; it is idolatry; and being such, it is a turning of your back on the Lord Jesus and a renouncing of him." " I would not," he says, " ye should have fellowship with devils. Ye cannot drink the cup of the Lord and the cup of devils; ye cannot be partakers of the Lord's table and the table of devils. The two things are altogether opposed to each other. You must give up one or the other."

And this reasoning, you perceive, will fully bear us out in viewing our attendance on the Lord's supper, as a profession on our parts of faith in Christ and allegiance to him. It is more so than baptism. That is done once and over, but this is continually recurring, and is like a continual confession of Christ, and a continual dedicating of ourselves to him. Besides, baptism has comparatively little reference to Christ. It speaks only of our pollution and of our need of spiritual washing; but the Lord's supper goes into the very heart of the gospel. It speaks of Christ crucified, and of all the mysteries of love and mercy, of grace and glory, connected with his crucifixion. It is a recognition of him as a dying and atoning Saviour; not simply a shewing forth of Christ, but a shewing forth of his death, and a shewing of it forth with approbation and delight. It is an avowal of our confidence in it, and of our having staked our all on it, and not regretting having done so. It is like saying, " We are not ashamed of Christ crucified;" it is something like a glorying in the cross.

This sacrament must have been, in the early church, a trial of the Christian's faith. "There," says Christ, "I leave you a memorial, not of my power and greatness, not of my glorious resurrection and ascension, but of my humiliation, my shame and dishonour, my death, my violent death, my death on a malefactor's cross. Now can you own me in my shame? Can you honour me in my seeming degradation? Are you willing to bear in the proud, scoffing world you are inhabiting, my reproach? That world hated me, and hates me still; can you in the face of it avow your love to me and call me your Lord?" And hence it was that this ordinance soon began to be designated by the word "sacrament." It signifies an oath, and refers to that particular oath which the Roman soldiers took to be faithful to their general. It represents us at the table of the Lord, as so many soldiers of Jesus Christ, enlisting under his banner, and binding ourselves in the most solemn manner we can, never to forsake him; to follow him whithersoever he may lead us, and to be faithful to him even unto death. Our church reminds us of this. It makes us say at his table, that we offer and present unto him there ourselves, our whole selves, our souls and bodies, to be a sacrifice unto him; to be regarded by him as altogether his; to be applied to any purpose he pleases, even, if need be, to be sacrificed for his sake. O that we could always at his table get this lofty language into our hearts! It is not enough to say there to Christ, "We take thee as our Saviour;" we must say too, "We avouch thee to be our Master and Lord. Let us feel at thy feet that we are thine; and when we go from thy feet into our families and the world, let us feel and act there as those who are thine. Thou hast promised to write thy name on our foreheads in thine own world; O give us grace to write it on our own foreheads in this."

IV. There is yet another point of view, in which the supper of the Lord is set before us in the text. It is *an emblem of our union one with another in Christ.* Men who feast together, and who voluntarily feast together, may be supposed to be men of one mind. If they are heathens and feast together in honour of any idol, they may be regarded as worshippers of that idol, and united to one another by their common attachment to him. The apostle takes up this idea. "We being many," he says, "are one bread and one body, for we are all partakers of that one bread." Here is a double use made of the same symbol. That bread, he says, represents the body of Christ. Now we who partake together of it, must all be considered as the followers of Christ, and bound one to another by our mutual participation of him; more especially as we not only eat together at the same table, but all eat of the same bread there; it is one and the same loaf, that is distributed amongst us all. And that loaf is an emblem also of ourselves. It consists of many distinct grains of corn, but these have been so kneaded and blended together, that they now form one mass. So also we, though many in number, are all one in Christ Jesus. We are brought together in him, and united. We are become one bread and one body. The bread we eat of is one, and we are one.

And this union of his followers with each other, seems to have been much in our Lord's mind when he instituted his supper. In the same night, he calls upon his disciples again and again to love one another; he prays that they may be one even as he and his Father are one. He appears, like this apostle, to associate in his thoughts their mutual love and fellowship with their mutual partaking of his supper. Do we associate them, brethren, in our thoughts? We thank God sometimes at his table for the assurance he gives us there, " that we are very members incorporate in the mystical body of his Son, which is the blessed company of all faithful people;" do we think of this blessed company and of ourselves as belonging to it? It is easy to say what feelings questions like these should excite in us. They are feelings of shame that we love one another so little, and feelings of wonder that professing to believe the gospel, we look at one another so little in the bonds of the gospel. We can come together for years to the same house of the Lord and the same table of the Lord; we can look around us there and regard one another as friends and neighbours, as fellow-men, and sometimes as fellow-sufferers, but some of us have scarcely once said to ourselves there, " These are my fellow-Christians." The communion of saints has a place in our creed, it is every sabbath day again and again in our mouths; O that it had the place it ought to have in our hearts!

We have now gone through the apostle's words, and, with them, his account of this sacred ordinance. It is clear that without turning it in the least from our Lord's original design in it, he has made a wide and extensive use of it. It is a memorial, he says, but a memorial that answers in the church many noble purposes—it is a setting forth of the dying love of Jesus, it is a feast of thanksgiving and gladness, it is a plain declaration by us of our own need of Christ, it is an open avowal of our faith in him and attachment to him, it is a bond of union and love. We see then that we need not go beyond holy scripture in order to attach a high importance to this rite. Other books may seem to exalt it more, but while doing so, they either obscure it till we know not what it is, or else they clothe it with absurdities and degrade it. May the Spirit of truth teach us to view this sacrament as he views it, and give us, with right thoughts of it, right feelings towards it. It is grievous to the soul that a blessed thing like this should become a subject of contention and dispute, and still more grievous to be ourselves obliged to enter into these disputes. It is like the sounds of discord at a feast of joy, and this a feast in a father's house among his children. We must guard against the disturbing influence even of such discussions as you have now heard; and the way to guard against them, is to lift up our thoughts above them; instead of erring men, to place before us a bleeding Saviour. "This do in remembrance of me"—what does this simple sentence say? It bids each of us say, "Lord, let me forget for a while all the world, that I may think of thee."

SERMON XVIII.

THE APPREHENSION OF CHRIST.

St. John xviii. 4, 5, 6.

"Jesus therefore, knowing all things that should come upon him, went forth, and said unto them, Whom seek ye? They answered him, Jesus of Nazareth. Jesus saith unto them, I am he. And Judas also which betrayed him, stood with them. As soon then as he had said unto them, I am he, they went backward, and fell to the ground."

The Lord Jesus had suffered much from men, but as yet he had never been in their hands. Now at last however his hour is come, and he gives himself up to them; he allows them to take and bind him, and do with him whatsoever they will. It is evident that he might have died for us without this, and been slain for us without it. The hand of violence might at once have struck him down. But no. "I am to be numbered with the transgressors," he says. "I will not only die a violent and miserable, I will die a shameful death for you, and the most shameful I can die—they shall crucify me as a malefactor. And before I am crucified, I will be tried and condemned. And I will not go of my own accord to be tried; they shall come out as against a thief and apprehend me. Every thing shall be done that can be done, to degrade me in my latter end."

It is this last mentioned indignity, his apprehension, that the evangelist brings before us in the text. Among the circumstances attending it, we may select four for our consideration.

I. *The manner in which he was employed when this multitude came upon him.*

St. John does not mention this. He merely states that they found him in a garden on the other side of the brook Cedron. But all the other evangelists tell us what he had been doing in that garden. It was the garden of Gethsemane. *He went there for prayer.* The time he spent there, he passed in prayer; and he did this with the full knowledge that his enemies were coming thither to take him. He waited for them praying. Prayer was his very last employment before his final sufferings began. Have we sufferings beginning? Do any of us see the clouds rising, and a storm of affliction threatening us? Our praying Master tells us here how to prepare for that storm. "Is any among you afflicted? Let him pray," says one of his apostles; but he says, " Pray before you are afflicted. Pray in the prospect of affliction. Let grief and trouble find you where they found me, at my Father's feet. He is your shelter from the storm; fly to that shelter before the storm bursts."

But our Lord was not merely praying at this time, *he was praying, and most earnestly, for that which was not granted him.* It is deliverance he is asking in that garden, deliverance from his approaching sorrows. "O my Father," he says, " if it be possible, let this cup pass from me." And he did not say this once only and then recal it, he pressed it; he said it again and again. And what was his Father's answer? In that very moment he mingled that dreaded cup for him, and sent it him. Judas and his companions were actually on their way to apprehend him, while he was on the ground entreating to be spared.

We hear much of the omnipotence of prayer, brethren, the great things it can obtain and the wonders it can accomplish. And our Lord himself ascribes something like omnipotence to it. " Ye shall ask what ye will," he says, " and it shall be done unto you." But we are plainly taught here that prayer is not omnipotent; that there is a limit to its power; that we may pray and pray fervently, as Christ did, and yet have our request denied. God allows us to feel and desire, and, like a tender father, he bids us pour out before him as freely as we will our feelings and desires; but we must not expect these things always to govern his conduct towards us. The wishes of such blind creatures as we are, are not to regulate the doings of the all wise Jehovah. He has so formed his plans for us as in the highest degree to promote our good. Generally by his Spirit, if we are his servants, he causes our prayers to fall in with these plans, and then he puts honour on prayer by sending us the blessings he designs for us as answers to it; but when our petitions would thwart his plans, he will not grant them. "Take this cup from me," says Christ. "No," he says, "I cannot; you must drink it. My will must be done. My purposes must be accomplished. My people. must be saved, and you must be their glorious Saviour." "I besought the Lord thrice," says the suffering Paul, "that it might depart from me;" but it did not depart from him; there the thorn still was, rankling in his flesh, impeding and vexing him. His Master would take him up unasked into the third heaven, would do any thing that was good for his faithful servant, but he would not remove from him the affliction he had prepared for him, though Paul so earnestly besought that it might go. And this gives the Christian a happy freedom in prayer. As long as I pray submissively, he says, ask what I will, my prayers can do me no harm. If I ask a blessing, my God, I am sure, will give it me, and if I ask an evil, I know he will withhold it.

II. Observe *the frame of mind in which our Lord received these men when they came to take him.* He met them with a wonderful calmness.

But a few minutes before he was in a state of great mental agitation; so perturbed with fear and racked with suffering, that for the first time he sought compassion. " My soul is exceeding sorrowful," he said to his disciples, as though he could no longer master or conceal his sorrow. " He was in an agony," we read; in an agony so intense, that he cast himself on the ground, like one broken down and overwhelmed. But look at him now. The thing he dreaded is come on him, and what a change! In an instant, not a trace is left on him of fear, or agitation, or weakness. He comes forth to meet this armed multitude as unappalled and calm, as though they were there to do him honour, instead of to apprehend him. Before the blow came, he shrunk and trembled; now it is fallen on him, he bears it as though it were no blow at all.

How like, brethren, to ourselves! Through God's abounding goodness, some of us have borne, and borne with calmness, the very troubles that in the distance we trembled to look at. "If we have to pass through those deep waters," we have said, "we must be overwhelmed;" but what have we said when we have been plunged into them? The strength within us has astonished us. We have scarcely been able to believe that our calamity has been real and we so quiet. We have said that with our God thus helping us, we could do or bear any thing. And how is this to be explained? We may trace it generally to the power of prayer.

Had we seen this multitude coming on our Lord, we should have said perhaps, and said it with wonder, "Those earnest supplications of his in that garden have been all in vain; his prayers there have been so many lost prayers." "But they are not lost," says God. "Earnest prayer from one I love, is never lost. There is my answer to those supplications of my dear Son, there in that shining angel I have just sent from heaven to strengthen him; and here in this calmness and fearlessness you now behold in him. I could not keep from him the cup he dreaded; but I have done something better for him—I have given him strength to drink it." So with us. We go to God imploring him to save us from this or that coming sorrow, and because he does not save us and the sorrow comes, we wonder; we are ready to say our prayers have not reached him. But what is the fact? We soon find that they have reached him. He gives us a better thing than the thing we asked for; not deliverance from trouble, but power to bear it, and grace to profit by it, and a heart to thank him for it.

And this shews us the chief value and use of prayer. It is not so much to alter God's purposes towards us, as to reconcile us to those purposes. It is not to keep away affliction, but to prepare us for affliction, and to quiet and strengthen us under it. We expect it to regulate God's providence; but, instead of this, it unlocks the treasures of God's grace, enriching us with them, bringing down comfort, and peace, and submission, and thankfulness, and all the precious gifts of his Holy Spirit, into our hearts. Some of us have yet to learn what prayer can do for us. Try it, brethren. It calmed your suffering Master, it can calm you. There is nothing like it for a suffering man. It can do and do in an hour, what thinking, and reading, and all the sympathy the world can give us, cannot do at all. " In the day when I cried," says the psalmist, the very same day, " thou answeredst me and strengthenedst me with strength in my soul.'

And he calls upon us in the same way to obtain the same relief. "Cast thy burden upon the Lord," he says, "and he shall sustain thee"—sustain thee; if he does nothing else for thee, he shall bear thee up.

III. Look now at *the marvellous effect produced by our Lord on these men.*

They are called here "a band of men and officers." Their number must have been considerable, for another evangelist calls them "a great multitude." Leaving the city in the dead of night, they come with lanterns, and torches, and weapons, into the garden where Christ was. Seeing them approach and well knowing their errand, he steps forth from the darkness, and shews himself to them. "Whom seek ye?" he quietly asks. In an instant, we should have said, Judas will point him out, and an arm will be upon him; but not so, they stand still and answer him. "Jesus of Nazareth," they say. Our Lord does nothing, and all he says is, "I am he," and yet the next moment that armed throng is prostrate before him. Officers of justice, soldiers, and perhaps brave Roman soldiers, a simple sentence uttered by the man they came to apprehend, strikes them all to the ground.

Now why this display of power? It is clear that there was nothing vindictive in it—the men were not injured. Neither was it intended for our Lord's rescue from them—there he stands waiting for them to rise. The purposes it was designed to answer, seem to be three.

1. *It vindicated Christ's greatness.*

He had just feared and trembled as a man, and as a man he was now going to suffer and die; but he was more than man: there was the infinite Godhead within him, and for an instant he discovers it; he lets the majesty of it beam forth. Without any effort, without any visible means, by the secret working of his omnipotence, he paralyzes the men before him, confounds them with awe and astonishment, and lays them down. It is a miracle of somewhat the same kind with that he wrought on the cross. There in a dying hour, the hour of his seeming weakness, he brought a hardened malefactor by his side to repentance, working on his mind none could see how; here he touches the minds of a whole multitude together, producing in them, not repentance indeed, but confusion and terror; thus plainly shewing us in both instances, that he can do with the mind of man whatsoever he will. And nothing manifests his greatness more forcibly than this. The darkness that surrounded his cross, the earthquake, the rending veil of the temple, the shivering rocks, all proclaimed his dignity, but that prostrate multitude makes us feel his Godhead. We see at once that this is his own mysterious act, and an act which declares him the Lord of man's soul, man's great Master, the mighty God.

2. And *it provided for the safety of his disciples.*

The hour of his sufferings was come, but not of theirs. They would have to suffer, and suffer enough, when he was peaceful in heaven. At present therefore he will not have one of them touched, nor even alarmed. These men seem to have come prepared to apprehend them together with him, but, " You must let them alone," he says; and the display he had just made among them of his power, placed him in a position not to ask, but to demand this of them. " If ye seek me," he says, " here I am, but let these go their way. The slightest attempt to stop them shall be at your peril." And such authority had he obtained over these men, that when the warm-hearted but rash Peter drew his sword and wounded one of them, they bore it, they did not retaliate; they appear to have stood like so many astonished children before our mighty Lord. And just as weak before him are all the enemies of his people. We cannot tell what the world would do with us, if he did not restrain it; nor need we be anxious to tell, he will restrain it. Our anxiety must be to bear calmly, as he bore, any ill usage we may experience from it. Here is a proof that in such a case the world has his permission so to use us—our rough treatment from it he could have hindered and he has not. But here is a proof too that his eye is on the world and on us. He would not let it touch a hair of our heads, move a hand or a tongue against us, were it not for some holy purpose; and when that purpose is accomplished, he will interpose between us and the world; compel it, with its weapons in its hand and perhaps its enmity strong as ever in its heart, to stand still and let us alone.

3. And this miracle *manifests also the voluntariness of our Redeemer's sufferings.*

He had said before, " No man taketh my life from me; I lay it down of myself;" and there was this remarkable circumstance in his past history to confirm this assertion—notwithstanding all their rage against him and all their cunning and power, his enemies had never yet been able to take him. For three years they had been making continual attempts to do so, but he had strangely baffled all their attempts, and escaped their hands. But had any one looked on him in this garden one short hour ago, beheld his agony there, and heard his earnest cries for deliverance, his impression when he saw him bound and led away, must have been, " There goes to prison and to judgment one who would have saved himself from both, if he could. He may be submissive, he may be patient, but he is submissive to a power he is not able to resist, and patient under sufferings he cannot escape." Our Lord therefore determines to counteract such an impression. He shews us at the very commencement of his sufferings, that it is of his own free accord he submits to them. He strikes down to the earth the men who come to apprehend him, and instead of withdrawing himself while they lie helpless before him, he waits till they raise themselves up again, and then with a dignified composure places himself in their hands.

And his conduct all throughout this scene harmonizes with this. He goes forth, the text says, to meet these men; by a second time asking them whom they seek, he seems to encourage them to fulfil their errand, intimating to them that they have no more to fear from him; and when Peter comes forward in his defence, he checks him, avowing more than a willingness, almost an eagerness, to go and suffer. " Put up thy sword into the sheath. The cup which my Father hath given me, shall I not drink it?" Just as he had said ages ago in the councils of eternity, " Lo, I come to do thy will, O God," so he speaks now, with that fearful will of

God immediately before him, with the cords that were to bind him within his sight, and the bitterness of death at hand.

And whence did this willingness to suffer and die proceed? It proceeded, brethren, from the love and pity of his heart; his own free, abounding, wonderful love to a world of sinners. Here and elsewhere indeed he represents himself as going to the cross simply in obedience to his Father's will, but this is to magnify his Father's love to us, not to conceal his own. " God so loved the world," he says, " that he gave his only begotten Son;" but that Son also loved the world; he was as willing to be given, as God was to give him; as willing to be sent into our world, as God was to send him. It is true that when here, the weak nature he had taken on him, shrunk for a moment from the awful scene before him, but it could not turn him back. " He loved us, and gave himself for us." And to think who he was that gave himself, even the Fellow, the Equal, of Jehovah, the Creator of this mighty universe, its Sustainer and its Lord; to remember what he went through on this vile earth; and then to be told that he was not surprised into any one indignity or pain he endured here, not hurried, as we often are, into one scene of misery after another, without any expectation of it, and hoping every new sorrow will be the last, but that he knew all things that should come upon him, had from the first the clearest and most comprehensive view of all he should suffer; and then to remember one thing more, that it was for you and me, and for others as mean and worthless as you and me, that this amazing effort of compassion was made;—what shall we say of the love of Christ? Shall we say, it is so great we cannot comprehend, we cannot measure it? We might as well say, we cannot comprehend infinity, we cannot measure eternity. Here is a love that tells us at once, it passes all understanding. It is of a character with that infinite Being whose love it is. We say that in heaven we shall understand it, and so we shall far better than we understand it here, but even there we shall know but little of it; we shall never know its boundless greatness, though for ever seeing more and more of it. It will still seem to us like an ocean we have scarcely begun to traverse. The question is, what do we know of this love now, brethren? What do we care about it? What value do we set on it? We have sought the love, the poor, straitened love of our fellow-worms; have we sought for ourselves the love, the exceeding great love, of our Master and only Saviour, Jesus Christ?

IV. We have yet one circumstance more to

notice. It is a painful, but yet an instructive one—*the conduct of this band of men towards our Lord after they had felt his power.*

In the seventh chapter of this gospel, a striking instance is related of an attempt to take him. The pharisees and chief priests are described as sending officers to him for this purpose. But to their vexation and surprise, these officers return without their prisoner. "Why have ye not brought him?" they ask. "Never man spake like this man," answered their servants. "We heard him talk, and we could not take him." Overcome by his wisdom and love, they dared not touch him. They preferred braving the anger of their rulers, rather than commit so great an outrage. In the passage now before us, officers and soldiers are again sent on the same errand. Endeavouring to seize our Lord, they are struck down to the earth at his feet; but after a while they rise up again, and now how will they act? Surely, we might have thought, just as the other officers acted, or better—they will cast themselves again one and all at his feet, and implore his mercy; they will rather die than touch him. But look—they seize him; they bind with cords the very man before whom a few minutes ago they shrunk away in terror.

See here then, brethren, the hardness, the amazing stupidity and senselessness, of the human heart. We talk of miracles. We think that were they wrought around us, unbelief would every where give way, all men must believe and be saved. Some even appear to think that by the power of miracles the kingdoms of the world will at last become the kingdoms of the Lord. But Christ was not only born among miracles and lived amongst them, he was despised and rejected amongst them, he was apprehended amongst them, he was crucified amongst them. All the signs and wonders that followed him from the manger to the tomb, seem to have produced no more effect on the mass of the people who witnessed them, than the passing of so many meteors through the air, or the fall of so many leaves to the ground.

These hearts of ours are tenfold harder than any of us think them. Feel they can and keenly too about earthly things, about man and man's concerns; but as for spiritual things, the things that concern Christ and God, the nether millstone is scarcely harder, a clod of earth is not more senseless. Learn from this history, if you will, the necessity of prayer, the power of prayer, the blessedness of prayer; learn from it the greatness of Christ, the love of Christ, and the security of the people of Christ; but whatever you fail to learn, let no one among us fail to learn this, that we carry about with us hearts that must be softened, and yet hearts that no judgments, no terrors, no startling signs and wonders, nothing earthly, ever can soften. Omnipotence is as needful to break and subdue every heart within these walls, as it was to build the universe or is now to destroy it. But here is our comfort—this omnipotence dwells in him who is our Saviour. Our hearts are as much under his command as any of us can wish them. In one moment he could lay us all down at his feet, not in fear and terror, but in penitence and prayer. Let every one of us look up to him and say, " Lord, lay me there. From all hardness of heart and contempt of thee and thy word, good Lord, deliver me."

SERMON XIX.

THE CHRISTIAN ENQUIRING FOR HIS ABSENT LORD.

Song of Solomon i. 7.

"Tell me, O thou whom my soul loveth, where thou feedest, where thou makest thy flock to rest at noon; for why should I be as one that turneth aside by the flocks of thy companions?"

We can read no part of God's word profitably without prayer. We cannot read this part safely without it. It is not food, it is poison, to the light and prayerless mind. Though given us by God, it comes under that class of things which will not bear to be trifled with. They are among the best when rightly used, but they become, when ignorantly or carelessly taken up, the very worst. May he who wrote this scripture for us, watch over us whenever we open it, and guard every feeling of our hearts.

The person addressed in that part of it now before us, is the Lord Jesus under the figure of a Shepherd. This anxious enquirer after him is the church in the character of his bride.

I. We may notice *the situation in which we find her*.

A faithful wife loves to be near her husband. She is never willingly separated from him. But this bride appears before us alone. She is at a distance from the Shepherd, and does not even know where he is.

And if ever wife had reason to cleave to her husband, the church of Christ has reason to cleave to him. We are dependent on him for all our soul's comfort and joy; yea, for all its needful provisions and safety. We live on him. We have nothing and are nothing without him.

And the Christian delights in being near his Lord, and his Lord also takes pleasure in having him near; but yet there are times when, like this woman, he feels alone. His Lord has not forsaken him; he is close to him as ever; he is supporting and guiding him every step he takes; but he does not reveal himself; the soul is not conscious of his presence; it holds no longer any communion with him; and the consequence is, it thinks him gone. It is like a man whose companion in a dreary night walks unperceived by his side; his guard, but not his solace; near to help, but silent as though far away.

And how, we may ask, does this happen? The text does not tell us; but had we asked this woman how it was that she was thus wandering alone, she would probably have said that her husband had left her; he was gone she knew not why. And so with the desolate soul. It often lays the blame of its loneliness on its Lord. " I long much as ever," it says, " to have him near, but he keeps himself far away from me. I seek him; O that I knew where I could find him! but it is all in vain; he will not be found of me. And his absence from me is as mysterious as it is painful. All I can say concerning it, is what one of old has said before me, " When he hideth his face, who then can behold him ?" And there are cases in which there may be a measure of truth in language like this. The Lord for a time may withhold his consolations from the soul, just as at other times he imparts them—after his own good pleasure; to teach the soul that its consolations and all its fresh springs are in him. But this is not the account he gives us of the matter. He lays the blame on us. We say, " The Lord hath forsaken me, and my Lord hath forgotten me;"

but he says, " No; I have never forsaken or forgotten one that is mine. This breach is all your own work; you have forsaken me. You have turned aside from me to lying vanities. Your iniquities have separated between you and your God, and your sins have hid his face from you."

And how true is this! and how easily explained! The enjoyment of Christ's presence with the soul, is a high and holy enjoyment. It requires therefore, in the mind that participates of it, a spiritual capacity and taste, and that mind must be at leisure for spiritual pursuits and delights. And more—the powers and affections of the soul must be in vigorous exercise, to enable the soul to rise up to this high enjoyment; and there must be no object any where on earth to impede them, to clog them or hold them down. When therefore the world with its turmoil and cares engrosses the mind, or some indulged sin benumbs and enfeebles it, or some earthly idol is allowed to bind all its thoughts and feelings round itself, what must follow? Can we wonder that after a little the soul has to complain of its happiness lost and its Saviour absent? We might as well wonder that an eagle with its wings broken, or fastened down by a chain to the earth, is not soaring as it was wont among the mountains, or getting through the mists and clouds into the sun's brightness. Communion with God, brethren, is not that light and easy thing some of us suppose it. There is nothing greater or higher we have to do on earth, than to keep it up. There is nothing more difficult to creatures such as we are, than, in such a world as this, to walk with God.

II. Let us look next at *the description this bride gives of her absent husband.*

In the new testament, the Lord Jesus is frequently described by his love towards us. Without naming him, his apostles bring him readily to our minds by speaking of him as " him that hath loved us." And this is a natural mode of pointing him out. None has ever loved us like him; none, in comparison with him, has ever loved us at all: he stands distinguished therefore from all others by the love he bears us. And this woman's language is as natural. She does not call her husband by his name; she does not mark him out by any thing peculiar in him; she describes him from her own feelings towards him, by the love she has for him. " O thou," she says, " whom my soul loveth." And herein she plainly shews us that she greatly loves him, and feels that she loves him.

1. *She greatly loves him.*

Had her husband been by her side and been giving her proofs of his affection and tenderness, this language even then, we should have said, is strong; but he is far away from her, and, as she conceives, has deserted her. Her words therefore are expressive of a most fervent attachment to him.

You remember what our Lord said to one of the Jews; "Thou shalt love the Lord thy God with all thy heart, and with all thy soul, and with all thy strength, and with all thy mind." He seems to heap words upon words in order to express the ardour of affection God requires from us. And when he tells us what kind of love he himself requires, he speaks in the same way, or, if possible, more strongly. It is a love, he says, that must equal the tenderest earthly affection the soul knows. "He that loveth father or mother more than me, is not worthy of me; and he that loveth son or daughter more than me, is not worthy of me." Nay, our love to him is to rise so high, that the love of a father for a child, or a child for its parent, may be called hatred when compared with it. As we read his words, we are ready to imagine that he does not mean what he says. He never had, we think, from any one on earth such love as this, and he could never expect to have it. But here it is. This short, simple address to him meets all he requires. "Thou shalt love me," he says, "with all thy heart and with all thy soul." "Lord," answers this disconsolate soul, " I do so love thee, and none but thee. Thou art he whom my soul loveth." There is a superlative love, you observe, expressed here. None could have uttered these words, without loving this great Shepherd intensely, supremely, better than all besides. And wonder not at this, brethren. He is the most glorious Being in the universe. Of all beings, he is the most deserving of our love, and, at the same time, the most capable of winning, preserving, increasing, and satisfying it. To love him once therefore is to love him for ever. To love him at all is to love him warmly, to love him supremely, to love him as none other on earth or in heaven can be loved. The Christian may seem to love others better, he himself may fear at times that he really does so; but let the man have to make a calm, deliberate choice between him and any other object—the strength of his affection for him will discover itself. He will not hesitate a moment, or, if he does hesitate one moment, he will wonder at himself the next, and say, " My Saviour is more to me than all the world. I renounce it all for him."

2. *This woman felt that she loved her husband.* She speaks strongly and unhesitatingly of her love for him, as though she felt it in her inmost soul, and could not possibly doubt the reality or strength of it. Peter's words, " Lord, thou

knowest that I love thee," do not express a stronger consciousness of love than she expresses. And there is this difference between her and Peter—he was in his Lord's presence when he uttered these earnest words, and had just received from him a wonderful instance of his kindness to warm his heart towards him; but this woman is away from her husband, and has received, she thinks, nothing from him of late but neglect and desertion; yet she says, " My soul loveth him." It is easy to say we love the Lord, when he is heaping what we call blessings on us. We are pleased with his blessings, and are ready to mistake the pleasure we take in them, for delight in him. The trial of our love begins when he removes from us his mercies or what we deem such. Too often when they go, our supposed affection for him goes with them. Who ever heard a worldly-minded man talk of his love for Christ under a keen disappointment or a bitter sorrow? But real love for him is often called into new life by sorrows and disappointments. The true Christian is seldom so conscious of his love for Christ, as when Christ withdraws from him the manifestations of his favour. Nor is this strange. While living in the habitual enjoyment of a friend's society and affection, we are sometimes hardly aware how dear that friend is to us. It requires some interruption of our friendship or intercourse, to discover to us the real place he holds in our mind. And so with the Christian. Let him walk in the light of his Redeemer's countenance, he feels that his Redeemer loves him, and is conscious perhaps that he too loves him, but let that light be withdrawn from him, and let the man's soul be still alive to spiritual things, it is easy to say what his feelings will soon be—he will feel as though he never loved his Saviour till now, and be half astonished at the strength of his affection for him. When were the disciples the most sensible of their love for their Master? When they were eating and drinking with him, or walking the streets of Jerusalem by his side? No; when he was lying, as they imagined, in his tomb, and they were talking together sorrowfully of his absence. And look at David. " As the hart panteth after the water-brooks, so," he says, " panteth my soul after thee, O God;" and when did he say this? When his soul was disquieted within him, and he was saying unto God, his rock, " Why hast thou forgotten me?" " He has forsaken me now," the Christian says, " but O the blessed fellowship that in time past I have had with him! He has been my companion, my guide, and my familiar friend. I have come up from the wilderness leaning every step on his arm. And shall I cease to love him, because now he has withdrawn himself from me? No; sooner could I cease to love a buried father, or the mother that bare me. He is gone, and my peace and joy are gone with him, and my hope is well nigh perished, but my love for him is still left me. It is almost the only thing that is left me; but here it is enthroned in my heart, and here in my heart I will cherish it. Come sorrow or come joy, come light or come darkness, here let me keep it, enthroned within me for ever."

III. We must turn now to *the language this woman addresses to her husband.*

And here we discover one blessed use the Holy Spirit sometimes makes of a real love for Christ. We frequently look at it as the mark whereby his true followers may be known, the best evidence of their faith in him. At other times it comes before us as the great spring of almost all the obedience they render him. And then again we see it enlivening and sweetening their intercourse with him. But it is presented to us here in a new light—it leads the Christian back to his Lord when he has wandered from him. For observe—the love of this wife not only appears in what she calls her husband, it shews itself as plainly in what she says to him. She is speaking and acting under its influence. Love for him is leading her to enquire for and seek him, and will eventually place her again by his side. What we have to do then, is to trace in her words the various steps whereby love for Christ brings back to Christ the soul that has forsaken him.

1. Mark in such a soul *a vivid remembrance of its past enjoyments in its Redeemer's presence.*

This wife does not say, " Tell me, O thou whom my soul loveth, where thou art;" but " where thou feedest, where thou makest thy flock to rest at noon." Her mind is evidently recurring to the abundance and tranquillity she had seen attend her husband's footsteps. She thinks of the scenes of enjoyment she had witnessed around him, of the plentiful pastures where he had fed his flock, of the still waters beside which he had led them, of the pleasant shades where in the noon-day heat he had taken them to lie down. As David, far away from Jerusalem, half envied the birds which built their nests in the tabernacle, so she almost envies the sheep that are now feeding or reposing in her husband's presence. And how natural is this! Look at the starving prodigal. The first thing he thinks of when he comes to himself, is his father's house, and the abundance that reigns in it. " How many hired servants of my father have bread enough and to spare, and I perish with hunger." Look at Job. " O that I were as in months past," he cries, " as in the days when God preserved me, when his candle shined upon my head, and when by his light I walked through darkness!" And what, brethren, has been one of the first feelings which have risen in your hearts, when you have looked around you and found your Saviour gone? It has been none other than this. You have thought, and thought with a cutting sorrow, of the blessedness you once enjoyed in him and have now lost. Are your minds even now recurring to that blessedness? Are past scenes of tranquillity, of holy delight and joy, rising up before you? Then keep them before you; cherish the remembrance of them. Painful indeed may be the contrast between them and the scenes into which you have now wandered, but it is good for you to see and to feel the contrast. " Then was it better with me than now," said backsliding Israel of old, and all began to be well with her again when she said this; so your first step towards the recovery of your lost happiness may be a remembrance and a bitter remembrance of this happiness, and of your folly and sin in losing it.

2. And see also in the returning Christian *a sorrowful dissatisfaction with all things while his Lord is absent.* "Why," says this woman, "should

I be as one that turneth aside by the flocks of thy companions?"

We may suppose her standing on a lofty rock or on a hill, whither she has climbed to look around for her husband. She sees the flocks scattered about in the vallies, and on the sides of the mountains around her, but which is her shepherd's flock and where he has led his sheep, she knows not. Bewildered and agitated, "Tell me," she says, "O thou beloved of my soul, where thou art. Why should I go wandering about in search of thee among the flocks of thy companions? The pasture may be as green where they are as where thou art, and the shade as pleasant; but that is nothing to me, and they are nothing to me. I want to rest where thou restest, and to walk by thy side." The translation in the margin adds somewhat to the force of the passage, without altering its sense. The word "veiled" is found there, and it has been supposed that in the original there is an allusion to the eastern custom of covering the head in seasons of humiliation and sorrow. Thus Jeremiah, in order to paint the distress of the people under a severe drought, says of them, "They came to the pits and found no water, they returned with their vessels empty, they were ashamed, and confounded, and covered their heads." And the sorrowful David, when fleeing from Jerusalem to escape his rebellious son, is described as manifesting his grief of heart in a similar manner. He " went up by the ascent of mount Olivet, and wept as he went up, and had his head covered; and all the people that was with him, covered every man his head; and they went up, weeping as they went up." So this woman is represented here with her head covered in the day of her sorrow. " Why," she says, " should I go veiled, veiled as a mourning widow or a divorced and degraded wife, among the flocks of thy companions?"

And every man who really loves Christ and has at any time found himself separated from him, can well understand this language. The world has allured and deceived him; it has led him astray; but it has not satisfied him, and it cannot satisfy him, and he has at last discovered that it cannot. With an aching conscience and an aching heart, " This will not do," he says. " I must seek my happiness in these wandering paths no more." And then his whole soul looks round again for its Lord. It feels as though it would fly for ever from the world, yea, and from itself, that it may once more rest in him. And nothing but Christ can calm and content it. Earthly comforts will no longer do; holy duties will not do; sermons and ministers will not do; angels, did angels come from heaven to comfort it, would not do;

they came to the weeping Mary when she had lost her Lord, and they could not dry one of her tears, they left her weeping. Let all the stars in the heaven shine brightly as they may above him they cannot supply to the traveller the loss of the sun's light; so neither can all the things the world contains, supply to the benighted soul the loss of its Saviour's presence.

3. This language intimates also *a readiness in the returning Christian to go any where or do any thing, so that he may find Christ.*

Why does this bride so anxiously enquire where the Shepherd and his flock are? That she may paint the scene to her mind, and delight herself with thinking of it? No; that she may fly to it and share its happiness. No matter how far off it may be or how toilsome the way to it, " Tell me where thou art," she says, " and I will come." In the third chapter, she is described as rising from her bed by night, and traversing the city to seek him, preferring his society to her rest, and heedless alike of toil and danger so that she may have it.

And where is the experienced Christian who does not understand this also? He will tell us that a departed Saviour is not easily found again. If we have slumbered and let him go, mere wishes and desires will not take us to him, nor bring him back. " My soul followeth hard after thee," said David to him when he had lost him; and he makes every one that loses him, say the same before he again meets him. Set a sorrowful wife to seek her husband among pathless mountains—there is a picture of a desolate Christian seeking his Saviour. He must be prepared for effort, prepared for disappointment, prepared to go hither and thither in his holy search, from sermon to sermon, from sacrament to sacrament, from prayer to prayer, and to do this, as he will often say, in vain; now and then catching a glimpse of his Lord, or thinking he does, and then losing him again,. and not knowing whither to turn. Above all, he must be prepared to leave every worldly and sinful path, however pleasant to him. He whom he is seeking, is without the camp, far from the world's pleasures and ways, and he must be content to go forth after him without the camp, bearing his reproach. And will he find him? Thus seeking him, assuredly he will. In some unexpected and perhaps disconsolate hour, the blessed Jesus will draw near to him, as he drew near to his sorrowful disciples on their way to Emmaus, and his burning heart shall say, as they said, " It is the Lord."

And what has done this? What has once more placed this wandering Christian by his great Shepherd's side? Love, we see, has done it. You may say, " That Shepherd's love for the man, which has never failed him, and has now at last drawn and restored him;" but we must say too, the man's own love for his Shepherd. The Holy Spirit has all along kept it alive, and now by calling it again into exercise, he has led him once more to his feet. Look then to your hearts, brethren. There is not one among you, who could condemn a religion of mere feeling too strongly. It is a delusion, enthusiasm, hypocrisy, or any thing bad you may please to call it. But see here what a religion without feeling is. It is without that which warms the soul when it is near its Saviour, and recals it to him when it has forsaken him.

Are any of you rejoicing now in his presence? Cherish your love for him, as you would cherish that joy itself. It not only sweetens your communion with him, it promotes it and keeps it up. "He that dwelleth in love, dwelleth in God, and God in him."

Have any of you left him? Is this lonely woman's situation a picture of your own? See here then what must lead you back to him.

What would this wife have done had her heart been cold towards her absent husband? Mere duty would never have prompted such language as this, nor led to such conduct. It might have kept her where she was, waiting his return; but this could not satisfy her. She loved him, and because she loved him, she enquired after him; she went wherever she could go, determined to find him.

And you, brethren, must have your love for Christ quickened again into life and feeling, before you can hope to see him again. It was a heart grown cold towards him, that turned him from you; and it is a heart warming again towards him, that must bring him back. And here is the difficulty —how shall our hearts be warmed? Consult your own experience. What led you at first to love this Saviour? It was a discovery of his own great love for you, his wonderful love in giving himself for a world of such sinners as you are, and dying for their sins. "We love him," you said, "because we know and feel that he has first loved us." To that point go back. Begin again to fasten your minds on him as a dying Saviour, and on yourselves as the sinners he has died for. Think less of the proofs you want of his love, and more of the amazing proofs of it he has already given you. You are going now to his table, and your prayer perhaps is, "Lord, meet me there. Lord, make thyself once more known to me there in breaking of bread." Without changing this prayer, add yet another to it; "Lord, reveal anew to me there thy love. I am going to commemorate thy dying for us; O let me remember thy exceeding great love in dying for us. Because thou didst love us, thou hast washed us in thy blood. Lord, impress this yet once again on my heart, and let my heart be again warmed and melted with love for thee."

But what shall we say to you, brethren, to whom all you have heard to-day is as nothing? Would that it were something to you! Would that you understood these things! Would that you cared about them! You must see that if you do not care about them, your religion and that of the men who give utterance to their feelings in holy scripture, are two very different things. They often talk in a way that you cannot comprehend, and it is love for their divine Lord, that leads them to talk so. Can you doubt then where the truth lies? It lies here—that heavenly Lord asked these men for their hearts, and they through grace gave them to him—from that moment their religion became a religion of the heart. He has asked you for your hearts, and where are they? Any where but with him. The Lord Jesus says to you, "Come to me, take me as your Saviour and your Friend, love me, walk with me." You say—what? "We have not time to do so;" or, "There is no need that we should do so. We will give thee our respect, and a little outward service with it, attend thy house and sometimes thy table, but as for our hearts, we will keep them to ourselves, or the world shall have them." And your religion corresponds with this. It is an altogether heartless thing. It leaves you towards the Saviour who has died for you, cold as a stone. O may the living God take compassion on you! May he lead you to take compassion on yourselves! Such a religion as this is a comfortless thing to live with; it is a worse to die with. Long for a better. Seek Christ in real earnest as a Saviour indeed for your guilty souls, and that one thing will do all the rest. You will soon love him; you will soon know what is meant by his favour and presence; you will soon say, "O let them be mine, for in his favour is life, and in his presence joy, the fulness of joy, and pleasures for evermore."

SERMON XX.

FELLOWSHIP WITH GOD.

1 St. John i. 3.

"Truly our fellowship is with the Father, and with his Son Jesus Christ."

THERE are a few expressions in our communion service of so lofty a character, as to be scarcely understood by some of us. They are such as speak of our dwelling in Christ and Christ in us, of our being one with Christ and Christ with us. The apostle's language in the text has nearly the same meaning. A right understanding of it therefore will help us to understand the other. It will do more—it will unfold to us one of those glorious privileges a mighty God has bestowed, in the riches of his grace, on the people he delights in, or rather the most glorious privilege of them all.

We must consider, first, the nature of this happy fellowship, and, secondly, the ends the apostle has in view in speaking so assuredly of his possessing it.

I. *The nature of this fellowship.*

It is fellowship, the apostle says, "with the Father, and with his Son Jesus Christ;" but we must not suppose that the eternal Spirit is excluded from it. He is the author, the very life and soul, of it. He does much at first to bring it about, and it is his peculiar province to keep it up, enliven and sweeten it. And hence it is that St. Paul calls it in one place "the fellowship of the Spirit," and in another "the communion of the Holy Ghost." Both words are in the original the same. Indeed throughout the new testament, the original word is translated indifferently fellowship or communion.

It comprehends in its meaning two distinct things.

1. *Partnership*, a sharing with another in any thing, the possessing of it in common with him. In this sense we have all fellowship one with another as Englishmen, we participate together in the many blessings a bountiful Providence has showered down on our native land.

In this sense too the merchant has fellowship with his partners in business—he has the same interests with them, he shares with them in the same gains and losses. And this is St. Paul's meaning, when he expresses his desire for " the fellowship of Christ's sufferings"—he wishes to partake with Christ in their blessed fruits and results. And the same idea also is in his mind, when he speaks of the Lord's supper as " a communion"—it is a common taking together by us of the bread and the cup, and a token of our common participation in the body and blood of Christ.

Now transfer this idea to the text. What a lofty declaration does it in one moment become! There is a fellowship, it tells us, between the great God and us, a partnership, a sharing together of the same things. And what things are these? They include every thing in which we can share with God, or God with us. There is no limit to this partnership, except that which our finite nature makes on the one hand, and that which his holy nature makes on the other. Our poverty is God's or has been his— " he became poor for us;" and his riches are ours or will be, " the unsearchable riches of Christ." He has borne our griefs and sorrows; he will make us inheritors of his joys. Our sins have been " on him," he bare them all in his own body on the tree; and now, the moment we believe in him, his righteousness is on us, his spotless, perfect righteousness; we can plead it for the justification of our guilty souls as though it were our own. Are we men, " partakers of flesh and blood?" " He himself likewise took part of the same;" the Lord himself also is become a man, uniting our nature to his own; not dwelling in it merely as a tabernacle, or wearing it for a little while as an outward dress, but connecting it closely and inseparably with himself, making it as much his nature as it is ours, so that long as he exists as the everlasting Father, so long will he exist as the real, the perfect and complete Son of man. And what nature does he give to us? You may say, a holy and heavenly one, the same that he has given to his angels who surround his throne; but he calls it a divine nature, he tells us that it is his own. He sends his Spirit down into our hearts to regenerate them, to impart to us a new and lofty existence; and then not to leave our hearts, but to dwell and rule in them—the same Spirit that dwells in his own heart, and rules in his own soul. We are raised in the scale of being or soon shall be, we know not how high, nearer to God than any other creatures, and made more like him. And with his nature, he gives us an interest in all his glorious perfections. Not only are his mercy and love ours, we may look on his wisdom, and power, and greatness, as ours. They are all exercised for our welfare, they are all pledged for our everlasting happiness. As certainly as he came into our world, we are to go into his; and as really as he shared here in our shame, degradation, and sorrow, so are we to share there in his exaltation, his kingdom and glory. " The day of his appearing," is to be the day of our " manifestation;" and when he shall appear, we are to be like him, to wear, not inwardly only as now, but outwardly and visibly, his form and likeness. Indeed the scripture carries this mutual participation between Christ and us, as far as words can carry it. He himself is said to be ours and we his. He is called our portion, and we his portion; we his inheritance, and he ours. We are represented as identified with him, as one with him, and he one with us. There is no union in all the universe so close as that which exists between the Lord and us, no bond so fast. The union of father and child, of husband and wife, is not half so intimate, no, not that of the most tender wife and the most loving husband that ever breathed. If we want a comparison for it, we must look to the limb that forms part of our body, or to the branch that grows out of the tree. But even this fails. That branch may be severed from that tree, this limb may be cut off from this body, but we, if we are really the Lord's, can never be severed from him. He could as soon lose his glory or his existence, as lose one of that happy people he has chosen and redeemed. Think of that union which binds together the Father and the Son. What it is we cannot tell, but our Lord seems to go high as that for an emblem of the union between his people and himself. He prays that they may be one with him, and through him one with his Father, just as he and his Father are one with each other; and this, he says, shall one day be a proof to all the world of his Father's love for them; and what can magnify the exceeding greatness of his love more?

2. The word "fellowship" has another sense. It signifies *intercourse*, converse, and a free and familiar converse. It is another word for what we call communion, an interchange between two or more persons of thought and feeling.

And can there be any thing like this going on between God and us? Yes, brethren, there can. In this sense also we have "fellowship with the Father, and with his Son Jesus Christ."

This apostle well knew what converse with Christ was. He had seen his face, and heard his voice, and sat by his side, and leaned on his bosom. In the first verse of this chapter, he evidently alludes to this. He speaks of having heard, of having seen with his eyes and looked upon, the Word of life. We might have expected him to say now, " O that I could look upon him again! O that I could again hold that blessed intercourse with him I once held!" But, instead of this, he says, " I do hold intercourse with him. Though I see him not, I am not separated from him. There is still intimacy, still converse, still fellowship, between me and my blessed Lord." But how can this be?

We make known our thoughts and feelings one to another by outward signs, chiefly by words. We have no other way of making them known. But suppose any one to possess the power of looking into our hearts, and seeing every thought there as it rises up, and this whether he is present with us or not, then words and outward signs would not be needed; we could speak to him within our own minds, and he would understand us, and understand us better than any one besides, more readily and fully. Now God does possess this power, and the Christian knows that he possesses it; and he acts like one who knows it. This fellowship consists, on his part, in the turning of his soul to God, in a habit he has acquired of speaking within himself to God, just as another man speaks by outward expressions to his neighbour or friend.

Naturally we know nothing of this fellowship.

Man in his innocence knew it and loved it. It was his highest joy even in his joyful paradise, to converse there with him who made him. But when man fell, God became his fear and dread. He fled from him. The dreariest solitude he could have found on the earth, would have been less terrible in his apprehension, than his once rejoiced in presence. When however the soul is recovered by Christ from its ruinous fall, it loses its dread of God. Its old feelings return. It begins again to long for God's society and friendship. It not only sees that it may draw near to him through a Mediator, but it does draw near to him, and wishes to draw nearer, and feels that it never can draw near enough. Would you know what a real Christian is? He is a man who goes through the world feeling that there is the living God by his side, and as a companion and friend by his side. He makes use of him as his friend, and of him above all others; consulting him in his difficulties, turning to him in his wants, taking to him his sorrows—some that he would never think of taking to his fellow-men, and telling him of his joys. His whole life, in the emphatic language of scripture, is a walking with God. He is to him as " the man of his right hand," and the friend of his heart. Ask him whether he has any thing to do with God —" I should be miserable and undone," he says, "if I had not. I have more to do with him than with any one beside. I sometimes almost wish that I had to do with him alone. If fellowship with God consists in the turning of an aching, thirsting, weary, and sometimes happy soul to him, then I have fellowship with God. My own soul longs as it longs for nothing else, to be ever with him."

But look now on the other side. There must be communications passing also from God to the soul, in order to constitute society or intercourse; and such communications really do pass to the Christian's soul from him. If you ask how they are made, we can scarcely tell you, without appearing to some of you to be speaking a strange language. It would be easy to say much concerning them, were you all the people of God. It would then be like speaking to a happy family of the pleasure of gathering round a happy father, and listening to his voice, and receiving tokens of his affection; but you must be in the number of those children, and love that father, before you can enjoy this pleasure, or even understand clearly what it is.

This however we may say, and this every one can understand—God speaks to his people here on earth by his holy word. He speaks thus indeed to us all, but in the case of these men, he communicates to his word a peculiar power, so that it comes to them with something like the force that the voice of God in heaven may be supposed to come to an angel in heaven : he makes them feel that it is a word addressed to them, and a word that he has spoken. The same with his glorious gospel. They hear the same sermons that others hear, but not as others hear them. God carries them home to their hearts. No mere preacher could do what many a poor sermon has done within these walls. No mere man could give the comfort, or impart the strength and hope, that have sometimes been received and enjoyed here. " The Lord is in this place," one and another has said as he has sat among us. " I am as sure that he has spoken to me to-day, as I am that I live and breathe."

And another thing we may say, that is almost as plain—just as God is able to read our hearts, so is he able to speak at once to our hearts. He can discern our thoughts and feelings without our expressing them, and, through the secret operation of his Spirit, he can as easily call up thoughts and feelings within us without his expressing them. And in this way he holds intercourse with his people. Not that in this way he ever reveals to them now any new truths, or brings them acquainted for the first time with any truths already revealed; this would be inspiration; but he recals to their memories the truths his holy word has taught them, he compels them to see how closely they concern themselves, and he penetrates their hearts with them. And this goes on within them let them be where they may. He can reach them any where and under all circumstances. They go up to his house, he meets them there and makes them joyful and sometimes sorrowful, as it pleases him, in his house of prayer; they go to his table, at his table he lets them know he is with them there also; they pray before him in secret, in secret he meets them again. He manifests his presence also and they discern his presence, in the varying occurrences of their lives. The bystander does not see his hand or hear his voice, but they do. In every gladdening dispensation of his providence, they recognize his tenderness, and when the sorrowful dispensation comes, the cloud and darkness and storm, then is the time when they know indeed how near he is to them. Then he makes his visits the most frequent, and his intercourse with the soul the closest and sweetest; for then the soul draws the nearest to him, and casts itself the most entirely on his love.

Communion with God—it is an abiding conviction of God's presence with us, and an occasional realizing of it, a " seeing him that is invisible." It is a sense of his love communicated to the soul, when all other love fails to satisfy it. In trouble of conscience, it is a sight of his abounding mercy; in darkness and perplexities, it is a new manifestation made to us of his unshaken faithfulness; in weakness, it is a springing up within us of his strength; in wants, it is the power of the Holy Ghost enabling us to say in the midst of our wants, " Our God shall supply all our need." In temptations, it is hearing a voice saying to us, " O do not that abominable thing which I hate;" in arduous duties, it is hearing the same voice promising us help; in bereavements and desolation, it is God telling us that he is with us; and in death, it is the same God assuring us again that he has not forsaken us, that he will continue to be with us even to the end. Is this enthusiasm? Is this delusion? God forbid, brethren, that any of you should think so! It is what the scripture calls " the power of godliness." It is true religion, religion, not in its outward dress, but in its reality and substance, in its strength and blessedness. God grant that you and I may know more and more of it!

We have now seen enough of this fellowship to explain, in part at least, the language to which I at first adverted. It consists of such a participation of all that God is and has, as may well be expressed by speaking of us as "one with him;" and of so close and constant an intercourse between him and us, as may justly be described by "our dwelling in him, and he in us."

And these two things are never separated. There can be no real communion between him and us, till we are spiritually united to him, and this union with him is never real, without leading at once to this intercourse and communion. A prayerless man may talk of his union with the Lord, but he knows nothing of it; and we shall never in prayer or in any other way hold converse with him, till our souls are once again brought nigh and made one with him.

And for both these things we are indebted altogether to the Lord Jesus Christ. In his human nature he stands nearer to us than his Father, and his Father has ordained him to be the one great Mediator between himself and us. "Through him we have access to the Father." United by a living faith to him, we become united with the Father, and through him all our intercourse with the Father is kept up. It is in him we find God a God present with us, and gracious unto us, and communing with us, and allowing us to commune with him; hearing our prayers, and sending us mercies in answer to them; pouring out blessings upon us, and listening with delight to the thanksgivings and praises we offer him.

II. We have yet to examine *the ends this apostle has in view, in speaking to us so assuredly of his possessing this blessed fellowship.* He asserts it, you observe, in strong terms, as though he were most anxious for us to believe it. " Truly our fellowship is with the Father, and with his Son Jesus Christ." Now why this?

1. *That we may desire to have our portion with him and the real followers of our Lord*

" Remember me, O Lord," says David, " with the favour that thou bearest unto thy people;" and some of us feel the prayer to be a natural and right one. We can see that the people of God are a favoured people, and, in the midst of all their trials and sorrows, a happy people. The world reviles, ill treats, and affects to despise them; but we can perceive that the world is really not worthy of them, that, with all their failings and mistakes, there is something about the men, which raises them high above it, and compels us often to say, " Would we were like them." And they themselves wish us like them. " I would to God," said the noble Paul to Agrippa, " that not only thou, but also all that hear me this day, were both almost and altogether such as I am." And here comes this affectionate

John telling us that he writes this epistle—why? "that ye also," he says, "may have fellowship with us." And why does he desire us to have fellowship with him? Because he had a high opinion of himself, and thought it a great thing for any one to be near him or like him? No; because he was happy in God his Saviour, and longed for all others to be happy in him. He wishes us to have fellowship with him, because his fellowship is with the Father, and with his Son Jesus Christ.

And precious indeed must this heavenly fellowship have been to his soul. Think, brethren, of the persecutions and sufferings he and his fellow-apostles endured. Trodden upon, buffeted and spurned, driven about an evil world as though not fit to live in it, they yet long to have others join them, and this, not to uphold or comfort them in their miseries, but to share their privileges, their honours and happiness. "None of these things move us," they say. "We do not care for them. We would at once plunge you into them, so that we might but bring you acquainted with our blessedness." And where is the real Christian who does not feel the same? Has he a higher wish for the friend of his heart, or the child that he loves, than this? No; he had rather have him the poorest, meanest, and most afflicted in the church of Christ, than see him out of that church high as the world can lift him.

And what a stamp of dignity this puts on the disciples of Christ and their condition! This very John says, " He hath made us kings on the earth." He speaks like one who feels his elevation, and can hardly find words to express it. " He hath raised us up together, and made us sit together in heavenly places," says Paul. Do any of you despise the Christian? Learn from this text that you despise you know not what—a man whose situation and character you are not able to understand, much less rise above. And do any of you admire him? Read this text and say, " From this hour we will pray and strive to be like him. We will go with him, for we have heard that God is with him."

2. Another object the apostle is here aiming at, is that *his fellow-believers in Christ may be happier in him.*

He thinks first of those who are far off from Christ. " We tell you," he says, " of this happy fellowship to bring you to desire it;" and then he turns round to those who are already near Christ, and says, " We tell you of it, that you may rejoice in it. These things write we unto you, that your joy may be full." He supposes them now to have some joy, but not all the joy they might have. " Think of this high privilege," he says, "and your joy will be greater; it will be as great as it can be on earth; it will be full."

We lose, brethren, half the sweetness of our spiritual blessings, by not being more mindful of the existence and extent of them. We know they are ours, and we live in the daily use of them, but we are content with making daily some use of them; they are not enough in our thoughts; we do not endeavour as we ought to discern their glory and greatness. We are like men who are in possession of a mine of gold, and who go to it for a little supply when their wants compel them; but who forget that it is a mine, and are often complaining of their poverty, when they are in fact abounding in riches. And in this way we treat this lofty blessing.

We should esteem fellowship with an apostle a privilege, especially with such an apostle as this beloved John. To be what he was, and to be side by side with him, sharing his employments and pleasures, his friendship and converse —this, we feel, would be no light thing; but what is this compared with that great thing every real Christian possesses? What is this compared with the presence and society of the infinite Jehovah, and as large a participation with him in his fulness as our nature will allow? Heaven is little more than this fellowship with him better understood, and more abundantly enjoyed, and all impediments to the enjoyment of it removed. Ask the happiest spirit there what makes his happiness; he will tell you it is nothing but this; and then turn to another world, and ask another spirit wherein consists his unutterable wretchedness; he will tell you it is only the want of this. And look around you in our world. Ask the Christian at one time why he is so peaceful and joyful; "My Saviour is near me," he says; "I feel that he is walking by my side." And then ask him at another time why he is so sorrowful; "My God is far from me," he answers; "I cannot find him." Go through the whole universe—it is every where the same. All the real happiness that is found in it, flows from this fellowship with the Father and with his Son; there is nothing any where but misery, dark, desolate misery, without it. Think of this, brethren, and you will soon feel that you have never yet prized this unspeakable blessing as you ought; nay, that you have scarcely prized it at all. You will feel like a man who has just discovered the immense worth of a treasure he has long possessed and but little valued, and now that he is acquainted with its value, can hardly believe it his own. Your language will be, "Lord, open thou mine eyes that I may see the abundance of that grace thou hast bestowed on me. If

I have fellowship with thee, O let me know it, and let me rejoice in it! And that I may rejoice in it, give me more of it; draw me nearer to thee; manifest thyself more to my soul."

3. The apostle has yet one end more in view— *to save us from self-deception.*

Almost in the same sentence in which he tells us that we have fellowship with Christ or may have it, he warns us against thinking it ours while we have fellowship with sin. "God is light," he says, "and in him is no darkness at all. If we say that we have fellowship with him and walk in darkness, we lie and do not the truth."

What different characters he addresses in so short a space! first, the stranger to Christ, then the real Christian, and now the hypocritical or self-deluded professor of the cross. And of these are all our Christian assemblies composed. Where among them, brethren, do we take our stand? Is there a man here who has been saying this morning within himself, "All is well with me for I know what union with Christ means, and have had many a strong feeling in my heart towards him?" And is that man living a life that he is obliged to shroud in darkness, a life he does not dare to lay thoroughly open to the gaze of his fellow-men? Is he day by day practising, or, if not practising, cherishing in his heart, some secret sin? This scripture plainly tells such a man what his supposed fellowship with God is worth. It is worth nothing at all, it is a wretched, fearful delusion.

Feelings, brethren, however strong and deep, are dangerous tests of character, are perilous things for a dying man to ground his hope on. They themselves, before we can dare to trust them, require to be brought to another standard. Do they lead to a holy and heavenly life? Does our daily conduct harmonize with them? Do they war with sin, and make us war with it, and give us no peace while any one evil thing has the mastery over us? We were once led captive by " divers lusts and pleasures;" can we say that, sinful as we still are, there is not a single lust or pleasure which, by God's grace, we have not conquered? that we can bear the light? that the whole world might see our lives, and our faces not be ashamed? Then may we indeed hope that we have fellowship with a holy God and his holy Son. Then may we venture to say there are feelings in us, that come from his Holy Spirit. Then have we ground to believe that of his abounding mercy he has formed us for himself, and is preparing us for his holy kingdom.

" And is there nothing in this text," some of

you may say, " for us who long for a share in this heavenly fellowship and cannot obtain it?" Yes, brethren, there is. It bids you dismiss from your minds the thought that you cannot obtain it. Why are you told of it? Were you starving, and did any one tell you again and again of the existence of food which others around you were freely taking and enjoying, would you not infer, if the food were his, that he meant you also to go and take it? So with this blessing. It may not be yours, it may not be mine, but for many years we have been continually told of it, and told of it by him in whose gift it is. He tells us of it again to-day; what is this but saying to us again to-day, " Come and accept it?"

Your error perhaps lies here—you have not sought this fellowship aright. It must begin with the Lord Jesus Christ, not with your receiving from him some pleasurable, joyful emotions, but with your embracing, under a deep sense of your own guilt and wretchedness, his great salvation. " Take me as your Saviour," he says; " believe in me as a Saviour; lie as sinners at my feet." It is there, brethren, fellowship with God begins, there in the dust when the soul is thinking perhaps nothing of this fellowship, but looking up to a once bleeding Jesus for the cleansing of his blood. It is faith in him as a Saviour, that makes us one with him. It is drawing near to him as a Saviour, that brings us into converse with him. It is when leaning on him as a Saviour, that he discovers to us he is our Friend.

SERMON XXI.

THE HOLINESS OF CHRIST.

Hebrews vii. 26.

" Such an High Priest became us, who is holy, harmless, undefiled, separate from sinners."

The Lord Jesus Christ is very God of very God. All the glorious perfections of the Godhead therefore are his; and, among them, transcendant, infinite holiness. But besides the holiness which shines in him as God, he possesses a holiness peculiar to himself as the Son of man. It is of this the apostle speaks in the text. The terms he uses in describing it, are all of nearly the same meaning. He multiplies them, not only to shew how completely and perfectly holy our Lord is, but also to inpress on us the necessity of his being so, in order to qualify him to be our High Priest or Saviour. Let us then consider, first, the reality of his holiness; secondly, its peculiar character; and, thirdly, its importance.

I. *The reality* of our Lord's holiness is most clearly and strongly declared in scripture.

1. We are told that he came into our world with *a holy nature*.

Though true and very man, he was not born, as we are, of a corrupt father; and consequently he was free from those seeds and elements of evil, which we inherit. His human nature was God's own immediate work. He prepared it for him, he says, created it specially for him; and like all that comes at once from that great Creator's hand, it was pure and holy. We accordingly find the angel who foretels his birth to Mary, connecting his holiness with his divine origin, calling him at once " that holy thing which shall be born of her," and " the Son of God;" and in like manner he is called twice over in the fourth chapter of the Acts, God's " holy child."

2. *His life too was holy*.

Our first father Adam had originally a holy nature. He too had God for his Creator and was formed in his image; but he defaced that image; he sullied the purity of his nature, and died a sinner. But the Lord Jesus never sullied the purity he was born with. He was as unpolluted in his dying hour, as in the first hour he breathed.

We have abundant evidence of this. God himself repeatedly declared from heaven, that he was "well pleased" with him. He himself challenged his angry enemies to lay the least sin to his charge. The man who betrayed him and who knew him well, publicly asserted his innocence; and the very judge who condemned him, said of him, and said it while condemning him, that he found in him "no fault at all." The heathen soldier who guarded his cross, was compelled to cry out at the very moment he saw him dying as a malefactor, "Certainly this was a righteous man;" and even Satan himself is forced to bear witness to him. "I know thee who thou art," said that vile blasphemer who would have exulted to proclaim him sinful if he could; "I know thee who thou art, the holy One of God." "He did no sin," the scripture says; "he knew no sin;" "in him was no sin." No language can be stronger. It proves him to have been, not only pure in his nature at the first, but pure in heart and life to the very last.

II. Let us now look at *the peculiarity* of his holiness.

This cannot consist simply in his freedom from sin; for though herein he differs from us, yet not from the angels. They, like him, have retained, and retained unimpaired through ages the purity they were created in. We must look farther then in order to discover the peculiar glory of the holiness he possesses.

1. It was *holiness amidst sin and temptation*, perfect holiness amidst abounding sin and the utmost possible temptation.

When man was holy, it was in a holy paradise; and even there the first hour in which he was tempted, he fell. And it is in a holy world too, that the angels are holy. If tempted at all, we are sure that it is in a slight degree only. Our own feelings tell us, they would not be the happy creatures they are, had they much temptation to sustain. But what had our Lord to sustain? Beyond doubt, more than any being before or after him ever bore. He "suffered being tempted," the scripture says; and that one expression declares plainly the exceeding greatness and multitude of his temptations. With his mighty power of withstanding them, they pained and distressed him. But this was all they could do. They never overcame him. He never once yielded to them. He was holy amidst all the efforts hell could put forth to make him unholy; and holy in this world of evil; and not shut up in it, or living alone, like John his great forerunner, in one of its wildernesses, but moving about in it, mixing with his fellow-men among its pollutions. It seems vile enough to defile any thing, but he passed through it, through all its mire and dirt, undefiled, without a spot or stain. He was with sinners, and yet separate from them, uncontaminated by them, unlike them.

2. His was holiness also *amidst weakness and suffering*.

We lose sight of this, brethren. We think of our Lord as living here much such a life as an angel might live here; with a nature like an angel's, or like Adam's in paradise. But he took not on him, we are told, an angel's nature; nor did he take on him our human nature such as it originally was in happy Adam. He took on him, the scripture says, " the seed of Abraham;" he was sent in the likeness, not of our holy, but of our " sinful flesh." Divest us as we are sitting here of sin and of all tendency to sin, all corruption, and then we may say the Lord Jesus was exactly like one of ourselves; like us in body and in soul; subject to our wants, to our weaknesses, to all our sinless infirmities. And yet in this nature, wounded and bruised as it is, low as it is brought, he was holy. Man in paradise became a sinner with this nature in its strength; this man Christ Jesus withstood all the powers of earth and hell to make him a sinner with this nature in its weakness.

And this constitutes the great peculiarity of his holiness. A sinless soul in a sinner's weak nature—that was the holiness of Christ; and what is an angel's holiness compared to this? Give the holiest angel in heaven the nature that our Lord had, and put him here, and we might safely say he would be a sinner in an hour.

And herein consists a great part of the glory of his holiness, and the glory of Jehovah's triumph in it. He shewed his universe in Christ Jesus that he can keep a creature standing, where there is every thing to throw him down; that he can keep him holy, not only amid sin and temptation, but in weakness, infirmity, and suffering. Satan had a triumph when he laid upright man low, but what was it? It was a poor one—the triumph of an angel beating down with an angel's strength a creature of inferior nature, a giant's triumph as he overcomes a child. But the triumph of Jehovah in the holiness of Christ was a great one. There was man in his weakness, almost on the ground where Satan had thrown him, withstanding Satan, coming unhurt from a fierce and long contest with him, and giving him at the end of it a blow that crushes him for ever. We speak of our Lord in his holy human nature as the light and glory of heaven; we might speak of him as the reproach, the shame, the sorest misery, of hell.

III. Let us come now to *the importance* of Christ's holiness. The character he had to sustain, and the work he had to perform, required it.

1. It was necessary *in order to constitute him a real manifestation of God.*

God is not only a holy Being, he is " glorious in holiness." His holiness is one of the highest and brightest perfections of his Godhead, if not the brightest of all. Now one main object he had in view in uniting himself in Christ to our nature, was to make himself and his glory visible to his creatures. In his own divine nature, he is invisible, " dwelling in the light which no man can approach unto," one whom no man or angel " hath seen or can see;" but it pleased him to come out of this unapproachable light and embody himself in the person of his Son, and so to bring himself within our sight and knowledge. Hence Christ is spoken of in scripture as " God manifest in the flesh ;" he is called " the image of the invisible God," his " express" or exact image, " the brightness" or shining forth " of his glory." We are to look into his face, and see reflected there the likeness and splendour of his

Father. It is plain therefore that had the least defilement sullied him, this great end of his incarnation would have been lost. We should not have seen God in Christ as God is. It would have been like looking at a glorious object in a mirror that is both tarnished and false—not only would the chief beauty of that object have been lost, but we should have ascribed to it the mirror's imperfections, and consequently have formed of it an erroneous and degrading notion.

2. This perfect holiness in our Lord was needful *to make him an effectual sacrifice for our sins.*

A blemished sacrifice would have availed us nothing. The law of God's universe is, " the soul that sinneth it shall die." Had the blessed Jesus therefore sinned, his death could not have answered his purposes of love towards us; he would only have paid by it the just penalty for his own transgressions. But being holy, his death becomes a new thing in God's universe. He is the only sinless being who ever died in it or ever suffered in it, and hence his sufferings and death take that conspicuous, and peculiar, and wonderful place in it for which they were designed. They become an immense atonement for the sins of a guilty world. They are like a mighty ransom paid by one who is not a captive, and who demands for that ransom the freedom of whom he will among enslaved millions.

The Jewish sacrifices prefigured this. They shadowed forth the holiness of Christ at the same time that they typified the shedding of his blood. They were all to be perfect animals. Let the slightest blemish be discovered in them, they were to be at once rejected. In the prophet Malachi's time, after their long captivity in Babylon, the people and the priests also forgot this command concerning him or despised it; they brought to the temple the "blind and the lame and sick." And what does God say to them? "This is worse than useless, it is evil. It is an insult offered to me. It is treating my table or altar with contempt."

We accordingly find the apostles, after our Lord's death, laying a great stress on his holiness when he offered himself a victim. "Ye were not redeemed with corruptible things as silver and gold," says St. Peter, "but with the precious blood of Christ;" and what made that blood so precious? He was "as a lamb without blemish and without spot." "He hath made him to be sin for us," says St. Paul, "who knew no sin, that we might be made the righteousness of God in him." And our church has not lost sight of this. In our communion service it says,

"He was made very man, and that without spot of sin, to make us clean from all sin."

And it is giving truths like these as they arise their due importance, that renders at last the Christian's confidence in his Saviour so firm. It does not rest on one thing only in him, it rests on many. And when the man, through unbelief or infirmity, is beaten off one thing, he goes to another, and stays himself there. It is now his Saviour's love that he leans on, now his power, now his faithfulness, and now his holiness; at one time God's appointment of him to be his Saviour, at another time God's delight in him as his Saviour, and sometimes on two or three of these combined. Any one of them is enough to support his soul, but when he feels several of them underneath him, he is like a house that has foundation upon foundation beneath it, rock upon rock — not only may the storm beat and the sweeping flood come, the earthquake may come, rending and shivering assaults, and the house will bear the shock.

3. But our Lord's office as our great Redeemer was not to end with his life on earth, he was to go into the eternal heavens in the same character that he bore here, and to carry on there, though in a different manner, the same work. We sometimes think of him as simply entering there into his glory and joy, but he

is intent on our salvation in the midst of his glory and joy; as much engaged in it on his throne, as he was on his cross. The apostle accordingly represents him in this passage as our High Priest in the heavens, " ever living to make intercession for us;" and tells us that it became him to be holy in order *to qualify him for this heavenly office and work.*

This too was typified under the law. The Jewish high priest was never to go before God in the temple, without bearing a plate of gold on his mitre with this inscription on it, " Holiness to the Lord;" and the reason is given us —the people were thus to be reminded that their " holy things," their gifts and services, had iniquity in them, and that it was only through the typical holiness of their appointed intercessor, that the Lord would accept them. And this inscription was to be placed on the " fore-front" of his mitre, the most conspicuous part of his whole person, doubtless with this intent, that the people might never lose sight of his holiness, and might feel that the God before whom he was to appear in their behalf, could not lose sight of it.

And who does not feel that he needs a better righteousness than his own, to make such worship and service as his acceptable? Who is not sometimes fearful and ashamed as he thinks, not of his sins, but of his prayers and praises? The godly man numbers these things among his sins. They give him often greater sorrow of heart, than all their transgressions together give to other men. " But think in your sorrow," the exalted Saviour says to him, " of me and my holiness. It is no typical holiness as Aaron's was; it is real and perfect, and it is conspicuous. I never appear in my Father's presence but my Father sees it in me; and I am always in his presence, and always pleading it there for you; pleading, not only the blood I shed on the cross to cleanse you, but this spotless righteousness of mine which I wrought out for you, which my Father never looks on but he deems it yours, losing sight in my holiness of your unholiness; or if not so, feeling and acting towards you as though he did." St. John understood this. " We have an Advocate with the Father," he says, " Jesus Christ," not the merciful or the compassionate, but " Jesus Christ the righteous."

4. *As the pattern and example to which all his people are to be conformed,* it was needful that our Lord should be holy.

It is his glory that he is the image of his Father, it is our glory that he is the image of our future selves. " We know that when he shall appear," says St. John, " we shall be like him." It is one of the eternal purposes of the divine mind, that every redeemed sinner shall resemble at last the Saviour who redeems him. " Whom he did foreknow, he also did predestinate"—to what? to live a bold, ungodly life for a few years on earth, and then to go in their boldness and ungodliness to heaven? No; " to be conformed to the image of his Son." That Son is not to stand alone in the universe, the same scripture says; he is to be the head of a large family all like him, " the first-born among many brethren." For this purpose the Holy Spirit is sent down into our hearts, not simply to lead us to Christ and to bring us through faith into union and fellowship with him, but to work day by day within us, to mould us into his likeness. And we ourselves are commanded to labour after conformity to him. We are to be " followers of him," to have " the same mind in us that was in him," and " so to walk even as he walked."

Now all this, brethren, is very glorious, but suppose our Lord to have come short in any degree of perfect holiness, what becomes of the glory of all this? Of what use would his example be to us? We should not know when we were right and when we were wrong in following him. There would be no peace of mind for us in following him. And as for looking forward to wearing his likeness in a future world, we should never do it; the prospect would not be glorious enough even for us. We must look higher, we should say. "Be ye holy, as I am holy," is our God's command to us. He sets his own lofty holiness before us, and bids us aspire to it; and his Spirit within us lifts up our desires to it. We want a perfection like his, the perfection of holiness, and earthbound as our affections sometimes are, nothing below this will satisfy us. But now there is this perfection in the holy Jesus, a sinless perfection. We cannot look higher. He is purity itself, the divine purity embodied. To be made like unto him comprehends in it all that is blissful and glorious. We feel that we shall indeed be satisfied when we awake with his likeness.

We must now see, brethren, the necessity, and with it something of the importance, of this attribute of the Redeemer. It is not a mere ornament of his mediatorial character, it was from the first an essential part of it; he could have answered none of the great purposes of his coming here without it. A sun without light could as easily make a day, as a Redeemer without holiness have brought us salvation.

Let us learn then, first, *to rejoice in his holiness, and admire and adore him for it.*

Any man can admire some things in Christ. His matchless condescension, his gentleness and patience, his kindness and love, his loftiness and greatness—these things when pressed upon the heart, must force even the unfeeling heart into something like admiration of him. But to adore him for his holiness, or even to take pleasure in thinking of it—none but a soul born of God and ripening for heaven ever does this. The reason is a mournful one. It lies in our own unholiness. When man lost his original purity, he lost with it his delight in purity, and almost his perception of it. The consequence is, that just as a shining star or a beautiful landscape is nothing to one whose sight is gone, so moral beauty and spiritual brightness are naturally nothing to us; we do not perceive them, or, if we perceive them, they do not attract us; we have no taste for or delight in them. And even when it pleases a sovereign God by the working of his Spirit to renew our souls, the soul does not all at once recover from its native blindness. It often rejoices in the mercies it receives from Christ, long before it begins to rejoice in Christ's great excellencies. But to this every renewed soul at length comes; and till we are brought to this, our spiritual condition must at the best be doubtful. Heaven is a world of praise, and before any one of us is warranted to think he is meet for heaven, he must have learned to admire and adore that holy Saviour who is for ever praised in it.

Let us seek for ourselves a share in this holiness of Christ.

All the perfections which he possesses as the incarnate Jesus, he derives from God. God imparted them to him; and this, not for his own sake only, to adorn his character or to qualify him for the work appointed him, but for our sakes. They are placed in him as in a treasure-house from which his church in all ages is to be enriched. This is what St. Paul means when he says, " It pleased the Father that in him should all fulness dwell," a fulness of every thing that we, his sinful, empty, destitute creatures, can require. This too is what he himself means when he says, " God giveth not the Spirit by measure unto him."

You see then, brethren, what we have before us. It is not simply a resplendent holiness that we are to admire, but a holiness of which we ourselves may partake. It is not a treasure which we are to contemplate and wonder at, and then go away heart-sick with our own poverty and need; it is a treasure thrown open to us, placed within our reach, and we are invited to take, freely and abundantly as we will, of its precious riches. O how little do we regard our blessed Lord in this light, as the great storehouse of all we want! We look to him for mercy and forgiveness, but he is as able to give us holiness as he is forgiveness. None other can do this. We are utterly unable to impart to others the smallest portion of the holiness God may have given us, but he can impart whatever he possesses. All he possesses has been given him to be communicated, and never is he so delighted to communicate of it, as when we lie down at his feet and implore him to give us of his holiness. "Blessed," he said, "are they which do hunger and thirst after righteousness, for they shall be filled;" and he well knew what he said when he promised them this. He has an abundance of righteousness to give, enough to fill and satisfy hungering millions. Lord, excite in us this blessed hunger, and teach us to look for our righteousness and holiness in thee.

And let us banish from our minds for ever the thought, that though living ungodly lives, we may yet be followers of this holy Saviour.
The thing is impossible, brethren, as impossible as that a man should follow the sun in its glorious course, and yet live in constant darkness, never see its light or feel its warmth. What is real religion in a sinner's heart? It is nothing else than fellowship with Christ, a union and communion with him, a partaking with him in

all that adorns and blesses him. It is a coming under his influence, and growing into a spiritual resemblance to him. What becomes then of our natural ungodliness? We must not say, what becomes of the darkness when the sun shines on it? but what becomes of the dampness and wretchedness of a dungeon, when the air and the light begin freely to enter it? They gradually disappear, and so will our unholiness most assuredly give way, when our hearts are thrown open to our holy Lord, and he enters and dwells in them.

It is hard to believe this. Nothing our minds seem naturally more determined to disbelieve. There is no notion however false, no absurdity however great, which we are not more ready to receive than this simple assertion of the living God, " Without holiness no man shall see me." How have men laboured to make the gospel of Jesus Christ contradict this! some taking its doctrines and privileges, others its sacraments and ordinances, and saying, "These set it aside; these shall carry us into God's presence; these shall be our substitutes for a holy heart and life." Brethren, there is no substitute for holiness of heart and life. Man has been at work for six thousand years endeavouring to find one, but all in vain. May none of us wish to find one! May we all love our God the better, for requiring holiness of us; and may we bless him every day we live that he has provided a holy Saviour to impart it to us! Would we have it? We must seek of him his Holy Spirit through whom he communicates or rather works it; we must put ourselves in his hands, submit to all his will and ways, take up any cross he lays before us, welcome any affliction he may send us; when we read his word, our prayer must be, " Lord, let thy word cleanse my heart;" and when at his table, it must be the same; " Lord, let me so behold thee here as to adore while I love thee, and long to be like thee, as well as with thee."

SERMON XXII.

CHRIST CONTEMPLATING HIS FUTURE BLESSEDNESS.

Psalm xvi. 9, 10, 11.

"Therefore my heart is glad and my glory rejoiceth; my flesh also shall rest in hope; for thou wilt not leave my soul in hell, neither wilt thou suffer thine holy One to see corruption. Thou wilt shew me the path of life: in thy presence is fulness of joy; at thy right hand there are pleasures for evermore."

In the former part of this psalm, David is speaking perhaps in his own person, but not so in this part of it. It is not true of David. It relates to the Lord Jesus Christ, and, in its full sense, to him only. So Peter told the Jews in the sermon he preached to them on the day of Pentecost. St. Paul also gives it the same interpretation. We must consider these words then as our blessed Master's own words, as much so as though they came from his own lips. They describe to us the feelings of his human soul while dwelling in a human body in our world. And this gives them a very high interest. We sometimes wish, brethren, that we could have followed him as he left his disciples and went alone into the desert or up some mountain, to pray. We think how elevating it would have been to stand near him at such a time, and witness the pourings out of his soul before his Father. In this scripture the Holy Spirit seems to meet this wish. " Here," he says to us, " is your beloved Master before you in exactly the situation you desire. He is holding secret communion with his Father, and you may draw near and listen to it. He is willing you should know it all."

I. We must begin with just noticing *the title our Lord applies here to himself.*

He calls himself God's " Holy One," and in so doing, he lets us see that he was not only really holy, but *eminently, conspicuously holy*. He is characterized by his holiness, called after it, known by it. " Thine holy One"—the words imply that of all living beings there is none so holy as he, not one who can be deemed holy at all in comparison with him. They convey the same idea that those lofty words in our communion service convey, " Thou only art holy."

And his application of this title to himself, shews us that *he deems it an honourable title,* that he is pleased with it and glories in it. Had David called him God's holy One, the name would have set forth only his holiness and David's admiration of it; but he is speaking here in his own person; he calls himself by this name; and he thus discovers to us his own admiration of holiness. He delights in it, he tells us, more than in any thing besides. It is not the compassion, or love, or tenderness of his human soul, that he most rejoices in, but the purity of that soul. He had rather be the holiest creature in the universe than the kindest, or the wisest, or the greatest, nay, than the most beloved. When his Father speaks to him from heaven, he designates him by the affection he bears him. His soul is full of love for him, and he calls him " his beloved, his well beloved Son." But when he speaks to his Father, dear as his Father's love is to him, he passes it by; he thinks of the holiness he has given him, and calls himself after that—" thine holy One." When, brethren, shall we value holiness as our holy Lord valued it? When we have more of his Spirit within us; when nature and self are more subdued within us, and grace reigns alone.

II. We must notice in the text *our Lord's resurrection*, or rather the prospect he had of it. And in speaking of this, he partially describes it, and, with it, the constitution of his own person and nature. " Thou wilt not leave my soul in hell, neither wilt thou suffer thine holy One to see corruption. Thou wilt shew me the path of life."

Now here we learn that our holy Lord, considered as the Son of man, *was made up, just as we are, of two parts, a body and a soul;* not a human body and a divine soul, but a human body and a human soul. Here is express mention made of his soul, and that a soul in God's keeping and at God's command, evidently a soul as distinct from God's, as our own souls are, though mysteriously united with it. His body indeed is not mentioned, but it is meant. He has it in his mind when he says he shall not see corruption.

And proceeding a step farther, we learn *that at his crucifixion these two parts of him were separated.* A real dissolution, and not merely the appearance of one, took place. He actually died, and just as we die; the flesh and the spirit were rent asunder; the one took its flight into what he calls " hell," that is, some part of the unseen world inhabited by disembodied spirits; the other sunk down on the earth an empty thing, a soulless, forsaken tenement of clay.

Thus far we all resemble our Lord, or shall do so; but now comes something peculiar to him —*his human frame*, we are told, *was saved from corruption*. It was forsaken of his spirit; it became quiet, and cold, and senseless when forsaken by it, as our own frames will one day become; it was buried; but there ended the matter. Destruction and the worm dared not come near it; the least taint of corruption never touched it. God, he intimates, would not suffer this. He speaks of it as though it were something that neither he nor his Father could endure. And why this?

We make light of death and of all its attendant circumstances. We can turn away from our acquaintance and friends and bury them out of our sight, leave them to the worms that cover them and the strange process that consumes them, almost without a shudder. The reason is, we are living in a world of death, and are familiarized with the dreadful thing. But did we look at this thing for the first time, as our first parents, for instance, looked on it when they buried Abel, or as angels and spiritual beings look on it now, our feelings concerning it would alter. It would be no longer a trifle that we pride ourselves on half scorning, we should see in the corruption of the grave something to be abhorred; a mark of more than God's displeasure against us, a token of his disgust with us; a fixed purpose on his part to degrade and degrade us to the utmost for our transgressions, as well as afflict and punish us. Had it been needful for our redemption, the Lord Jesus would doubtless have borne even this for us; have suffered his body to be eaten of worms, as readily as he suffered it to be nailed to the cross; have become an abomination for us, as well as a curse; but this was not needful. God's broken law was satisfied when his body and spirit were once rent asunder; divine justice required no more; and that sacred frame shall consequently never know corruption.

But we learn more here. *The resurrection of Christ consisted mainly in a re-union of his body and soul.* This is not indeed stated in the text, but it is implied. "Thou wilt shew me the path of life," he says, and he says this immediately after he had said that his soul was not to be left in hell nor his body to undergo corruption; plainly intimating that his soul is to be brought back again from the spiritual world whither it had fled, lodged once again within his uncorrupted frame, and then life is to ensue, life of the same kind that he had lived before. He is again to be a being made up of a human body and soul, and the same body and soul that were his before.

And here comes out again that wonderful truth, the eternal manhood of the divine Saviour. Death made no essential change in him. He rose from the grave as really and perfectly the Son of man, as he was when he sunk down with agony in the garden or bled on the cross. We have not an High Priest in the heavens, who is a stranger to us. He is allied to us and one of us. There is a human form, brethren, on the throne of Jehovah, and within that form a human soul and heart. That mighty God whom in his spiritual essence no eye hath ever seen or can see, is still God united to our nature and manifest in our flesh. Angels and archangels lie down before him, they are as worms of the dust in comparison with him, but " he is not ashamed to call us brethren;" he is as truly our Brother as he is the infinite Jehovah, our everlasting God. We may well say, wonderful is his condescension. It is as much above our comprehension as his power or his greatness is above it. He surpasses our thoughts in every thing, as much when he humbles as when he exalts himself—never so much as when he stoops down to manifest the riches of his love to the sinful children of men.

But here we may ask why this re-union of our Lord's human body and soul took place. Why this immediate bringing of them together again after they had been separated? They seemed to have done their work; why then not throw them for ever aside, or leave them alone to sink into nothingness? One answer to this question we may find in the text. It seems to intimate that there was something in the character which the great Speaker of it sustained, that prevented God from acting thus towards him. "I am thine holy One, and thou wilt not suffer thine holy One to see corruption. My holiness will withhold thee from giving me up to destruction."

"The righteous Lord," we are told, "loveth righteousness." It is congenial with his nature, of a piece with himself; he loves it more than he loves any thing else. And he shews his love to it wherever he finds it. There is not a holy creature in his universe, who has not visibly on him the stamp of his approbation. And whatever is holy in his universe, he preserves. Nothing pure does he ever suffer to perish. While he allows the stream of time to sweep away with it all that is polluted, he rescues from it all that is undefiled; so that time and its stream, roll on long and resistless as they may, will never destroy one particle of that which is good, never permanently injure one holy being or thing. Now here in Christ's human nature is something pre-eminently holy, a soul without a spot and

D D

a body without a stain. And what though they might have answered the purposes for which they were created, though they might have done their work, it would not have harmonized with God's usual proceedings to leave them to perish. No holy frame had ever yet known corruption, or the slightest touch of it. Christ's holy frame therefore shall never know it. God will not allow any thing so pure to be thus degraded. He will not " suffer his holy One to see corruption."

But we well know that all the ends for which the Son of God had become incarnate, were not yet accomplished. He had made in our nature an all-sufficient atonement for his people's sins, and had purchased for them in it all the blessings of grace and glory, but they had not yet received these blessings, and it was his Father's will that they should receive them from no other hands than his. He was to wash them in his blood, as well as to shed it for them; to cover them with his righteousness, as well as work it out for them; to dispense to them salvation, as well as to purchase and obtain it; to lead them to the heaven he had opened for them, and to make them meet for it. Besides he was to be enthroned in heaven as the world's great Governor. God was, as it were, to step aside, and leave the administration of all things in his wide dominions to this Son of man. He was to reign in heaven, and continue to reign there, till all the divine purposes towards this world of sinners were fulfilled. Now he could not have done this had he remained in the grave. He could not have done it so visibly and gloriously, had a part of him only been taken into heaven. God therefore raised him up at once, re-united at once his body and soul, and sent him up a perfect man to his heavenly throne. Hence St. Peter tells the Jews soon after his resurrection, " Him hath God exalted with his right hand to be a Prince and a Saviour, for to give repentance to Israel and remission of sins." And the consequences of his exaltation were soon apparent. The church he had left on earth, soon felt it had a mighty Helper. It discovered with joy and wonder that its risen Lord was wielding all the power of the spiritual world, dispensing its gifts and blessings as it pleased him, doing what he would with their hearts and the hearts of all men, bruising Satan underneath their feet, reigning over earth, heaven, and hell. The once crucified Nazarene was known and acknowledged as " Head over all things for his church," " God over all blessed for evermore."

III. The text sets before us *the view he had of his heavenly blessedness.*

That heaven is meant in the last verse of this

psalm, there can be no doubt. The path of life it speaks of, is a path that leads farther than from the grave back again into this world; it passes through this world into another; it is a path from the grave into the regions of life and happiness. And the first thing that strikes us in our Lord's description of this happiness, is the perfect absence from it of every thing peculiar to himself. Not one word does he say in it of his lofty exaltation, of the honour that is to cover him as the author and finisher of our salvation, or of that wonderful delight which the sight of his redeemed church all at last faultless and glorious before his throne, is to impart to him. He places himself in this scripture on a level with his people, and looks forward to no other blessedness than that they are to share.

Observe, first, *the nature* of this blessedness. It is not rest as he sometimes calls it, nor yet peace; it rises above this; it is "joy," happiness of the highest kind. And it is not one strong feeling of joy; it is termed "pleasures," a happiness made up of many joys, flowing into the soul through many channels.

And then notice *the perfection* of this blessedness. It is "fulness of joy." There is as much of it as the soul can possibly hold, or desire, or conceive of. It is a joy that fills the soul to overflowing, and could fill numberless souls to overflowing, were their desires and powers ever so much enlarged.

And we are told too of *the duration* of this happiness. It is constant, everlasting happiness. The pleasures that compose it, are " pleasures for evermore," pleasures that are never interrupted and will never have an end.

And the text discovers to us also *the source* of this happiness. On first reading it indeed, we do not perceive this. When it tells us of joy in God's presence and pleasures at his right hand, we imagine that it points out to us simply the place where this joy and these pleasures are to be found; but St. Peter, in quoting the passage, assigns to it a higher meaning. He represents our Lord as saying to his Father, " Thou shalt make me full of joy with thy countenance. I shall not only be happy in thy presence, thy presence shall make me happy. My joy shall flow from it, my fulness of joy."

Now some of you, brethren, can understand this. There is something in your minds, that responds to it. You so love your glorious God, that you long to be with him; and you have already experienced so much delight in his favour and friendship, that once with him, you feel you shall be blessed. He is now your portion, the chief source of your happiness, far away as he at times seems and always out of your sight.

There have been moments perhaps in which you have felt him near you, and then you have been ready to say, "This is enough. None on earth and scarcely any in heaven can be happier than we." But to see his face as well as have him near you, to be with him in his own kingdom immediately before his throne, to hold and hold for ever an uninterrupted, intimate, communion with him, more intimate than you have ever yet held with any one of your fellow-men—you can feel that there is happiness in this, the perfection of happiness. You can think of nothing higher, and you do not wish to think of any thing more. And this is the happiness which you know is awaiting you. The blessedness our Lord here describes, is a blessedness he has taught all his people to expect, as well as long for. It is the very blessedness he has prepared for them in heaven. They are all to partake of it there. It is common property there. This fulness of joy in God's presence, these pleasures at his right hand for evermore—there is not a redeemed soul in heaven, that is not overflowing with them.

Here then we learn that *we and our beloved Lord shall be sharers together in the same happiness in his kingdom.* We shall not only inhabit the same world, we shall partake of the same blessedness in it. He himself tells us that we are to eat and drink at his own table, and to enter into his own joy. Not that our joy will be equal to his. As God, he possesses a boundless happiness which none but a boundless mind, like his, can contain; and as man, his happiness, though of the same nature with ours, will doubtless far surpass it. Our joy will be full. It will be as abundant as our glorified spirits can hold. But the powers of his soul are larger than ours, and capable of receiving more abundant joy. His union too with the Father, the fountain of all happiness, is closer than ours. And he is his Father's holy One, the holiest of all created beings, and therefore the happiest. "Thou lovest righteousness and hatest wickedness," says the psalmist to him; "therefore God, thy God, hath anointed thee with the oil of gladness above thy fellows. That happy oil shall be poured out on every head around thee, but not in that abundance wherewith the eternal Jehovah shall pour it upon thine." And thus in all things he is to have the pre-eminence. He bore on earth a heavier weight of suffering than we, he shall bear in heaven a more exceeding weight of glory. The Spirit was given him here in greater measure to sanctify him, it shall be given him there in greater measure to gladden him. His fellowship with us, and yet his superiority to us, are both provided for. We are to sit at the same table with him in his kingdom, but he is to sit at it in a higher place. We are all the Father's children, but he is the Father's first-born. We shall all be in our Father's presence, but he will be the nearest to him, and have a double portion of his joy and pleasures.

IV. We may now advance another step. We have seen our Lord anticipating his heavenly blessedness; let us look now at *the effects which his anticipation of it produced in him.*

And here we must place him before us as he was on earth amid griefs and sufferings. In the eighth verse of the psalm, he tells us that he is sustained and carried on in these sufferings by his Father's presence with him, and his own constant reliance on his succour. " I have set the Lord always before me; because he is at my right hand I shall not be moved." But then he goes on to speak in the next verse of far higher feelings than those of confidence; and these he traces, not so much to the presence of God then with him, as to something before him—to the view he had of that joyful resurrection and that heavenly blessedness we have now been contemplating. He had heaven in his sight, and, " Therefore," he says, " my heart is glad and my glory rejoiceth, my flesh also shall rest in hope."

1. *Joy* then we may say, gladness of heart,

was one effect produced in our Lord's mind by his anticipated happiness.

We are accustomed to think of him, as experiencing nothing on earth but unmingled sorrow. We picture his path to ourselves as a path overhung with the thickest darkness, through which no ray of cheerful light ever reached him. And dark indeed his path was, darker than our imaginations have ever painted it. But yet many a gleam of heavenly light pierced through that darkness. Our Lord's sufferings, we have reason to believe, were not unmingled. They never ceased perhaps, no, not for a single moment; but they were alleviated by many secret consolations, and sometimes, the text seems to intimate, overbalanced by them. Here is gladness and heart-felt gladness spoken of in the very midst of them, and spoken of by our suffering Lord himself.

And he describes this inward gladness as so great, that his heart cannot contain it. "My glory rejoiceth," he says, and St. Peter explains this; "My tongue was glad." His joy vented itself in joyful language. It was not kept secret. It was so great that it could not be kept secret; it burst forth in exultation and praise.

And if we trace our Lord's history, we shall find such to have been really the case. We read in the tenth chapter of St. Luke, that he "rejoiced in spirit," and the next moment we see that joy expressing itself in a holy thanksgiving. His last interview with his disciples indicates a soaring and rejoicing, as well as a sorrowful mind. You remember that burst of triumph which came from him when Judas at last went away to betray him. There is no complaining of his treachery, no mourning over faithless friendship and cutting ingratitude, there is not a tear or a sigh; there is exultation and joy. " Now is the Son of man glorified," he cries, " and God is glorified in him." St Matthew describes him as singing a hymn with his disciples but a few minutes before his final agony began. And how at last did he leave the world? With something like a conqueror's shout. " It is finished," he cried; and perhaps never were any words uttered in our world, so joyful as those. The battle, he felt, was fought, the victory won, and the agonies of death could neither master nor silence his triumphant gladness.

2. Another feeling he expresses here is *hope*; and he expresses this in very strong terms; " My flesh shall rest in hope."

He has evidently his death in view, and he describes the hope he has within him as reconciling him even to that. And just as David describes his longing after God as so intense, that his soul will not contain it, it runs over and finds its way into his bodily frame, so does this blessed Jesus speak here of his hope in God as pervading his mortal flesh, and accompanying it even to the grave. It takes away from the grave its terrors. It enables him to anticipate it with a fearless calmness.

When Lazarus died, he did not speak of him as dead. He used a milder term, as though he looked on death almost with complacency, regarding it as something pleasurable and desirable, like a lying down at the end of a weary day. " Our friend Lazarus sleepeth." Similar is his language here. " Death," he says, " will be to me a rest; the grave I am going to, a bed for my wearied, aching body to be quiet in; and the eternity I am about to enter, a place of repose for my tired spirit. I have no fear either of the one or of the other. I know well that they can do me no harm, and I know as well what is to follow them. I am God's holy One, and he will not leave my soul and my body long asunder. After a little while I shall breathe again the air of this lower world, and then a little longer and I shall breathe a purer air, and enter into my blessedness. Hope has carried me peaceful and sometimes joyful through a sorrowful life, it shall carry me peaceful through a yet more sorrowful death. I will lie down in my grave like one who lies down in his bed, looking for a morning of light and joy."

We have now, brethren, gone through this scripture. There is a happiness set before us in it, that the highest Being in the universe and the holiest is content to share, nay, a happiness that he is represented as looking forward to with desire and hope, and with a hope so delightful, that it keeps his heart glad and rejoicing under circumstances of the most extreme misery, and with a death before him of unequalled anguish. It is clear then that such a happiness must be immeasurably great, inconceivably exalted in its nature, and unutterably desirable and precious. And we have reason also to believe that this wonderful happiness is not a happiness peculiar to this holy and lofty Being. It is a joy that is common to him with an immense multitude of sinful men whom he has redeemed, as open at this moment to you and me as it was to him.

Now what are we thinking of all this? Nothing at all? Then, brethren, we are not acting as reasonable men. We are not feeling as our own judgments and consciences will tell us we ought to feel. There must be something mournfully wrong in the state of our minds to allow us to remain thus senseless and indifferent with things like these before us. The scripture speaks of some who are " dead in trespasses and sins," whose souls have no more spiritual feeling or life than a corpse. May the God of all mercy grant that if any such are now within these walls, they may go out of them conscience-stricken, humbled, and ashamed.

Are any of you saying, " Would that this happiness might be ours?" It certainly may be yours, brethren. Nothing but sin keeps any rational creature in the universe out of it, and this holy One of God has been manifested to take away your sins. All the sufferings he went through in his way to this happiness, he went through for you, to remove sin from you and cleanse you from the guilt of it. You have only to believe this, and heaven will be yours. A simple faith in him as your atoning Saviour will in one moment give you an interest in his sufferings, and ensure to you his happiness. "What," you may say, " faith only without any thing else?" I answer, faith without any thing else. "And will faith do this," you may say again, " for such sinners as we are?" I answer again, it will do it for any sinner, the most guilty and polluted that walks the earth. And do you once more ask, " What is to become then of those good works and that holiness, without which, we are told, no one can see the Lord?" Ask the man who is casting the seed into the ground, what is to become of the future harvest; or ask another man, as he is planting a tree in the earth, where we are to look for the pleasant fruit. That simple faith will produce those good works which God requires of you; it will secure that holiness without which you can never see him. It is the seed of all that is good, all that is holy, and all that is happy, for it brings the soul into union and fellowship with its holy and happy Saviour.

Is this precious faith already yours, and this Saviour yours? Then learn to think of him as a sometimes rejoicing Saviour.

It may be that, like him, you are stricken and afflicted. Suffering and sorrow may be laid on you, till you are ready to sink under the heavy weight of them. Or you may have some hour of trial before you; a cross may be coming on you, which you dread to bear, or death may be drawing near. And in these circumstances you may have little to cheer you; the consolations you expected from the Spirit the Comforter do not come. Now you are the persons to whom the Lord Jesus especially speaks in this text. He bids you look at him. He is anticipating here the feelings of his own soul in a situation very similar to yours, only far more distressing, and what are they? Gladness and joy. And whence do they spring? Simply from hope. His chief joy on earth, he says, his gladness of heart, comes not from any peculiar consolations he receives from his Father; descending angels do not bring it him; he is looking forward; he is rejoicing in hope; for the joy that is set before him he endures the cross. The same source of gladness is open to you. The same joy is set before you, and there is the same faithful God to make it yours. Do you believe this, brethren? Then try to feel and act as though you believed it. Do not say, "We must wait for our troubled life to be over, or this affliction to be gone, or that dark hour to be passed, before our hearts can rejoice." Lift up your hearts to heaven, and let them rejoice now. Look beyond dark hours and troubles, beyond life itself; put present things often aside, and bring a glorious eternity near. You admire your blessed Master's submission and patience in his sufferings you would not think yourselves his disciples, if you did not in some measure imitate them; admire his joyfulness also, and imitate that. Think of him at his table to-day, as one frequently happy even on earth, and abundantly happy now. Aim to realize more your fellowship with him, to see and to feel more of the deep interest you have in him, in his joys as well as his sorrows, in his glorious resurrection and ascension as well as his bitter death. He came out of the grave for you, as really as he went down into it for you. He is gone into heaven for you. He is as much your Saviour on his throne, as he was on his cross.

SERMON XXIII.

THE FOUNTAIN OPENED.

ZECHARIAH XIII. 1.

"In that day there shall be a fountain opened to the house of David and to the inhabitants of Jerusalem, for sin and for uncleanness."

It is pleasant, brethren, to look back on the types and prophecies which revealed a Saviour to the ancient church. It is like looking in the morning at the lights which guided the mariner, in the dark and stormy night, to the sheltering haven. And there is often instruction for us as well as pleasure, in contemplating these early revelations of the blessed Jesus. Dim and obscure as they may seem, many of them throw light even now on the way of salvation God has laid open for us through him.

The prophecy before us is of this character. It calls our attention, first, to the fountain it speaks of; then to the persons for whom this fountain is to be opened; and then to the day when the opening of it to them is to take place.

I. We have before us *a fountain*.

The imagery of scripture is naturally drawn from the habits of the people among whom it was written. Their country was a warm one, and water was consequently much used and valued among them. There was also occasionally a want of it, and a want that was most painfully felt, and this circumstance must have served to raise it still higher in their estimation. We must not wonder then that spiritual blessings are so often exhibited to us in scripture under images borrowed from water. These images found their way at once to the understanding and feelings of Jewish men. Did this prophet speak to them of their coming Saviour as a fountain? The word immediately presented him to them as one much needed, and much to be rejoiced in and prized.

That the Lord Jesus is meant in the text, there can be no doubt. The concluding verses of the preceding chapter make this plain. But he is represented in it as a fountain for a particular purpose; not for the thirsty to drink from, but for the unclean to wash in, " a fountain for sin and for uncleanness."

And here again the text carries us into eastern climes. Bodily ablutions are much more common there than among us. With the Jews too they partook sometimes of a sacred character. Within their temple stood a large cistern or " molten sea," in which the priests were obliged daily to wash before they entered on their sacred duties; and besides this, there were ten other smaller cisterns, wherein all such things as were intended for sacrifices, were washed before they were presented to the Lord. " And there shall be a sacred laver opened for you," the prophet says, " when your Messiah comes; a fountain in which not your priests only, but all the sinful and polluted among you may wash and be clean."

He mentions two things, sin and uncleanness, but he has one thing only in his mind—sin under the figure of uncleanness. And it is a very expressive figure.

Does uncleanness degrade whatever it touches? So has sin degraded us. Man was in honour when he had nothing to do with it, but where is he now? Down in the dust, " a worm and no man," fallen and debased. And is uncleanness a disgusting and loathsome thing? If there is a disgusting thing in the universe, it is sin. When

God calls sin by this name, he represents it as something which he cannot bear to look upon. The expression implies not a mere disapprobation of it, but a detestation, an utter abhorrence, of it. And thus, in another place, he speaks of it as " that abominable thing which he hates."

And every one of you, brethren, will feel the same towards sin, whenever you are brought to see it in its true character. It will appear to you as loathsome as ever it has appeared attractive. You will hate it more than you have ever loved it. And you will loathe and hate yourselves because you have suffered yourselves to be defiled with it. Job did so. " I abhor myself," he says. David did so. He compares sin to the most disgusting objects his imagination can conceive, to a loathsome disease, to putrefying flesh, to corrupt and offensive wounds. He speaks of it as though he scarcely knew how to bear the presence or even the thought of it. And this the prophet Ezekiel tells the Jews is to be their feeling towards it, when the Lord their God, in the latter days, shall bring them to repentance. " Ye shall loathe yourselves in your own sight," he says, " for your iniquities and for your abominations."

And now comes in the text the remedy for this hateful evil. It is *a suitable*, a real, effectual remedy for it. It is a fountain, the prophet says; water; something which can remove uncleanness, and is intended to remove it, " a fountain for sin and for uncleanness."

This fountain is nothing else than the precious blood of God's own dear Son. That blood was shed for us. It was designed by God to be "a propitiation for our sins;" that is, to remove from us the guilt of them, to save us from the punishment of them, to bear them away and " make an end" of them. Hence the sinner who by faith obtains an interest in this propitiation, no longer stands before God as a guilty, condemned creature, but as a pardoned creature; as one who has not a single sin imputed to him, but has all his multiplied sins completely and for ever cancelled. The apostle accordingly says, " The blood of Jesus Christ cleanseth us from all sin." Just as water removes uncleanness from the body, so does this blood remove the guilt of sin from the soul. It does away with it, frees the soul from it, makes our condition as safe and in the end as happy, as though we had never sinned.

Think of a garment polluted and offensive. " I will have nothing to do with it," says the owner. " It is not meet for my use. I cast it away." There is a picture of man as man is in his natural, defiled condition. But plunge that garment in water and cleanse it—its owner takes it again; he uses and values it. There is a representation of the sinner when Christ has once washed him from his sins in his own blood. That blood has removed from him the degrading and loathsome thing which made his God reject him. He calls him now to himself; he delights in having him in his presence; he employs him in his service; he becomes his treasure and his joy.

Or think of a Jew under the law incurring some ceremonial defilement. He was cut off from the congregation and camp of Israel. No one was to associate with him, or have any communication with him. He was an outcast. But when he had gone through certain purifications, his uncleanness was considered as done away with; he was admitted again among his brethren, and restored to his former privileges. Now man as a sinner is an outcast. He is " far off," the scripture says, far off from God, and from every spiritual enjoyment and mercy. But the blood of Christ applied by faith to his soul, removes the evil thing that cuts him off from his happiness. It puts an end to his exclusion and banishment. It throws open to him the church below and the church above. No more a stranger and foreigner, he becomes " a fellow-citizen with the saints and of the household of God." It is in this sense that the word " uncleanness" in the text, is rendered in the margin of our bible " separation for uncleanness."

And this effectual remedy for sin is described

here as *an abundant, lasting* remedy. The lavers made use of in the temple to remove uncleanness, were cisterns merely, vessels that might be exhausted if many came to them, and that, left to themselves, would in time become dry. But here is " a fountain," the prophet says, a sacred laver which can never be exhausted. No one can possibly be disappointed who comes to this to be cleansed. Thousands may wash in it, and it will be overflowing as ever, able to cleanse thousands and thousands more. And its abounding fulness is not to last for a year or an age; as long as there is a sin in his church to be done away with, so long shall this blessed fountain for sin which God has opened, continue full. It is our misery, brethren, and our shame, that we are perpetually contracting fresh defilement, but it is our unspeakable comfort, sometimes the only comfort we can find to cheer us, that the blood of Jesus Christ always "cleanseth from all sin." We went to it yesterday to be cleansed, we may go to it again to-day, and when to-morrow comes with its stains and its sins, again we may experience its cleansing power. And our children after us may go to it, and generations yet unborn. Think of the sun that is now shining in the heavens. It shone on Adam in paradise, on Noah in his ark, on Abraham in his tent, on Israel in the wilderness, on David in his palace, on Paul and Peter as they preached; and shine it will till the earth no longer needs its light. So with the blood of Christ. It began to cleanse almost from the foundation of the world, and it will continue to cleanse till the number of God's elect is accomplished and his kingdom full. O may every one of us be cleansed by it from every iniquity, spot and stain!

II. We have now to see *for whom this fountain is intended.* The text says, " for the house of David and the inhabitants of Jerusalem ;" in other words, for the Jews; not for them only, to the exclusion of all others, but for them before all others, and above all others. And this shews us,

1. *The utter insufficiency of all rites and ordinances to cleanse the soul from sin.*

Who were these men? The very men to whom pertained the law with all its sacrifices, and the temple with all its rites and ordinances; men who apparently had fountain upon fountain for sin, and all of God's providing; and men living, not at a distance from these fountains, in some remote parts of the land, but close to them, " the inhabitants of Jerusalem." When guilt oppressed or conscience disquieted them, they could in a few minutes be in their temple, and sharing in its sacrifices and service. But look at the text. It addresses them as it would address the very heathen. It seems to lose sight of their temple and all that belongs to it. It promises them a fountain for sin, as though they were utterly without any remedy for sin, had no where to turn for the removal of one transgression. And such was really the fact. All their legal ordinances could no more expiate their guilt, than a painted sun could dissipate the gloom of midnight. The best of them were but types and representations of that great propitiation which Christ was to offer. Attended on with a sense of guilt, an application for mercy, an humble and simple reliance on Jehovah's promises, they were accepted of God, and so were the men who joined in them; but trusted in, viewed as real atonements for transgression, put in the place of Jehovah's mercy and promises, these ordinances were altogether worthless, and worse than worthless—they were offensive to God, they aggravated, rather than removed, the guilt of those who came to them. Does this seem to any of you strong language? Then turn to the first chapter of Isaiah. God speaks there with indignation of all such sacrifices and worship. They are " vain oblations," he says, " an abomination" unto him, he " cannot away with them," his " soul hateth them," " they are a trouble" unto him, he is " weary to bear them."

And it is just the same, brethren, with our

Christian sacraments. God has ordained them in his church for exactly the same ends as he ordained of old these Jewish rites; not to take away sin, but to keep us mindful of it, and of that blood which can take it away. They are intended to beget in us, through his Spirit, such feelings as become us in our fallen and guilty condition, deep compunction of soul, an earnest and entire casting of ourselves on his free mercy, abounding thankfulness for the glorious Saviour he has given us, and joy in that Saviour, such as we have never known and never can know in any thing else. Christ wants at his table men who feel that his table can do nothing, nothing whatsoever, to cleanse them; and all other men who go there, he will not accept. They may eat the bread and drink the wine which shadow him forth, but this is really all they do. They touch not his body and blood. They obtain not the remission of their sins, nor any other benefit of his passion. They might as well have eaten the same bread and drunk the same wine elsewhere, and better, for then they would not have dishonoured the Lord who bought them; they would not have put aside the great sacrifice he has offered, and either ignorantly or presumptuously set a shadow of it in its place.

2. We are taught here *the all-sufficiency of Christ's blood to cleanse the soul.*

To see this, we have only to ask again who these inhabitants of Jerusalem were. They were the murderers of the Lord of glory, the very guiltiest men on the face of this guilty earth; men whom God bore with as he never bore with any other people, and then, when they had worn out his patience, punished as he never punished any others. For nearly eighteen hundred years, they have been spectacles to the wondering nations of his displeasure. Yet what does this prophet say? For them a fountain shall be opened for sin and for uncleanness. It shall be opened for all the world, but these are the men for whom it shall be said to be opened, they shall be first invited to it, they shall have a peculiar property in it, it shall be seen to be emphatically theirs.

And so it was. Our Lord, when he came, preached his own gospel among these men; he offered himself up for their sins in their very sight; the last command he gave his disciples, was to open their commission among them, to declare his salvation at Jerusalem before they proclaimed it to any other creature. And scarcely was he seated on his throne, when, by the outpouring of his Spirit, he brought multitudes of these men to the fountain he had opened for them. In one day three thousand of them washed in it, and were made clean. The first sinners the ascended Jesus saved, were sinners of Jerusalem, the greatest sinners in our world he could find to save.

And so it will be. We think of the Jews as cut off for ever from the Redeemer's mercy. Their condition, we say, is lost and hopeless. Some of us look with almost scorn on any effort that may be made to raise them out of it. But for them has this glorious fountain been opened, for them it is still designed, and before the end comes, the nations shall wonder again at these men; they shall see in them as astonishing a display of Jehovah's mercy, as they see now of his awful vengeance.

And what does all this proclaim to us? It tells us plainly that there is no guilt too great for the blood of Christ to wash out, no sinner whom he cannot recover and save. The sins of Jerusalem were full when the men of it had crucified him, but "Wait a little," he says, and before the wrath of his Father goes over it, he takes thousands upon thousands out of it, and makes them the trophies of his grace and power. When he converted Paul, he did it, Paul tells us, for the encouragement of others. "He came into the world," he says, "to save sinners," and how shall he let the world see that he is able to save them? "He took me," the apostle says, "me the chief of sinners, and held me up in the world's sight converted and saved. He made me an example and pattern of what he was able to accomplish." This is like a physician's coming among the sick and diseased, and to bring them to place themselves in his hands, healing in their sight the most diseased of them all, the very dying. Is there a man here whose sins appear to him too great for any mercy to pardon, whose condition seems to him too miserable and lost for any power to deliver him out of it? Let him think this day of guilty Jerusalem. Let him see a fountain opened in the midst of it for its sin and uncleanness; and then let him say with humble faith, with hope and joy, " That fountain can cleanse me."

III. And now comes before us in the text *the time when this fountain shall be opened to these sinful men.* " In that day," the prophet says, and the expression may refer to the day predicted in the end of this chapter, the day of our Lord's crucifixion. Then may this fountain be said to have been opened, when the sword of Jehovah smote him, when the nails pierced his blessed hands and feet and the spear his side, and his precious blood was actually poured forth.

But these words seem connected rather with the preceding chapter. They point out a day yet to come, that long promised and long looked for day, when the Jews as a nation shall be brought to repentance and the reception of Christ. By the opening of this fountain to them, we may understand the discovery of it to them; not the first bursting forth of it, but their beholding it, the making of them acquainted with it. There was a fountain near Hagar in the wilderness, but she knew nothing of it, it did her no good, she sat fainting by its side. It was not till the Lord shewed it to her, that she drank of it and rejoiced. So with the Jews. They hear of salvation for sinners through the blood of Christ, but they do not see it, they do not understand it, it is to them a hidden salvation. But it shall not always be thus, the Lord says. "I will pour upon the house of David and upon the inhabitants of Jerusalem the spirit of grace and of supplications, and they shall look upon me whom they have pierced, and they shall mourn; and then, when I have done this, when I have these guilty men praying and weeping before me, in that day there shall be a fountain opened to them for sin and uncleanness. Their eyes shall see my salvation, see it as a salvation provided for them and open to them, and with joyful hearts they shall accept it. He whom I have made already a light to lighten the Gentiles, shall be at last more than the light, the glory, of my people Israel."

But how far does this apply to ourselves? In

the spirit of it, quite as much as to these Jews. God does not promise to make known his salvation to them because they are Jews, but because they are brought to feel their need of salvation, because they are sinners, and are become, through his grace, humbled, contrite, and mourning sinners. We learn then,

1. *There can be no real knowledge of Christ without repentance.*

We might have supposed that when God had provided for this wretched world a remedy for its sins and wretchedness and told the world of it, he had done enough, that all the guilty and miserable would at once have had recourse to it. But such is not the case. Thousands hear of this remedy all their life long, and know no more of it at last than they knew at first; they know of its power to cleanse and comfort the soul nothing at all. Brethren, what do you know of it? For many years, from the days of your childhood perhaps, you have been continually hearing of this fountain for sin; have you ever once looked on it in its real character? Have you ever seen in it a remedy for your own sin and uncleanness? Have you beheld in the crucified Jesus a Saviour for your own guilty souls? If not, this text plainly intimates to you the reason. You are not the men, it says, to whom a spiritual discovery of Christ is ever made. The state of your hearts, it tells you, will not admit of such a discovery being made to you. There is a glorious salvation near you, as open to you as to any man living, and as free as God's grace can make it; but it will never be yours, you will never really understand any thing of it, till you yourselves are changed. The Jews know nothing of a Saviour from sin now, and why? They feel nothing of their own great need of one. They would embrace the gospel to-morrow, could you pierce their hearts with true repentance. Humble them, and you would at once convert them. It was so with their fathers in the days of old. "Crucify him, crucify him," they cried; but when, through Peter's preaching, the Holy Spirit pricked them in their heart, and constrained them to ask in trembling guiltiness, "What shall we do?" in that very same day the fountain was opened to them, they "gladly received" the apostle's words and were baptized in the name of Jesus Christ. And let that Spirit prick you to the heart, the result would be the same. Your indifference to the gospel would go, your prejudice against it would go. It now perhaps seems to you as a mere ideal thing, a something that you cannot lay hold of; it would then become to you a reality, and a reality of overwhelming importance. All you see around you, all worldly things, would appear as shadows in comparison with it. You would in one hour count them all but loss, so that you " might win Christ and be found in him."

Learn then this morning your need of what we mean by repentance, a deep sense of your own sinfulness and great sorrow of heart on account of it. Learn the importance of this repentance, and the utter impossibility of your ever being pardoned or saved without it. It cannot save you, it can do nothing towards obtaining a pardon for you, no more than a criminal's hearing his death-warrant read, and trembling as he hears it, can bring him a pardon; but God will never save you till he has given you this, nor even reveal to you fully how you may be saved. His gospel will be a riddle or a mere tale to you, till you possess this. He will never save your soul, till he has first smitten and broken your heart. May we all be willing to have our hearts smitten! May we this very moment lift up a prayer to this mighty God to come down and thoroughly break them!

2. We are reminded too here that *wherever there is real repentance, there also will God give in the end a real knowledge of his salvation.* Does your state of mind, brethren, correspond with that of these mourning Jews? Are you at this moment heart-stricken under a sense of your enormous sin against your God and Saviour? Are you filled with a self-loathing and abhorrence you could hardly find words to express, at the sight

of your inward pollutions? Then this promise in the text is intended for you; you are as much interested in it as any inhabitant of Jerusalem ever was or ever can be. God tells you plainly here, not that there is an abundant remedy for sin provided for you and within your reach, but more than this—that he will sooner or later make you acquainted with this remedy. He says that as surely as he has shewn you your own misery, he will shew you eventually his mercy; that you shall see the fountain he has opened for sin and uncleanness, as clearly as you now see your own great need of it; that you shall know as much and feel as much of Christ's power to cleanse, as you know and feel now of the power of sin to defile. He will not leave you for ever in the suffering condition in which he now finds you. " I have torn," he says, " and I will heal you; I have smitten and I will bind you up." " After two days will he revive you, in the third day he will raise you up, and you shall live in his sight."

Would, brethren, that we might all learn from this scripture to seek for ourselves a deeper consciousness of sin, a more heart-felt and abiding sorrow on account of it! We talk of contrition and we know perhaps a little of it, but O how little! These Jews are to mourn over sin, the prophet says, " as one mourneth for his only son ;" to mourn secretly, and bitterly, and long. And something like this is what we want. We want to feel, not once or twice in our lives, but every day we live, that we are miserable sinners. We want to have the remembrance of our sins often grievous unto us, and the burden of them intolerable. We want to see the sin that defiles us, and to hate and loathe it every hour we breathe. This would not make Christ's mercy more open to us or us more welcome to it, but it would make it ten-fold more precious to us; it would keep us living in a sweeter enjoyment of it. We should experience more of its elevating, its constraining and sanctifying power. There would be a life, a reality and power, in our religion, of which it is now often destitute, and there would be in it too an unspeakable blessedness. It would be more than a preparation for heaven, it would be sometimes a foretaste of it. The tear and the song would go together. We might weep for sin, but we should be glad to weep for it; there would be a joy mingled with our weeping, which would be more than earthly. We should understand at last that a broken heart is the only happy one.

BY THE SAME AUTHOR.

A SERIES OF PRACTICAL SERMONS, for every Sunday in the Year. Second Edition. Vols. I and II. Price 8s. each. Vol. III. *in preparation*.

SERMONS, preached in St. James's Chapel, CLAPHAM, Surrey. Fifth Edition. Price 10s. 6d.

PAROCHIAL SERMONS, preached at GLASBURY, Brecknockshire. Seventh Edition. Price 10s. 6d.

SERMONS, preached in the Parish Church of HIGH WYCOMBE, Bucks. Tenth Edition. Two Volumes. Price 21s.

PSALMS and HYMNS, selected and arranged for Public Worship. Fourth Edition. Price 2s. 6d.

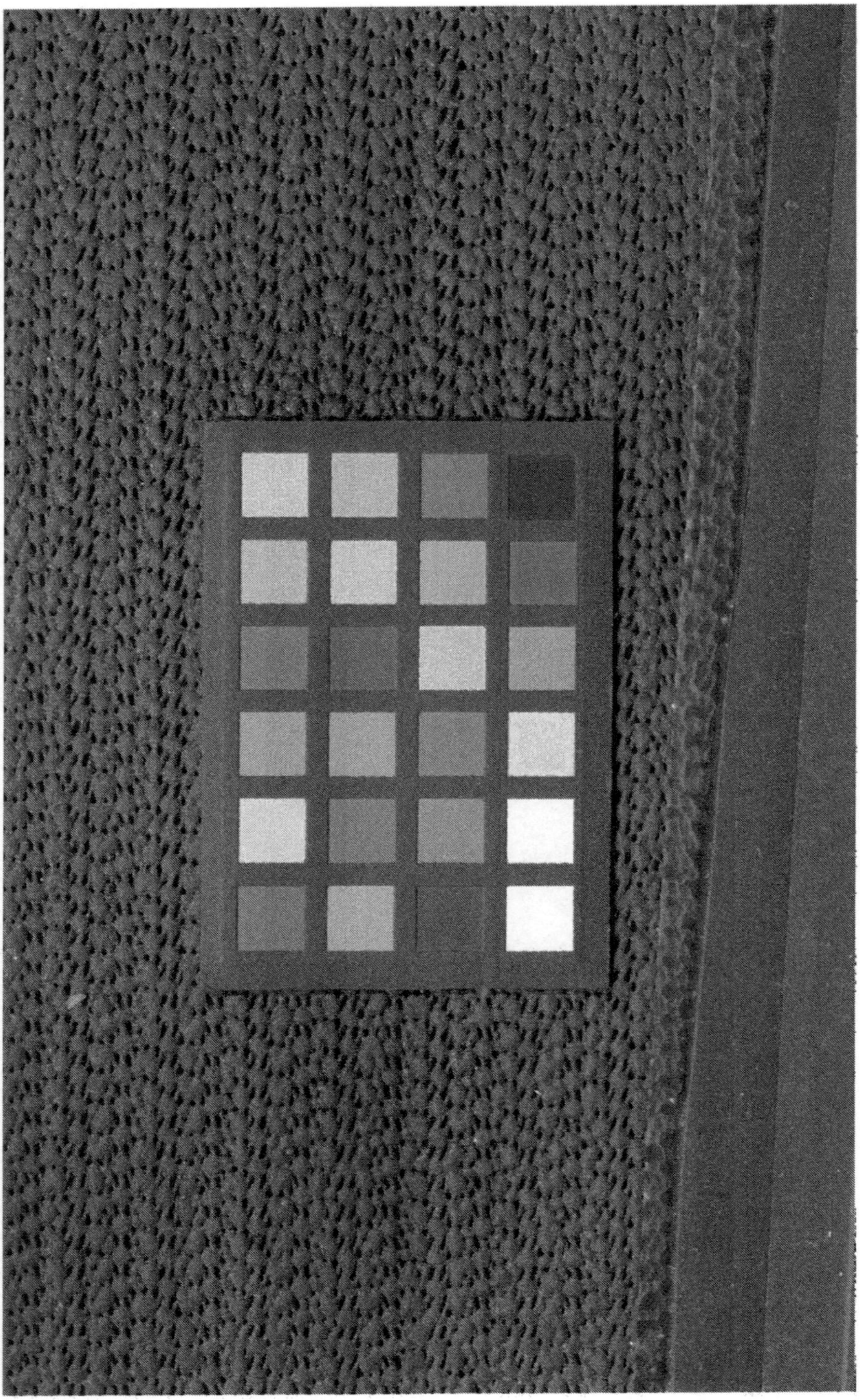

Ingram Content Group UK Ltd.
Milton Keynes UK
UKHW022257010523
421066UK00005B/388